Vikki + John

GOURMET
Our Way

Cascia Hall Preparatory School
A Catholic, Augustinian School
Cascia Parent Faculty Association
Tulsa, Oklahoma
1995

Cover Art

Original Watercolors by P. S. Gordon

Mr. Gordon received a National Endowment for the Arts Grant in 1979, and he was selected to paint the 1992-1993 Season Poster for the Metropolitan Opera Company of New York. He has been featured in several prestigious art books.

Works by P. S. Gordon appear in several art galleries and private collections throughout the country. Mr. Gordon resides in Tulsa. His daughter, Emily, graduated from Cascia Hall in 1998.

Cover Design

Johnny King
Desktop Design, Incorporated

Illustrations

Annette Rosenheck

Special thanks to Lu Celia Wise, author of THE BLENDING OF MANY CULTURES.

Copyright © 1995
2nd Printing Copyright © 2002
Cascia Parent Faculty Association
Tulsa, Oklahoma

Library of Congress Catalog Card Number 95-070244
ISBN 0-9643143-0-4

GOURMET OUR WAY is a collection of tasty recipes designed to use fresh ingredients in simple to prepare, imaginative dishes for any occasion. The recipes contributed are from kitchens of the "Cascia Family", friends and professional Tulsa chefs.

Creative menus offer suggestions for family meals and celebrations that produce garden fresh soups and salads, flavorful pastas, savory entrees and luscious desserts. GOURMET OUR WAY balances the concerns of the novice cook and the more seasoned cook.

Reflections of our Tulsa lifestyle and Oklahoma heritage together with the history of Cascia Hall Preparatory School are featured. The Cascia Parent Faculty Association provided the funds for publication of GOURMET OUR WAY. The association promotes the educational, spiritual, physical, cultural and social development of Cascia students. Proceeds of this cookbook will be donated to the Cascia Hall Charitable Trust.

Enjoy GOURMET OUR WAY

DEDICATED to the Cascia Hall Preparatory School tradition of truth, unity and charity.

Cookbook Committee
Co-chairmen
Sybil Zikmund
Catherine Doyle
Linda Lambert

Word Processing
Beverley Wayman
Beverly Gooch

Writers
Ronnie Donnelly
Cherry Bost

Illustrator
Annette Rosenheck

Cookbook Committee

Pam Cremer
Sally Dutton
Mary Elliott
Pam Eslicker
Katherine Frame
Jill Sulliven-Freeland
Marge Gaberino
Edie Gregory
Sharon Grimm
Marion Heatherman
Bonnie Henke
Blossom Horton
Margie Huffman
Kathryn Kenney

Kathy Miller
Kris Nichols
Mary Niedermeyer
Rhonda Pederson
Sally Rippey
Michelle Rooney
Susan Schloss
Laurine Schuler
Jan Scott
Rita Singer
Barbara Taylor
Anita Thomas
Barbara VanHanken

2002 Cookbook Committee
Co-chairmen
Jane Higgins
Annabelle Miller

Committee
Bonnie Chrisman
LaDonna Cullinan
Mary Husband
Tracy Moellers
Denise Piland

4

Table of Contents

Memorable Cocktail Buffet

Festive Wine Punch

California Torta

Sun-Dried Tomato and Cheese Bruschetta

Spinach Strudel

Avocado Mousse Ring

Marinated Green Golf Balls

Lemon Shrimp with Rosemary

Satay

Herb Ravioli Pockets

Kahlúa Bars

Tulsa Truffles

Football Sunday

Black Bean Salsa

Chalupa

Greens with Honey-Lime Cilantro Vinaigrette

Peppermint Brownies

Caramel Crunch Ice Cream Squares

Candlelight for Eight

Spinach Crêpes Stuffed with Tomato-Pesto Cheese

Tipsy Tomato Soup

Greens with Jícama, Almonds and Oranges

Herb Crusted Lamb in Wine

Parmesan Scalloped Potatoes

Chocolate Nut Torte to Diet For

Bridal Shower Luncheon

Mother's Day Strawberry Orange Soup

Shanghai Shrimp and Pasta Salad

Angel Biscuits

Coconut Lemon Pound Cake

Chilled Zucchini Bisque

Crunchy Oriental Chicken Salad

Sour Cream Banana Bread

Frangipane Tart with Strawberries and Raspberries

Alfresco Dining

Baked Garlic with Sun-Dried Tomatoes
Elegant Wild Rice Salad
Grilled Hoisin Pork
Chocolate Orange Sorbet

Garden Fresh Gazpacho
Very Caesar Salad
Grilled Salmon with Sun-Dried Tomato Sauce
Rhubarb Raspberry Crisp

Fourth of July Picnic

Beach Bum Iced Tea
Picnic Carrots
Garden Bean and Potato Salad with Balsamic Vinaigrette
Chicken and Ham Wrapsodies
Peach Upside-Down Cake

Busy Day Supper

Spinach, Strawberry and Bleu Cheese Salad
Sherried Chicken with Artichokes
Apple Yoda

Sunshine Confetti Salad
Fettuccine with Broccoli and Chicken
Lip Smackin' and Teeth Chompin' Cookies

Soup's On

Sirloin Steak and Winter Vegetable Soup
Wild Rice Bread
Lemon Cloud

Viva Tomato Soup
Mediterranean Stuffed Bread
Crème de Cocoa Cheesecake

Oklahoma Sunrise

At the invitation of Bishop Kelley, representatives of the Augustinian order traveled from Villanova University in Pennsylvania to Tulsa and opened Oklahoma's first Augustinian prep school. From it's 1926 initial enrollment of 25 boys, Cascia Hall has successfully educated and graduated over 3,000 young men and women. The Order of St. Augustine's vision and commitment to the pursuit of knowledge and Christian values has endowed Tulsa with excellence in education.

The continued generosity of Tulsa families has enabled Cascia Hall to expand its facilities, which include a high school, library, chapel, middle school, tennis complex, two gymnasiums, numerous playing fields and a running track. Cascia's 40-acre campus, featuring clinker brick, slate roofed buildings of Neo-French-Norman architecture, sits comfortably encircled by residential neighborhoods in the heart of Tulsa.

Educating youth according to the philosophy of St. Augustine of Hippo has been the Augustinian's resolve. On its athletic fields and in its classrooms, Cascia strives to instill respect, responsibility, critical thinking, teamwork perseverance, intellectual curiosity and an awareness of God's place in each life.

Cascia Hall's challenging curriculum and academic requirements have ensured both success and recognition for the students. Each year 99 percent of its graduates enter colleges, universities and military academies of their choice. Over the years they have distinguished themselves in careers of business, medicine, law, engineering, politics, teaching, religious life and theater.

Through its innovative January minimester program, junior and senior students may gain on-the-job experience in a variety of careers. This investigative period enlightens and stimulates while preparing students for life's choices.

An integral feature of Cascia Hall student life is the inclusion of students from surrounding Oklahoma communities as well as from various foreign countries. Young people from Latin America, Europe and Asia share their customs, perspectives and friendships with Cascia students, families and faculty.

Cascia Hall is actively supported by the Augustinian community, alumni and the Cascia Parent Faculty Association. The Association sponsors two annual fund raisers, the Cascia Christmas Walk and Celebrate Cascia. The Augustinian and lay board of directors has maintained a constant presence and an academic beacon that Cascia Hall represents, in Oklahoma and beyond.

Oklahoma
Sunrise

BREAD & BREAKFAST
Our Way

Breads

Blueberry Bundt Cake 19
Blueberry-Poppy Seed Bread 17
Johnny Appleseed Bread 17
Mediterranean Stuffed Bread 23
Peach Mini-Loaves 16
Rise and Shine Sausage Bread 24
Sour Cream Banana Bread 18
Strawberry Pecan Bread 16
Swedish Tea Ring 20
The Duke's Corn Bread 24
The Great Pumpkin Bread 19
Wild Rice Bread 22

Muffins, Biscuits and Scones

Angel Biscuits 21
(Don't Tell the Kids These Are) Vegetable
   Muffins 15
Fresh Ginger Muffins 14
Harvest Pumpkin Apple Muffins 15
Orange Cranberry Muffins with
   Honey Butter 13
Scottish Scones 18
Sunday Morning Biscuits 21

Breakfast Specials

Apple-Pecan Pancakes 27
Bed and Breakfast Cream Cheese Pancakes 26
Christmas Morning Brunch Puff 27
Dutch Baby with Fruit Topping 25
Gourmet Granola 29
Grandma's Boy-Raisin' Waffles 25
Great Grits 28
Quick Cheese Blintzes 28
Swedish Pancakes 26
The Queen's Oats Granola 29

Professional Chefs

Lavosh 30
Tomato Basil Boules 31

Orange Cranberry Muffins with Honey Butter

18 muffins

- 2 cups flour
- 1 cup sugar
- 1½ teaspoons baking powder
- ½ teaspoon baking soda
- 1½ teaspoons ground nutmeg
- 1 teaspoon ground cinnamon
- ½ teaspoon ground ginger
- ½ cup solid shortening
- ¾ cup fresh orange juice
- 1 tablespoon vanilla
- 2 teaspoons grated orange peel
- 2 large eggs, slightly beaten
- 1½ cups coarsely chopped cranberries
- 1½ cups chopped walnuts, divided

- In medium mixing bowl combine dry ingredients. Cut in shortening until mixture is the consistency of coarse meal.
- Combine juice, vanilla, orange peel and eggs. Stir into flour mixture until ingredients are moistened.
- Gently stir in cranberries and 1 cup of walnuts.
- Spoon batter into 18 paper lined or greased and floured muffin pans. Sprinkle with remaining walnuts.
- Bake in preheated 350° oven 25 to 30 minutes or until done.
- Serve warm with Orange Honey Butter.

Honey Butter

- ½ cup butter
- 2 tablespoons honey
- 1 tablespoon grated orange peel

- In small bowl, beat butter until fluffy. Gradually beat in honey and orange peel

Oranges and cranberries make a great combination.

Fresh Ginger Muffins

16 muffins

- 1 **piece fresh ginger, 4 to 5 ounces, unpeeled**
- ¾ **cup plus 3 tablespoons sugar**
- 2 **tablespoons finely grated lemon zest**
- 2 **cups flour**
- ½ **teaspoon salt**
- ¾ **teaspoon baking soda**
- ½ **cup unsalted butter, at room temperature**
- 2 **eggs**
- 1 **cup buttermilk**

- Cut the unpeeled ginger into large chunks. Finely mince in food processor fitted with a metal blade. This should yield about ¼ cup. In a small saucepan combine the ginger and ¼ cup of the sugar. Cook over medium heat, stirring, until the sugar melts and mixture is hot, about two minutes. Set aside to cool.
- Stir the lemon zest and 3 tablespoons sugar together. Let stand for a few minutes, then add to the ginger mixture. Set aside.
- Mix flour, salt and baking soda. Set aside.
- In a large bowl, beat the butter until smooth. Add the remaining ½ cup sugar and beat until blended. Add the eggs and beat well. Add the buttermilk and mix until blended.
- Add the combined dry ingredients and stir just until blended. Stir in the ginger-lemon mixture.
- Spoon into greased muffin tins, filling about ¾ full. Bake in preheated 375° oven 15 to 20 minutes. Cool in tins for 10 minutes, then remove.

Moist and spicy.

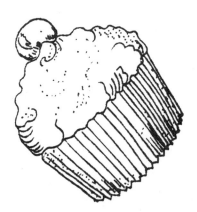

(Don't Tell the Kids These Are) Vegetable Muffins

8 muffins

- 1½ **cups flour**
- 1½ **teaspoons baking powder**
- ½ **teaspoon cinnamon**
- ¼ **teaspoon baking soda**
- ¼ **teaspoon salt**
- ¼ **teaspoon ground coriander**
- ¼ **teaspoon ground ginger or allspice**
- 1 **egg**
- ¾ **cup shredded zucchini**
- ½ **cup grated carrots**
- ½ **cup brown sugar**
- ⅓ **cup lowfat milk (or ¼ cup milk and ¼ cup peach tea)**
- ¼ **cup butter, melted and slightly cooled**
- ¾ **cup walnut pieces**

- Place baking cups in muffin pan.
- In medium bowl, combine dry ingredients and set aside.
- In large bowl, beat egg, stir in vegetables, brown sugar, milk and butter until well combined. Add flour mixture to zucchini mixture and stir just until dry ingredients are moistened. Add walnuts.
- Bake in preheated 350° oven 10 minutes or until golden brown.

This can be doubled and freezes well.

Harvest Pumpkin Apple Muffins

24 muffins

- 2½ **cups flour**
- 2 **cups sugar**
- 1 **tablespoon pumpkin pie spice**
- 1 **teaspoon baking soda**
- ½ **teaspoon salt**
- 2 **eggs, lightly beaten**
- 1 **cup canned pumpkin**
- ½ **cup vegetable oil**
- 2 **cups peeled, finely chopped apples**

Streusel Topping

- 2 **tablespoons flour**
- ¼ **cup sugar**
- ½ **teaspoon cinnamon**
- 4 **teaspoons butter**

- In large bowl, combine dry ingredients. Set aside.
- In medium bowl, combine eggs, pumpkin and oil. Add liquid ingredients to dry ingredients; stir just until moistened. Stir in apples.
- Spoon batter into greased or paper lined cups, filling ¾ full. Sprinkle streusel topping over batter.
- Bake in preheated 350° oven 35 to 40 minutes.

- In small bowl, combine flour, sugar and cinnamon. Cut in butter until mixture is crumbly.

15

Peach Mini-Loaves

8 to 9 small loaves

3⅓ cups flour
3 cups sugar
1 teaspoon nutmeg
2 teaspoons soda
1 teaspoon salt
1 pound frozen peach slices
4 eggs
1 cup vegetable oil
1 cup pecans, chopped
¼ cup water
1 teaspoon vanilla

- Mix dry ingredients.
- Chop frozen peach slices into half-inch pieces. Add eggs, oil, pecans, water and vanilla.
- Stir until all ingredients are moist.
- Fill buttered 8-ounce pans with ⅞ cup batter.
- Bake in preheated 350° oven 45 minutes or until peaches are golden.
- Turn from pans immediately. Cool on racks.
- Glaze and decorate if desired.

Strawberry Pecan Bread

2 loaves

3 cups flour
1 teaspoon baking soda
1 teaspoon cinnamon
2 cups sugar
1 teaspoon salt
2 10-ounce packages frozen strawberries, thawed and sliced, reserve ½ cup juice for spread
1¼ cups vegetable oil
4 eggs, well beaten
1 cup chopped pecans

- Mix dry ingredients. Make a hole in center of mixture. Add strawberries, juice, oil, eggs and pecans.
- Pour into 2 greased and floured 9 x 5-inch pans. Bake in preheated 350° oven 40 to 60 minutes.

Spread

½ cup reserved strawberry juice
1 8-ounce package cream cheese
1 tablespoon powdered sugar

- Mix together and spread on cooled sliced bread.

Johnny Appleseed Bread

1⅓ **cups flour**
¾ **teaspoon baking soda**
1 **teaspoon cinnamon**
¼ **teaspoon cloves**
1 **cup plus 1 teaspoon sugar**
½ **cup vegetable oil**
2 **eggs**
1 **teaspoon vanilla**
2 **cups coarsely chopped and peeled cooking apples (4 medium)**
½ **cup raisins**
½ **cup chopped pecans**
6 **pecan halves**

- Combine flour, soda, cinnamon and cloves in a bowl. Set aside.
- Mix 1 cup sugar with oil in large bowl. Add eggs and vanilla, then stir in apples, raisins and pecans. Add flour mixture and stir until blended.
- Grease 9 x 5-inch pan and line with waxed paper. Bake in preheated 325° oven 50 to 60 minutes. After 20 minutes gently pull out of oven, sprinkle with 1 teaspoon sugar and decorate with pecan halves. Continue baking.

This is a moist spicy bread that is delicious in the Fall made with Jonathan apples.

Blueberry-Poppy Seed Bread

4 **eggs, beaten**
1 **cup vegetable oil**
2 **cups light brown sugar**
3 **cups flour**
1 **teaspoon salt**
1½ **teaspoons soda**
2 **teaspoons vanilla**
1 **can evaporated milk**
1 **ounce poppy seeds**
2 **cups frozen blueberries**

- Combine eggs, oil and brown sugar.
- Sift dry ingredients and add to mixture. Blend in vanilla, milk, poppy seeds and blueberries.
- Bake in two 8 x 4½-inch loaf pans in preheated 300° oven 1 hour or until knife comes out clean.

Sour Cream Banana Bread

1 loaf

- ½ cup butter
- 1⅓ cups brown sugar
- 2 eggs
- 2 cups flour
- ½ teaspoon salt
- 1 teaspoon soda
- ¼ cup sour cream
- 1 cup mashed bananas
- 1 tablespoon vanilla
- ½ cup chopped pecans

• Cream butter with brown sugar. Add eggs.
• Slowly beat in flour, salt, and soda.
• Add sour cream, bananas, vanilla, and pecans.
• Pour into one greased and floured 9 x 5-inch loaf pan
• Bake in preheated 350° oven 1 hour.

Scottish Scones

16 pie-shaped slices

- 3 cups flour
- ½ cup sugar
- 1 tablespoon baking powder
- ½ teaspoon salt
- ½ cup plus 1 tablespoon cold butter
- 1 cup raisins or 1 tablespoon freshly grated lemon or orange peel
- 2 eggs
- ⅔ cup buttermilk

• Measure dry ingredients into bowl and stir with whisk.
• Cut butter into the dry ingredients. Stir in raisins or peel and set aside.
• Mix eggs and buttermilk. Gradually add flour mixture into the buttermilk mixture. If it is too moist and sticks to your hands or beater blade, add sprinkles of flour.
• Work with the dough as little as possible for a soft, pliable ball. Vigorous kneading will toughen the bread. Use dough hook at low speed for less than a minute.
• Divide the dough into two circles about ¾-inch thick. Place on ungreased baking sheet and with knife lightly score into the desired number of pieces. Brush lightly with melted butter or egg mixed with a tablespoon of milk to brown it nicely.
• Bake in preheated 375° oven 18 to 20 minutes or until golden brown.

Serve these at tea time.

Blueberry Bundt Cake

1 bundt cake

2½ cups sifted flour
1 teaspoon salt
1 teaspoon baking soda
1 teaspoon baking powder
½ cup butter, softened
1 cup granulated sugar
½ cup packed brown sugar
2 eggs
1 teaspoon vanilla
1 cup buttermilk
1 cup sour cream
1 cup fresh blueberries
1 cup chopped pecans
1 cup sifted powdered sugar
1 tablespoon milk
1 tablespoon finely chopped pecans

- Combine flour, salt, baking soda, and baking powder.
- Cream butter and sugars. Beat in eggs and vanilla.
- Add dry ingredients alternately with buttermilk and sour cream, beating well after each addition.
- Stir in blueberries and pecans. Pour batter into greased 10-cup bundt pan.
- Bake in preheated 350° oven 1 hour. Cool thoroughly in pan. Remove. Combine confectioners' sugar and 1 tablespoon milk. Drizzle over cake. Sprinkle with chopped pecans.

The Great Pumpkin Bread

3 loaves

1 cup vegetable oil
3 cups sugar
2 cups canned pumpkin
4 eggs
⅔ cup water
3½ cups flour
2 teaspoons baking soda
1 teaspoon cloves
1 teaspoon cinnamon
1 teaspoon nutmeg
1 teaspoon allspice
1 cup chopped pecans
1 cup raisins

- Combine oil, sugar and pumpkin. Add eggs and water.
- Add dry ingredients and spices.
- Add pecans and raisins.
- Mix well and pour into three greased 8 x 4½-inch loaf pans.
- Bake in preheated 350° oven 45 to 60 minutes.

This bread stays fresh and moist for several days.

Swedish Tea Ring

Serves 10 to 12

1 **cup milk**
1 **package granulated yeast**
1 **egg, well-beaten**
¼ **cup sugar**
1 **teaspoon salt**
¼ **cup melted shortening, cooled**
3 **cups flour, sifted**

- Scald milk. Dissolve yeast in one tablespoon of lukewarm water. When milk is cool, add the yeast and well-beaten egg.
- Add the sugar, salt, and shortening. Add flour. Knead. Let dough rise until doubled in size.

Filling

2 **tablespoons of soft butter**
¼ **cup brown sugar**
½ **package dates, ground**
½ **cup walnuts, ground**

- Combine butter, sugar, and dates. Add a little water and warm slightly to form a paste.
- After dough has risen, roll out to 15 x 24-inch rectangle. Spread with date mixture and sprinkle with walnuts.
- Roll tightly, jelly-roll style from the long side. Pinch sides to seal, and form a ring.
- Place on greased cookie sheet.
- With kitchen scissors, cut slashes 1½-inch deep and ½-inches apart.
- Cover dough and let rise until doubled in size. Bake in preheated 350° oven 35 to 40 minutes. Drizzle with icing.

Icing

1 **cup powdered sugar**
1 **teaspoon freshly squeezed lemon juice**
water or milk

- To powdered sugar, add lemon juice plus enough water or milk to make thick frosting. Beat with whisk until smooth and creamy.

Sunday Morning Biscuits

4 to 6 biscuits

   1 **cup sifted white flour**
  ½ **teaspoon baking soda**
   1 **teaspoon baking powder**
  ½ **teaspoon salt**
 2½ **tablespoons solid shortening**
  ½ **cup buttermilk**

- Sift dry ingredients.
- Work in shortening until it looks like cornmeal.
- Add buttermilk gradually until dough holds together.
- Roll out, cut and place on a greased baking sheet.
- Bake in preheated 400° oven 12 minutes.

Each recipe makes four to six three-inch biscuits. I make three or four batches for Sunday breakfast. Recipe can be easily doubled or tripled.

Angel Biscuits

12 to 16 large biscuits

 4 **cups flour**
 4 **tablespoons baking powder**
 2 **teaspoons salt**
 2 **teaspoons sugar**
½ **teaspoon baking soda**
½ **cup shortening**
 1 **16-ounce carton sour cream**

- Blend dry ingredients and shortening. Add sour cream. Knead and roll out on floured board.
- Cut with biscuit cutter and place in greased pan.
- Bake in preheated 400° oven 20 minutes until brown.

These are delicious with flavored butters, such as strawberry or lemon.

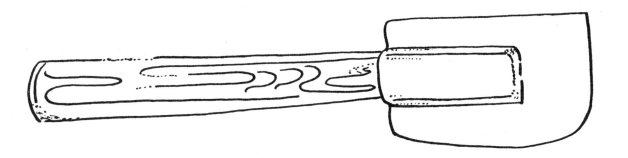

Wild Rice Bread

2 loaves

⅓ **cup wild rice (cook in 1 quart water for 1 hour; drain and save liquid)**
2 **packages yeast, dissolved in ¼ cup warm water**
2½ **cups liquid from rice**
¼ **cup brown sugar**
1 **tablespoon salt**
¼ **cup potato flakes**
¼ **cup molasses**
¼ **cup soft butter**
2 **cups whole wheat flour**
1 **cup white flour**

- Prepare rice and set aside.
- Combine the yeast and water in a large mixing bowl, stirring until dissolved. Blend in liquid from the rice, brown sugar, salt, potato flakes, molasses and butter.
- Beat in whole wheat flour to make a smooth batter. Gradually add remaining flour to make a soft, workable dough that pulls away from sides of the bowl.
- Turn out on a lightly floured surface and knead 10 minutes.
- Place dough in a warm, buttered bowl, turning to coat top. Cover loosely with plastic wrap and a towel. Let rise until doubled, about 1 to 1½ hours.
- Punch down and divide in half. Knead dough and let rest 10 minutes.
- Butter two 8 x 4½-inch loaf pans. Shape dough into loaves and place in pans. Cover and let rise to tops of pan, about 1 hour.
- Bake in preheated 375° oven 45 to 50 minutes. Brush with melted butter while warm.

Serve with Viva Tomato Soup, page 64.

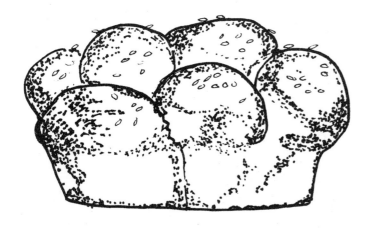

Mediterranean Stuffed Bread

2 loaves

Dough

    2⅔ **cups lukewarm water**
    2 **envelopes yeast**
    2 **teaspoons honey**
    2 **teaspoons salt**
6 to 7 **cups flour**

- In large bowl mix water, yeast, honey and salt. Stir briefly and let stand 5 to 10 minutes until it begins to foam.
- Stir 3 cups flour into yeast mixture and beat well. Gradually add remaining flour until you have a soft dough. Do not add more flour than the dough can absorb.
- Turn dough onto a lightly floured board and knead until no longer sticky, about 2 minutes. Place in oiled bowl and turn to coat. Let rise in a warm place 30 minutes.
- Punch down dough and let rest for 10 minutes.

Filling

    ½ **cup mayonnaise**
    8 **ounces grated cheddar or Monterey Jack cheese**
    1 **cup chopped onion**
    1 **teaspoon oregano**
    1 **teaspoon basil**
    4 **tablespoons olive oil**
    2 **tablespoons mint**
    1 **egg, beaten**

- Divide dough in half. Roll out on floured board. Spread with mayonnaise leaving 2-inch border. Top with cheese, onion, and spices.
- Fold dough over to form a seam. Use cold water to seal seam. Bake on greased baking sheet, seam side down. Slash tops to allow steam to escape. Brush top with beaten egg.
- Bake in preheated 425° oven 35 minutes. After 20 minutes reduce heat to 400° if browning too fast.
- Transfer bread to racks to cool. Cool 20 minutes before cutting.

The aroma and taste will bring rave reviews!

The Duke's Corn Bread

Serves 10

- 1 **cup corn meal**
- ½ **teaspoon soda**
- ¾ **teaspoon salt**
- 1 **small to medium onion, chopped**
- 1 **glove garlic, chopped**
- 1 **cup cream-style corn**
- ¼ **cup bacon drippings or vegetable oil**
- 2 **eggs**
- 1 **cup sour cream**
- 1 **small jalapeño pepper, minced**
- 1 **cup grated cheddar cheese**

- Combine corn meal, soda, salt, onion, garlic, corn, oil, eggs and sour cream. Beat well.
- Spread half of mixture in greased 10-inch iron skillet or baking pan. Spread pepper and cheese over batter. Cover with remaining batter.
- Bake in preheated 350° oven 45 minutes. May be made ahead of time and reheated before serving.

John Wayne's Recipe.

Rise and Shine Sausage Bread

Serves 12

- 1 **cup raisins**
- 1 **pound hot sausage (raw)**
- 1½ **cups brown sugar**
- 1½ **cups white sugar**
- 2 **eggs**
- 1 **cup pecans, chopped**
- 3 **cups flour**
- 1 **teaspoon ginger**
- 1 **teaspoon pumpkin pie spice**
- 1 **teaspoon baking powder**
- 1 **teaspoon baking soda**
- 1 **cup cold coffee**

- Simmer raisins in water (covered) for five minutes and drain
- Combine sausage, brown sugar, white sugar and eggs. Stir in pecans and raisins.
- Combine flour, spices and baking powder in separate bowl.
- Stir soda into coffee. Blend coffee and flour mixture into sausage mixture.
- Pour into a greased and floured 12-inch tube pan (Bundt pan). Bake in preheated 350° oven for 1½ hours.

Unique and oh so tasty!

Grandma's Boy-Raisin' Waffles

Serves 8

2 eggs, separated
3 cups flour
½ cup sugar
4 teaspoons baking powder
1 teaspoon salt
2½ cups milk
¼ cup vegetable oil
1 teaspoon real vanilla extract

- In a small bowl, beat egg whites until soft peaks form. Set aside.
- In another bowl, blend egg yolks and remaining ingredients until relatively smooth.
- Fold in egg whites.
- Bake in preheated waffle iron.

Batter will keep for a couple of days in the refrigerator, or bake the whole recipe, wrap well and reheat in a 375° oven. Serve with warm maple syrup.

These are a big hit the "morning after" you've had a lot of kids spend the night!

Dutch Baby with Fruit Topping

Serves 2 to 4

Pancake

½ cup flour
2 tablespoons sugar
¼ teaspoon salt
½ cup milk
2 eggs
2 tablespoons butter

Fruit Topping

½ cup sugar
1 tablespoon cornstarch
½ cup freshly squeezed orange juice
2 tablespoons orange-flavored liqueur or orange juice
3 cups sliced fruits and/or berries

- In medium bowl, combine all pancake ingredients except butter. Beat until smooth.
- Place butter in 9-inch pie pan and melt in 425° oven just until butter sizzles, 2 to 4 minutes. Remove pan from oven and tilt to coat bottom of pan with melted butter. Immediately pour batter into hot pan.
- Bake in 425° oven 14 to 18 minutes or until puffed and golden brown. Some butter may rise to the surface of pancake during baking.
- While pancake is baking, mix fruit topping. When pancake is cooked, top with fruit and serve immediately.

Delicious the next day, if any is left.

Swedish Pancakes

Serves 3

3 eggs
1¼ cups milk
¾ cup sifted flour
1 tablespoon sugar
½ teaspoon salt
  grated lemon rind

- Beat eggs until thick and lemon-colored. Stir in milk.
- Sift dry ingredients into egg mixture. Mix until smooth. Drop by tablespoon onto buttered griddle. Flip when bubbles appear on surface.
- Serve topped with fresh strawberries or blueberries and whipped cream.

Father's Day Favorite.

Bed and Breakfast Cream Cheese Pancakes

Serves 2

1 8-ounce package cream cheese
3 eggs
1 tablespoon flour
1 teaspoon sugar
  powdered sugar and fresh fruit for garnish

- Place cream cheese in a food processor or blender. Blend to soften.
- Add eggs, flour and sugar. Blend until smooth.
- Pour three-inch cakes in a lightly buttered and heated frying pan. Flip when bubbles appear on surface.
- Serve sprinkled with powdered sugar and fresh fruit.

Recipe is easily doubled, tripled, etc. These reheat well in a microwave oven. "Light cream cheese" may be substituted for cream cheese, but they will not be quite as creamy.

Apple-Pecan Pancakes

Serves 4

2 **eggs, beaten**
4 **tablespoons sugar**
4 **tablespoons vegetable oil**
1 **teaspoon vanilla**
¼ **teaspoon salt**
2 **cups flour**
4 **teaspoons baking powder**
1½ **cups milk**
1 **apple, grated**
½ **cup chopped pecans**

- Combine all ingredients and mix until smooth. Cook batter on lightly greased griddle, turning each pancake when bubbles form. Serve with butter and hot syrup.

Christmas Morning Puff

Serves 12 to 15

2 **sticks of margarine**
1 **cup butter**
¼ **cup sugar**
4 **eggs**
1½ **cups milk**
2 **teaspoons baking powder**
1½ **cups flour**
　 pinch salt

- Cream butter and sugar. Add eggs, one at a time. Blend in milk.
- Mix baking powder, flour and salt together. Add to egg mixture.

Filling

2 **pounds ricotta cheese**
4 **tablespoons butter, melted**

- Mix filling ingredients together. Set aside.
- Spread half of the batter in a buttered 9x13-inch baking pan. Carefully spread the filling over the batter and top with remaining batter. Cover and refrigerate overnight.
- Bake in preheated 350° oven 45 minutes or until golden. Cut into squares and serve with sour cream and jelly or jam.

Quick Cheese Blintzes

5 dozen

1 pound loaf diet, thin-sliced white bread
1 8-ounce package cream cheese
2 egg yolks
½ cup sugar
1 teaspoon or more cinnamon
½ cup or more brown sugar
½ cup butter, melted

- Remove crusts from bread. Roll each slice very thin.
- Cream together cream cheese, egg yolks and sugar. Spread on bread and roll up each slice.
- Mix cinnamon and brown sugar. Roll blintzes in butter and brown sugar/cinnamon mixture. Refrigerate several hours. Cut in thirds.
- Bake in preheated 350° oven, 15 minutes or until brown and crisp.

Great for a morning coffee!

Great Grits

Serves 6 to 8

4 cups water
½ teaspoon salt
1 cup quick grits
1½ cups grated Monterey Jack with jalapeño peppers
½ cup butter, cut in small pieces
2 cloves garlic, pressed
dash of Tabasco Sauce
3 eggs

- Bring water and salt to a boil in a heavy saucepan. Stir grits slowly into boiling water. Return to a boil, reduce heat and cook 10 minutes, stirring occasionally.
- Remove pan from heat. Whisk in cheese, butter, garlic and Tabasco. Stir until cheese melts. Let cool slightly.
- In large bowl, lightly beat eggs. Add ½ cup of grits mixture to eggs and beat well. Add remaining grits and blend.
- Pour grits into a buttered 2-quart casserole dish and bake in preheated 350° oven 45 minutes to 1 hour, or until set. Serve hot.

An Oklahoma specialty.

Gourmet Granola

10 cups

8 cups rolled oats
1½ cups unsweetened coconut
1 cup wheat germ
1 cup chopped pecans or
almonds
1 cup hulled sunflower seeds
½ cup sesame seeds
½ cup bran
1 cup ground toasted soybeans
(grind in food processor)
½ cup oil (almond oil if
possible)
½ cup honey
1 to 2 teaspoons of vanilla

- Mix dry ingredients and place in a large shallow pan.
- Heat oil, honey and vanilla.
- Pour over dry ingredients and bake in 375° oven 20 to 30 minutes. Stir every 10 minutes.
- Raisins or other dried fruit can be added after baking. Makes a large amount. Keep in an air tight container and use like any other dry cereal.

Place half in a plastic bag and store in freezer for future use.

The Queen's Oats Granola

8 to 10 cups

8 cups regular rolled oats
1½ cups firmly packed brown
sugar
1½ cups regular wheat germ
½ cup walnuts
1½ cup unprocessed bran
½ cup vegetable oil
¾ cup honey
2 teaspoons vanilla
raisins or chopped dried
fruits

- Stir to blend oats, sugar, wheat germ, walnuts and bran.
- In a small pan, heat oil, honey and vanilla, stirring until boiling.
- Thoroughly mix liquids with dry ingredients.
- Divide between two greased 10 x 15-inch baking sheets and bake at 325° until brown.
- Add raisins or chopped fruits when cooled.

Start the morning in a healthy style.

29

Lavosh

3 ounces yeast
4½ cups warm water
6 tablespoons sugar
6 teaspoons salt
9 cups sifted flour, all purpose
2¼ cups olive oil

- Add yeast to water and let rise.
- Add oil. Reserve 3 tablespoons.
- Mix sugar, salt and flour and add to the liquid.
- Mix well and let sit until it doubles in size, approximately 1 hour.
- Place on floured board or bench. Divide into 4 pieces. Roll each to ⅛ to ¼-inch thick, or a little thinner if possible. Lift and place on an oiled cookie sheet. Brush top with oil or small amount of butter.
- At this point, put your favorite seasoning on lightly, (onion flakes, seasoning salt, fennel, red or green peppers, sesame seeds, poppy seeds, etc.). Cook in oven for approximately 20 minutes or until brown and crisp.

Bill Chambers, Executive Chef, Oaks Country Club

Tomato Basil Boules

4 Boules

1 **tablespoon dry yeast**
¼ **cup warm water**
3 **cups bread flour**
1 **teaspoon kosher salt**
1 **tablespoon honey**
2 **tablespoons olive oil**
¾ **cup marinara sauce**
1 **tablespoon fresh basil
  leaves, chopped**
1 **tablespoon cornmeal**

- Proof yeast and water 20 minutes until frothy.
- Mix all ingredients except basil in food processor or mixer fitted with dough hook. Mix slow at first, then aggressively until dough is homogeneous and cleans the sides of the bowl. Add basil and pulse or mix until incorporated. Set aside to rise in a greased bowl covered with a sheet of plastic. Refrigerate overnight, if time permits.
- Punch down. Roll into a log. Cut into four pieces. Let rest 5 minutes. Roll each piece into a smooth round ball. Flatten to look like a hamburger bun. Cut an "x" to score the top. Brush with milk or egg white. Place on wax paper sprinkled with 1 tablespoon cornmeal. Let rise in warm place until doubled.
- Bake in center of 350° to 375° oven until just lightly brown, about 35 minutes.

Chef Tim Fitzgerald

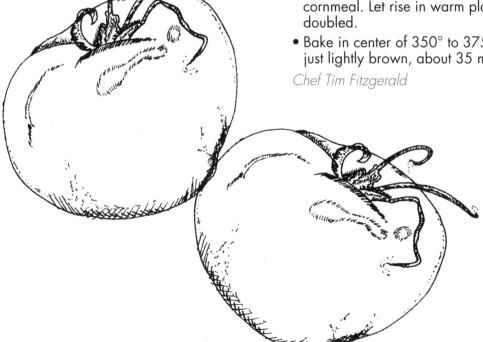

Sooner Savories

The City of Tulsa credits its founding to the Lockapoka Creek Indians who were relocated by the federal government's removal plan from the southeastern states to Oklahoma. On their long trip, the Lockapokas carried with them ashes from the sacred fire at tulsey, or old town, in Alabama. Under what has become a revered Tulsa landmark, the Council Oak Tree, the Lockapokas rekindled their ceremonial fire and established their new home in Indian Territory.

Remarkably resilient, the Creeks soon owned farms, cultivated crops and raised cattle, horses, hogs, poultry and sheep. In 1848, Lewis Perryman, a prominent Creek, established a cattle ranch and the first trading post near the Lockapoka settlement. Perryman's son, George, later opened a mail station to serve Tulsa at his family's store.

After the Civil War, the western sector of the Indian lands was ceded to the United States as unassigned lands or Oklahoma Territory. Townsites and 160-acre allotments became the goal of settlers. In 1889, Congress passed legislation authorizing the first opening which was a gigantic run on April 22, 1889. The first settler to reach an allotment on the unassigned lands could stake a claim and more than 50,000 participated. At the opening the "Boomers" were those who entered the territory at the "boom of the gun". The "Sooners" were the settlers who "jumped the gun" early. Between 1889 and 1906, land openings and runs brought colonization to over half of the State of Oklahoma.

As the complexion of the western half of the state underwent change, the eastern portion known as Indian Territory also changed. The government's plan to break up tribal land systems into individual allotments began with the Dawes Severalty Act in 1887.

The promise of land, coupled with the extension of the Frisco Railroad to the Arkansas River in the Creek nation, assured Tulsa a steady influx of settlers. The railroad, including the bridging of the Arkansas River in 1883, brought Tulsa to prominence, as ranchers from across the territory brought their herds to local stockyards for shipment to the Northeast.

The demand for statehood required joining Indian Territory and Oklahoma Territory. When put to a vote of the people in 1907, statehood passed and Oklahoma became the nation's 46th state.

Sooner
Savories

CHAT^au
LONGUEVILLE
Pauillac - Medoc

1990

Bordeaux

France

APPETIZERS & BEVERAGES
Our Way

Cheese and Spreads

Artichoke Quiche Nibblers 49
Avocado Mousse Ring 39
Baked Garlic with Sun-Dried Tomatoes 36
Baked Raspberry Brie 40
Bleu Cheesecake 41
Boursin Stuffed Endive 40
California Torta 37
Cheesy Chokes 50
Pecan Cheese Wreath 41

Finger Foods

Caramel Corn 53
Gougère 42
Guadalajara Black Bean Mexican Pizza 35
Marinated Green Golf Balls 48
Minted Fruit Kabobs 48
Spinach Crêpes Stuffed with Tomato-Pesto
    Cheese 38
Spinach Strudel 39
Summer Time Bruschetta 35
Sun-Dried Tomato and Cheese Bruschetta 36
Veggie Pizza 37
Zucchini Puffs 49

Meat and Seafood

Ceviche 45
Chalkboard Liver Pâté 42
Chicken Ham Pinwheels 43
Crab Cakes 46
Crabbies 47
Lemon Shrimp with Rosemary 45
Marmalade-Glazed Chicken Wings 44
Puffed Chicken Pockets 43
Satay 47
Shrimp Bundles 46

Salsa and Dips

Anaheim-Jalapeño Salsa 51
Bean Guacamole with Tortilla Chips 50
Black Bean Salsa 51
Green Tomato Relish 53
Humus Tahini 52
Italian Flag Dip 52
Jezebell Sauce 53
Salsa Fresca 52

Beverages

Banana Punch 54
Beach Bum Iced Tea 55
Civil War Egg Nog 54
Margaritas 54

Professional Chefs

Dungeness Crab Cakes 57
Festive Wine Punch 55
Guacamole 58
Herb Ravioli Pockets 56
Papaya Mango Relish 56
Salsa 59
Tapanada 58

Guadalajara Black Bean Mexican Pizza

Serves 2

- 1 15-ounce can black beans, drained and rinsed
- 3 tablespoons olive oil
- 2 tablespoons cilantro
- 1 teaspoon ground cumin
- 1 teaspoon Tabasco Sauce
- ½ teaspoon minced garlic
- 1 large Boboli pizza crust
- 1 cup shredded Monterey Jack cheese
- 1 cup shredded cheddar cheese
- 1 2¼-ounce can sliced ripe olives, drained
- ½ cup diced red bell pepper
- ¼ cup sliced green onions
- ½ cup sour cream
- ¼ cup taco sauce
- 1 cup thick and chunky salsa

- In a food processor combine beans, oil, cilantro, cumin, Tabasco and garlic. Process until smooth, scraping down sides of bowl.
- Heat oven to 425°. Place crust on lightly greased pizza pan.
- Spread bean mixture over crust. Sprinkle with cheeses, olives, pepper and onions.
- Bake for 8 to 12 minutes or until cheese is melted.
- In a small bowl, combine sour cream and taco sauce. Serve pizza with sour cream mixture and your favorite salsa.

Olé! Perfect after game snack.

Summer Time Bruschetta

Serves 6 to 8

- 18 thick slices crusty bread
- 2 tablespoons minced garlic
- ⅓ cup olive oil, reserve 1 tablespoon
- 2 tablespoons minced shallots
- 6 large, firm ripe tomatoes, peeled, seeded and chopped salt and pepper, to taste
- 1 teaspoon freshly squeezed lemon juice
- 1 cup fresh basil leaves, coarsely chopped

- Preheat the broiler. Arrange the slices of bread on a baking sheet and broil until lightly browned. Turn and brown other side.
- Combine the garlic and olive oil and brush the mixture on one side of browned bread slices.
- In a skillet, heat remaining 1 tablespoon olive oil over medium heat, add shallots, tomatoes, salt, pepper and lemon juice. Toss 1 to 2 minutes just until the tomatoes are warmed. Stir in basil.
- Top the bread slices with tomato mixture.

Perfect with a glass of wine on a summer evening.

Sun-Dried Tomato and Cheese Bruschetta

Serves 8

1 baguette, in ¼ inch slices
olive oil for bread slices
¼ pound goat cheese with herbs
¼ pound ricotta cheese
¼ pound mozzarella cheese, grated
1 large garlic clove, minced
pepper
1 8-ounce jar sun-dried tomatoes, drained

- Arrange sliced bread on cookie sheet, brush with olive oil and bake at 300° until brown, about 5 minutes.
- Blend cheeses with garlic and pepper with an electric mixer. Food processor grinds too finely.
- Place spoonful of cheese mixture on baguette slice, top with a sun-dried tomato and cover with another teaspoon of cheese.
- Bake at 350° until melted, approximately 7 to 10 minutes.

Baked Garlic with Sun-Dried Tomatoes

Serves 6

4 large garlic heads, unpeeled
2½ tablespoons butter, thinly sliced
¼ cup olive oil
2 cups chicken broth
2 cups sun-dried tomatoes
¾ tablespoon dried fines herbes
freshly ground pepper
6 ounces goat cheese, sliced
fresh basil leaves
1 large loaf Italian bread, sliced

- Slice ¼ inch off tops of garlic heads (opposite root end). Remove any loose outer papery skin. Place garlic with cut side up in medium baking dish. Arrange butter slices evenly over garlic. Drizzle with oil. Add 2 cups broth to dish.
- Arrange sun-dried tomatoes around garlic. Sprinkle with fines herbes and season with pepper.
- Bake in preheated 375° oven until garlic and tomatoes are tender. Baste with broth every 15 minutes. Add more broth if necessary to maintain some sauce in pan. Bake about 1 hour and 15 minutes.
- Arrange goat cheese on tomatoes. Bake about 10 minutes or until melted.
- Garnish with basil and serve on Italian bread.

To eat: Pierce a garlic clove, press to release from the skin and spread on the bread with melted cheese and sun-dried tomato mixture.

California Torta

Serves 10 to 12

- **2 8-ounce packages cream cheese, softened**
- **8 ounces goat cheese**
- **2 cloves garlic**
- **2 tablespoons olive oil**
- **2 teaspoons dried thyme leaves, crushed**
- **3 tablespoons pesto, well-drained**
- **⅓ cup roasted red peppers, drained and chopped**

- Line 1-quart soufflé dish or loaf pan with plastic wrap.
- Place cream cheese, goat cheese and garlic in food processor. Process until well blended.
- Add oil and thyme; blend well.
- Place one-third of cheese mixture in soufflé dish and cover with pesto. Layer one-third of cheese mixture and cover with red peppers. Top with remaining one-third cheese mixture. Cover with plastic wrap. Chill.
- Unmold. Smooth sides.
- Garnish with fresh herbs and additional red pepper if desired.
- Serve with assorted crackers.

Sun-dried tomatoes may be substituted for red peppers.

Use Fresh Pesto Sauce, page 198.

Veggie Pizza

3 dozen

- **2 packages crescent rolls**
- **1 8-ounce package cream cheese**
- **1 cup mayonnaise**
- **1 package ranch dressing mix**
- **10 strips bacon, cooked and crumbled**
- **1 cup shredded cheddar cheese**
- **1 cup chopped broccoli**
- **1 cup chopped cauliflower**
- **1 cup chopped green onions**
- **1 cup chopped olives**
- **1 cup chopped tomatoes**

- Lay out crescent rolls flat on greased cookie sheet. Pinch seams together. Bake according to package directions.
- Mix together cream cheese, mayonnaise and dressing mix. Spread on cooled crust.
- Top with remaining ingredients. Refrigerate. Cut in 2-inch squares and serve.

Low fat variation: Use low-fat mayonnaise, cream and cheddar cheeses with the ranch dressing mix. Use turkey bacon.

Spinach Crêpes Stuffed with Tomato-Pesto Cheese

6 dozen spirals

Crêpes

- **3 eggs**
- **1½ cups milk**
- **1 cup flour**
- **½ teaspoon salt**
- **½ teaspoons freshly ground pepper**
- **½ pound fresh spinach, cooked and chopped**
- **1 cup finely chopped scallions**
- **1 tablespoon vegetable oil**

- In a food processor, combine eggs, milk, flour, salt and ½ teaspoon of pepper. Process until well blended, about 1½ minutes. Pour the batter into large bowl and whisk in the spinach and scallions.
- Warm a 10-inch skillet over moderate heat and brush lightly with oil. Pour about ¼ cup of the batter into the hot pan, tilting to coat evenly with a thin layer of batter; pour out any excess. Cook until lightly browned on the bottom, about 2 minutes. Flip the crêpe and cook until brown spots begin to appear on the second side, 15 to 30 seconds longer. Remove the crêpe from the pan and let cool. Repeat with the remaining batter and oil to make 12 crêpes.

Cheese Filling

- **2 8-ounce packages cream cheese, at room temperature**
- **½ cup finely chopped fresh basil**
- **1 tablespoon vodka**
- **2 teaspoons grated lemon zest**
- **4 garlic cloves, minced**
- **1 teaspoon freshly ground pepper**
- **½ cup sun-dried tomatoes, drained and finely chopped**
- **½ cup toasted pine nuts**

- In a medium bowl, stir together the cream cheese, basil, vodka, lemon zest, garlic and pepper.
- Lay the crêpes, spotted-side up, on a flat surface and spread each with about 2 tablespoons of cream cheese-basil mixture.
- Sprinkle each with sun-dried tomatoes and pine nuts.
- Roll the crêpes tightly and wrap in plastic wrap. Refrigerate for at least one hour.

The recipe can be prepared to this point up to 1 day ahead. Refrigerate until ready to slice.

- When ready to serve, trim the ends of each crêpe roll. Cut on the diagonal into 6 slices. Serve at room temperature or slightly chilled.

Well worth the time—beautiful, elegant, delicious and easy to prepare ahead of time.

Spinach Strudel

2 strudels

- 2 10-ounce packages frozen spinach, thawed and squeezed dry
- 1 8-ounce package cream cheese
- 1 cup feta cheese, crumbled and drained
- ¼ cup chopped parsley
- ½ cup chopped green onions
- 2 eggs, slightly beaten
- ¼ tablespoon fresh dill weed ground pepper
- ¼ cup freshly grated Parmesan cheese
- 8 sheets phyllo dough, thawed
- 2 tablespoons butter, melted

- For spinach filling, combine all ingredients except dough and butter. Set aside.
- Unroll phyllo dough. Grease cookie sheet.
- Layer 4 sheets of dough on pan brushing each sheet with butter. Don't worry about rips in dough.
- Spoon half of spinach filling down long edge, and roll jelly-roll fashion.
- Cut ½ way through in 1-inch slices. Drizzle with melted butter.
- Repeat process with remaining phyllo dough and spinach filling.
- Bake in preheated 400° oven 20 to 30 minutes.

Delicious! Freezes well. Just heat 5 minutes in hot oven to serve.

Avocado Mousse Ring

Serves 8

- 2 envelopes unflavored gelatin
- ¼ cup cold water
- ¼ cup chicken broth
- 3 to 4 ripe avocados
- 1 tablespoon grated onion
- 2 teaspoon Worcestershire sauce
- ¼ cup mayonnaise horseradish or Tabasco Sauce to taste
- ¼ cup whipping cream, slightly whipped

- Oil a ring mold. Soak gelatin in cold water five minutes. Add boiling chicken broth and stir until dissolved.
- Peel and quarter avocados, mash with fork. Add gelatin liquid, onion and Worcestershire. Cool mixture. Fold in mayonnaise, horseradish or Tabasco and slightly whipped cream. Pour into prepared mold and chill.

This is good served with shrimp mixed with a dressing of four parts mayonnaise to one part cocktail sauce. Unmold avocado mousse and put shrimp mixture in center. Garnish mousse with minced parsley. Serve as an appetizer before dinner on small plates.

This is wonderful at Christmas time with champagne cocktails.

Boursin Stuffed Endive

20 endive leaves

- 2 **6-ounce wheels Boursin cheese**
- 1 **8-ounce package cream cheese**
- 1 **tablespoon cracked pepper**
- 1 **shredded carrot**
- 1 **green pepper, chopped**
- 1 **bunch chopped scallion greens**
- 2 **heads Belgium endive, trimmed washed and separated**
  capers, red peppers and parsley

- Place cheeses and cracked pepper in food processor and process until smooth. Add carrot, green pepper and scallions and pulse until coarse.
- Place mixture in a pastry tube fitted with large fluted opening and pipe mixture attractively onto endive leaves.
- Garnish with capers, red peppers and parsley.

May add crab to mixture for variation.

Baked Raspberry Brie

Serves 10 to 12

- 1 **sheet frozen puff pastry**
- 1 **8-ounce round Brie cheese**
  raspberry preserves
- 1 **large egg, lightly beaten**

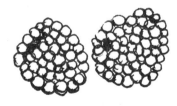

- On a lightly floured surface, roll out pastry sheet to ⅛-inch thickness. Cut in half. Using Brie as a guide, cut out one round the size of the Brie. With cookie cutters, cut out decorations from trimmings. Set aside.
- Transfer remaining half of pastry to a shallow baking pan. Spread pastry with a thin layer of raspberry preserves. Place Brie round on pastry. Without stretching pastry, wrap up over Brie and trim excess to leave a one-inch border on top of Brie. Brush border with some egg.
- Use reserved pastry round to top the Brie, press edges firmly to seal. Brush top of pastry with remaining egg and arrange cut outs decoratively. Lightly brush tops only of cut outs with egg.
- Bake in preheated 375° oven 20 minutes or until golden brown.

Serve with water crackers and seedless grapes.

Bleu Cheesecake

Serves 16 to 20

¾ **cup cracker crumbs, wheat thins or buttery crackers**
2 **tablespoons melted butter**
2 **8-ounce packages cream cheese, softened to room temperature**
10 **ounces bleu cheese**
1 **cup sour cream**
3 **eggs**
⅛ **teaspoon freshly ground pepper**
¼ **cup sherry**
⅓ **cup milk**

- Combine cracker crumbs and melted butter and press into the bottom of an 8-inch springform pan. Bake 5 to 8 minutes or until very lightly browned.
- Mix remaining ingredients in food processor. Pour mixture into crust in springform pan. Wrap bottom and sides of pan in a double thickness of aluminum foil and then place inside a larger pan, adding enough hot water to the larger pan to come halfway up the sides of the springform pan.
- Bake in preheated 350° oven 50 to 55 minutes. Do not overbake or brown. The cheesecake is done when a knife inserted in the middle comes out clean.
- Chill and serve.

Serve with bagel chips, thin slices of French bread or apple slices. May use non-fat dairy products with the same results.

Pecan Cheese Wreath

Serves 12

1 **pound extra sharp cheddar cheese, shredded**
1 **pound Colby and Monterey Jack cheeses, shredded**
1 **small onion, grated**
1 **cup mayonnaise**
1 **teaspoon red pepper**
1 **cup chopped pecans**
1 **jar strawberry preserves parsley sprigs**

- Combine cheeses, onion, mayonnaise and red pepper. Mix well. Sprinkle about ¼ cup pecans in a oiled ring mold, and press cheese mixture into mold. Chill until firm.
- Unmold on platter and pat remaining pecans onto cheese ring.
- Serve cheese ring with preserves in center, surrounded by crackers. Garnish with parsley.

A unique holiday first course.

Gougère

Serves 6 to 8

- **1 cup water**
- **6 tablespoons butter**
- **1 teaspoon salt**
- **⅛ teaspoon pepper**
- **1 cup flour**
- **4 eggs**
- **1 cup finely diced Gruyère cheese**

- Heat water, butter, salt and pepper in saucepan until butter melts and mixture comes to a boil.
- Add flour all at once. Stir until ball forms, about 1 minute.
- Remove pan from heat and beat in eggs, 1 at a time. Blend each egg completely before adding next egg.
- Stir in Gruyère, minus 2 tablespoons.
- Place rounded teaspoons of dough in an 8 to 9-inch circle on lightly greased cookie sheet. They should be lightly touching.
- Sprinkle reserved 2 tablespoons cheese on top.
- Bake in preheated 425° oven 30 to 35 minutes until golden brown and puffy.

Wonderful as an appetizer served with wine. Also great served with luncheon soup or salad.

Chalkboard Liver Pâté

1 cup

- **½ pound chicken livers**
- **1 teaspoon salt**
- **pinch cayenne**
- **½ cup butter**
- **¼ tablespoon nutmeg**
- **1 teaspoon dry mustard**
- **2 tablespoons finely minced onion**
- **1 teaspoon garlic powder**

- Cover chicken livers with water and bring to a boil.
- Simmer 15 to 20 minutes.
- Drain and process in blender until smooth.
- Add remaining ingredients and blend.
- Pack in crock and chill.

Serve with bread, crackers, sweet gherkins and onion on the side.

Chicken Ham Pinwheels

24 slices

2 chicken breasts, skinned and boned
⅛ teaspoon dried basil, crushed
dash of pepper
dash of garlic salt
3 thin slices cooked ham
2 teaspoons freshly squeezed lemon juice
dash paprika

- Place chicken breasts skinned side down on board and pound to ¼ inch thickness. Combine basil, pepper and garlic salt. Sprinkle on chicken.
- Place 1½ slices ham on each chicken breast to cover. Roll up lengthwise with ham inside.
- Place both rolls, seam side down, in 2-quart baking dish. Drizzle with lemon juice and sprinkle with paprika.
- Bake in 350° oven 35 to 40 minutes or until chicken is tender. Chill and cut into ¼ inch slices.

Puffed Chicken Pockets

18 pieces

6 ounces cream cheese
6 tablespoons butter, melted
4 cups chicken, cooked and cubed
½ teaspoon salt
¼ teaspoon freshly ground pepper
4 tablespoons milk
2 tablespoons chopped pimento
1 to 2 tablespoons fresh dill, chopped
1 box frozen puff pastry, thawed
1½ cups bread crumbs

- Blend cream cheese and 4 tablespoons butter. Add chicken, salt, pepper, milk, pimiento and dill.
- Roll out each sheet of puff pastry to yield nine 3-inch squares. (One box of 2 sheets will yield 18 dough squares.)
- Place 1 to 2 tablespoons of chicken mixture in center of each square and pinch opposing sides together at center.
- Baste with remaining butter. Roll in bread crumbs. Bake in 350° oven 35 minutes, or until squares are puffed and brown. Serve hot.

These chicken squares can be made ahead and stored unbaked frozen. Do not need to thaw before baking.

Marmalade-Glazed Chicken Wings

Serves 8 to 10

3 pounds chicken wings
½ cup Tequila
½ cup chopped cilantro
½ cup lime or lemon marmalade, divided
¼ cup olive oil
4 tablespoons freshly squeezed lime juice, divided
1 tablespoon coarsely ground pepper
2 medium cloves garlic, minced
2 teaspoons Tabasco Sauce
1 teaspoon salt
1½ teaspoons grated lime zest, divided
2 limes, cut into wedges sprigs of fresh cilantro

- Cut each chicken wing into 3 parts, discarding tip portions. Rinse chicken and pat dry. Place in shallow dish.
- Combine Tequila, cilantro, ¼ cup marmalade, olive oil, 2 tablespoons lime juice, pepper, garlic, Tabasco, salt and ½ teaspoon lime zest. Mix well and pour over chicken. Cover and marinate overnight, turning occasionally.
- Drain chicken, reserving marinade. Arrange chicken in large shallow baking dish. Bake in preheated 350° oven 30 minutes, turning after 15 minutes.
- Strain reserved marinade into saucepan. Cook 5 minutes or until reduced by half, stirring occasionally. Add remaining ¼ cup marmalade, remaining 2 tablespoons lemon juice and remaining 1 teaspoon lime zest. Boil for 1 minute.
- Brush over chicken. Broil in preheated oven until crisp and brown, turning and basting with marinade several times. Place on serving platter with lime wedges and cilantro sprigs.

This can be prepared ahead of time and reheated in 300° oven. A good party dish.

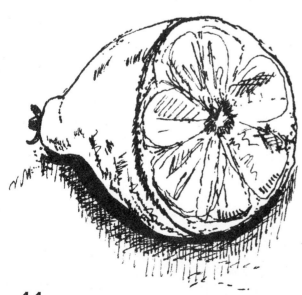

Ceviche

Serves 8

1 pound small scallops, fresh
1 cup freshly squeezed lime
  juice
1 large white onion, chopped
2 medium tomatoes, chopped
30 stuffed Spanish olives
20 capers
⅛ teaspoon cumin
¼ cup olive oil
  salt and pepper to taste
  dash Tabasco Sauce
1 tablespoon parsley, chopped
1 teaspoon oregano

- Place fish in a glass bowl. Cover with lime juice and marinate 4 or 5 hours in the refrigerator. Drain in colander, then blot off excess juice.
- Combine all remaining ingredients and the scallops in a glass bowl. Mix well. Cover and refrigerate until cold.

Small bay scallops work well for this, the pieces should be approximately "dime-sized". If pieces are too large, kitchen shears make nice clean cuts.

Serve as a first course on Bibb or red leaf lettuce, or with cocktail plates and forks. It is easy and looks pretty, especially in the summer heat when nobody really wants to turn on a stove.

Lemon Shrimp with Rosemary

Serves 4

¼ cup dry white wine
2 tablespoons fresh rosemary
  leaves or 1 tablespoon dried
2 cloves garlic, minced
2 tablespoons freshly squeezed
  lemon juice
  salt and pepper to taste
⅓ cup olive oil
1 pound medium shrimp,
  peeled and deveined
  fresh lemon wedges
  fresh rosemary sprigs

- In small bowl, mix wine, rosemary, garlic, lemon juice, salt and pepper. Set aside.
- In large skillet, heat oil over high heat. Add shrimp and stir until shrimp turns pink, about 3 minutes. Remove from heat and add rosemary mixture.
- Transfer shrimp mixture to shallow dish and marinate in refrigerator for at least one hour.
- Serve on a platter with fresh lemon wedges and rosemary.

Shrimp Bundles

20 to 22 bundles

8 **ounces medium shrimp in shells**
green onion tops
1 **tablespoon Dijon mustard**
2 **tablespoons white wine**
1 **tablespoon Worcestershire sauce**
20 to 22 **small mushroom caps**

- Peel and devein shrimp, leaving tails intact. Butterfly the shrimp by cutting to, but not through, the other side.
- Place onion tops in boiling water for 1 minute, remove and cool. Cut into thin strips 8 to 10 inches long. Set aside
- Mix mustard, wine and Worcestershire until blended.
- For each bundle, lay one shrimp butterflied side down over mushroom cap stem side down. Tie onion strip around bundle to secure shrimp. Brush bottom sides of bundle with mustard mixture. Place in a 12 x 7-inch baking dish. Brush tops with mustard mixture. Cover and refrigerate 2 hours.
- Place bundles on broiler pan. Broil 4 to 5 minutes or until shrimp are just cooked. Serve hot.

These look so impressive on your buffet table. To save time, buy the shrimp already shelled and deveined. The seafood shop will even butterfly them!

Crab Cakes

Serves 4

1 **pound lump crab meat**
1 **teaspoon parsley**
1 **teaspoon salt**
½ **teaspoon pepper**
1 **heaping teaspoon prepared mustard**
2 **tablespoons mayonnaise**
1 **egg**
3 **slices bread, crumbled**

- Remove any shells from crab meat and put meat into large bowl. Add all other ingredients and mix lightly so as not to break up lumps.
- Form into 4 cakes. Bread or cracker crumbs may be used as coating but are not necessary. If crumbs are used, Old Bay Seasoning can be added to taste.
- Fry cakes in butter. When one side is brown, turn and brown the other side.

These are delicious, and when eaten, you know they are crab cakes.

Crabbies

48 wedges

1 6-ounce package frozen crab meat
1 6-ounce jar Old English cheese spread
½ cup butter
1 teaspoon Worcestershire sauce
6 English muffins, fork split

- Combine all ingredients and blend well.
- Spread mix on half of each English muffin.
- Freeze on cookie sheet 30 minutes.
- Cut each half into quarters and bake 10 minutes at 400° or until lightly browned.

Freezes well.

Satay

Serves 6

1 pound lean pork, chicken or shrimps, cut in 1-inch cubes
2 cloves garlic, minced
lemon grass
4 tablespoons roasted sesame seeds
2 tablespoons soy sauce
2 tablespoons sugar
½ teaspoon salt and pepper to taste
4 tablespoons sesame oil
2 tablespoons melted butter

- Combine ingredients and marinate for 30 minutes. Thread a few pieces of chicken, shrimp or pork on top half of each satay stick or skewer. Broil in oven or over charcoal. Baste with marinade while broiling.

Peanut Sauce

1 cup coconut milk
4 tablespoons peanut butter
2 tablespoons brown sugar
1 teaspoon salt
2 tablespoons freshly squeezed lemon juice

- Combine coconut milk and peanut butter, and bring slowly to a boil.
- Add sugar, salt and lemon juice. Stir well.
- Pour over or dip each satay before serving.

This sauce should have a salty, sweet, and slightly sour taste. Chicken satay makes an excellent appetizer.

Minted Fruit Kabobs

16 kabobs

1 20-ounce can pineapple chunks, juice pack
⅓ cup honey
2 tablespoons orange liqueur
1 tablespoon freshly squeezed lemon juice
2 teaspoons snipped fresh mint
2 medium red apples, cut into bite-sized pieces
3 cups whole strawberries
1 6-ounce package dried apricot halves

- Drain pineapple, reserving ½ cup juice. Set aside. In a 9 x 13-inch baking dish combine reserved pineapple juice, honey, orange liqueur, lemon juice, and mint. Stir until well combined.
- Thread an apple cube, pineapple chunk, whole strawberry, and apricot half onto each of sixteen 6 inch wooden skewers. Arrange skewers in the baking dish. Brush generously with pineapple juice mixture.
- Cover and refrigerate 2 hours, brushing and turning occasionally.
- Transfer skewers to a serving platter and garnish with whole mint leaves.

Easy and very tasty served anytime of year!

Marinated Green Golf Balls

Serves 6

1 10-ounce package Brussels sprouts
½ cup Italian dressing
1 teaspoon dill weed
1 teaspoon garlic powder
toothpicks for serving

- Cook Brussels sprouts until done but not soft. Immediately drain.
- Combine remaining ingredients. Add sprouts and marinate in the refrigerator at least 12 hours.

Have plenty of toothpicks ready for the "noshing".

Don't tell Brussels sprout "haters" what these really are. These will surprise you!

Zucchini Puffs

36 slices

2 large zucchini
⅓ cup mayonnaise
⅓ cup freshly grated Parmesan cheese
1 teaspoon basil

- Cut zucchini into ¼-inch thick slices.
- Combine mayonnaise, cheese and basil.
- Top zucchini with mixture. Broil until bubbly and golden.

Artichoke Quiche Nibblers

12 squares

3 6-ounce jars marinated artichoke hearts
1 clove garlic, crushed
½ cup chopped onion
4 eggs
¼ cup seasoned bread crumbs
8 ounces sharp cheddar cheese, grated
1 tablespoon minced fresh parsley
⅛ teaspoon dried oregano
¼ teaspoon salt
⅛ teaspoon pepper
⅛ teaspoon Tabasco Sauce
watercress or parsley sprigs

- Drain marinade from 1 jar of artichoke hearts into a skillet and gently heat. Sauté garlic and onion in oil for 5 minutes and set aside.
- Drain and discard marinade from remaining jars of artichoke hearts. Chop all hearts finely and set aside.
- Beat eggs until foamy and blend in bread crumbs, cheese, parsley, oregano, salt, pepper and Tabasco Sauce.
- Add the finely chopped artichoke to egg mixture and gently stir. Add onion and garlic.
- Mix well and spoon into a greased 9 x 9-inch pan. Bake in a preheated 325° oven for 30 minutes. Cool well before cutting into 2-inch squares.
- Before serving, place in a 325° oven 10 to 12 minutes, then place on a warmed serving plate garnished with watercress or parsley sprigs.

Cheesy Chokes

48 wedges

1 13-ounce can artichoke hearts, drained and chopped
1 4-ounce can chopped green chilies
1 cup freshly grated Parmesan cheese
1 cup mayonnaise
¼ cup Dijon mustard
6 English muffins

- Combine artichokes, chilies, Parmesan, mayonnaise, and mustard. (Mixture may be prepared to this point up to several days ahead and refrigerated.)
- When ready to serve, preheat oven to 350°. Split English muffins and spread mixture on each half.
- Bake for 30 minutes until browned. Cut each half into quarters to serve as bite-sized pieces.

Muffin halves may be served whole as a luncheon entrée.

Bean Guacamole with Tortilla Chips

1 cup

1 cup dried white beans, soaked in water to cover overnight or 2 cups cooked beans
1 to 2 large cloves garlic, minced salt and freshly ground pepper
1½ tablespoons freshly squeezed lime juice
2 tablespoons chicken broth or water
2 tablespoons extra-virgin olive oil, divided
1 to 2 fresh jalapeño peppers, cored, seeded and minced
2 scallions, minced
¼ cup finely chopped cilantro, plus several sprigs for garnish
1 pound package corn tortillas

- Boil the soaked beans for 20 minutes or until tender. Puree the beans, garlic, salt and pepper in a food processor, adding lime juice and enough broth or water to obtain a smooth, thick puree. Add 1½ tablespoons oil.
- Stir in the peppers, scallions and cilantro. (It is best to do this by hand. If you use a food processor, the dip will turn green.) Garnish with sprigs of cilantro.
- Lightly brush tortillas on both sides with olive oil. Cut each tortilla into 6 wedges. Arrange the wedges on a baking sheet and bake in preheated 350° oven 10 to 15 minutes, or until crisp, turning once. Let cool on a wire rack.
- Serve the chips on the side for dipping.

Olé!

Black Bean Salsa

6 cups

- 2 15-ounce cans black beans
- 2 cups chopped fresh tomatoes
- 1 15-ounce can white corn
- 1 2¼-ounce can sliced black olives
- 2 bunches green onions, tops only, and chopped
- 1 bunch cilantro
- 1 4-ounce can chopped green chilies
  juice of 2 lemons
  juice of 2 limes
- ¼ cup olive oil
  garlic salt to taste
  fresh jalapeño peppers to taste, chopped

- Drain ingredients well and combine.

This is good on any tortilla chip or served with grilled meats.

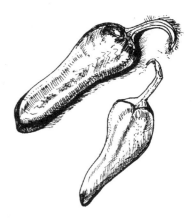

Anaheim-Jalapeño Salsa

3 cups

- 1 pound Roma tomatoes, seeded and chopped
- 1 bunch green onions, sliced
- 1 Anaheim pepper, seeded and chopped
- 1 jalapeño pepper, seeded and chopped
- 1 clove garlic, minced
- 2 tablespoons chopped fresh cilantro
- ⅛ teaspoon salt
- 4 tablespoons freshly squeezed lime juice

- Combine vegetables and sprinkle with salt and lime juice.
- Refrigerate.

Serve with tortilla chips. Also good as a topping on baked potatoes or grilled chicken breasts! Want it hotter? Just add more jalapeño peppers! Yes, it is worth all that time you spent chopping!

Salsa Fresca

6 cups

3 cups diced firm ripe tomatoes
1 cup diced yellow onion
⅓ cup chopped cilantro
1 cup crushed canned tomatoes
1 cup whole peeled canned tomatoes, chopped
¼ cup chopped green chilies
1 teaspoon granulated garlic
1 teaspoon salt
⅓ cup chopped jalapeño peppers, or to taste

- Mix all ingredients and chill.

Humus Tahini

2 cups

2 15-ounce cans garbanzo beans, drained, reserving ¼ cup liquid
2 large cloves garlic, sliced
1 teaspoon salt
2 tablespoons Tahini, sesame seed paste
1 cup freshly squeezed lemon juice

- Place beans, garlic, salt and Tahini in food processor. Add reserved liquid and half of lemon juice. Blend until smooth, adding lemon juice as needed for taste, and water in small amounts if needed for smooth consistency.
- Serve with carrots, celery, broccoli, cauliflower, chips or crackers.

Italian Flag Dip

2 cups

16 ounces sour cream
1½ packages dry Italian dressing mix
2 tablespoons freshly squeezed lemon juice
1 tablespoon mayonnaise
1 tomato, chopped
1 avocado, chopped

- Combine sour cream, dressing mix, lemon juice and mayonnaise. Stir well.
- Fold in tomato and avocado.
- Chill and serve with chips.

Jezebell Sauce

5 cups

1 18-ounce jar of apple jelly
1 18-ounce jar of apricot preserves
1 5-ounce jar of horseradish, drained
1 ounce dry mustard

- Mix together and place in jars. Refrigerate.
- Serve over a block of cream cheese with crackers.

This is an easy and quick hostess gift or Christmas present!

Green Tomato Relish

12 pints

1½ gallons green tomatoes, quartered
1 quart onions, cut in 6ths
1 cup fresh hot peppers
1 quart bell peppers, cut in 6ths
8 cups sugar
¼ cup plain (not iodized) salt
1 quart vinegar

- Place all ingredients in a non-aluminum pan. Simmer until onions are clear. Do not boil. Put into clean, hot jars, and seal with hot lids.

Great with meat loaf. Makes a good gift.

Caramel Corn

5½ quarts

2 cups light brown sugar
1½ cups butter
½ cup white corn syrup
1 teaspoon salt
½ teaspoon soda
5 quarts popped corn
2 cups dry roasted peanuts

- Bring sugar, butter, syrup and salt to a boil. Boil five minutes.
- Add soda and stir.
- Pour over popped corn and peanuts. Mix well.
- Place mixture on cookie sheets. Bake in 250° oven 1 hour, stirring every 15 minutes.
- Store in plastic bags or metal tins.

Civil War Egg Nog

2 quarts

3 **cups sugar**
12 **eggs, separated**
Southern Comfort whiskey
1 **quart whipping cream**

- Beat sugar and egg yolks until mixture looks like mayonnaise.
- Drip whiskey slowly into sugar mixture to your own taste.
- Whip 1 quart whipping cream
- Beat 6 egg whites until stiff. Fold cream and egg whites into sugar mixture. If too thick, add milk.

As a family tradition Dad made this on Christmas. Today his grandsons make the egg nog, their dad makes the omelets and Mother makes the biscuits.

Banana Punch

25 servings

5 **cups sugar**
4 **cups water**
5 **bananas**
2½ **cups fresh orange juice**
juice of 2 lemons
4 **6-ounce cans unsweetened pineapple juice, not frozen**
4 **32-ounce lemon-lime sodas or gingerale**

- Boil 5 cups sugar and 4 cups water for the syrup. Cool.
- Process bananas in blender. Mix with orange juice, lemon juice, and pineapple juice and add to syrup.
- Freeze in molds. When ready to serve, unmold into punch bowl.
- Pour soda or gingerale over and serve.

Best made two days ahead! Punch is a yellow color.

Margaritas

6 servings

1 **6-ounce can limeade concentrate**
6 **ounces water**
3 **ounces Triple Sec**
9 **ounces Tequila**
2 **ounces orange juice**
salt for glasses

- Combine all ingredients thoroughly and serve in salt-rimmed glasses over ice.

Measure ingredients in empty limeade can.

Beach Bum Iced Tea

10 servings

10 cups water
3 oranges
2 lemons
6 tea bags, plain or herbal
¾ cup sugar
   mint leaves

- Bring water to rolling boil.
- Squeeze oranges and lemons, reserving rinds. Set juice aside.
- Add rinds and tea bags to boiling water. Let steep 1 hour.
- Remove rinds and tea bags and add juices and sugar.
- Serve over ice with fresh mint leaves in a 5-quart pitcher.

Festive Wine Punch

12 servings

2 bottles Kabinett German Wine (see note), chilled
1 bottle dry sparkling wine (Cordoniu Brut Classico, Ferrari Brut or Piper Sonoma)
1 jigger Cointreau or brandy
   mint leaves
   lemon slices

- Prepare an ice ring mold the night before with mint leaves and lemon slices suspended inside. The rest is easy to assemble.

Note: Kabinett Designation is the first of a series of ripeness selections in German wine vocabulary (ex., Graff Urzinger Riesling or Wehlener Riesling). Consult your wine merchant.

Chef Tim Fitzgerald

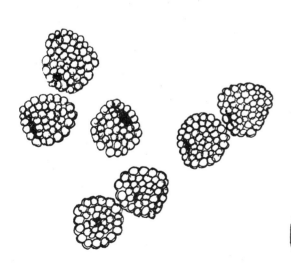

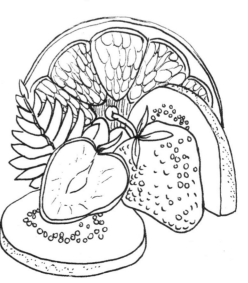

Papaya Mango Relish

Serves 6 to 8

- 1 **cucumber, peeled, seeded and diced**
- 2 **tomatoes, peeled, seeded and diced**
- 1 **papaya, diced**
- 1 **mango, diced**
- 1 **red pepper, diced**
- 1 **green pepper, diced**
- 2 **tablespoons extra virgin olive oil**
- 1 **tablespoon fresh dill, chopped**
- ½ **bunch mint, chopped**
  salt and white pepper to taste

- Add oil, dill, mint, salt and pepper to diced ingredients.
- Let marinate 24 hours before serving.

Serve on or with grilled, baked, or broiled fish, pork chops or chicken breasts.

Chef Cindy Payne, Summit Tower

Herb Ravioli Pockets

Serves 6

- 1 **package wonton wrappers (purchased at store)**
- 1 **8-ounce package Feta cheese**
- 2 **cloves garlic, minced**
  fresh dill
- 4 **ounces walnut oil**
- 1 **cup canned or fresh diced tomatoes**
- 1 **ounce fresh cilantro**

- Take wonton wrapper and place 1 teaspoon Feta cheese, pinch garlic, and sprig of dill moistened on all four sides with water. Place other wrapper on top and press to make it seal. Fold all four sides to tighten the seal. Freeze for 5 minutes.
- Poach in boiling salted water for 5 to 6 minutes.
- For sauce, simmer garlic, diced tomatoes, and walnut oil. Season with salt and pepper. Add chopped fresh cilantro.
- Top ravioli with sauce.

Chef Robert Kennedy, Southern Hills Country Club

Dungeness Crab Cakes

6 cakes, 4 ounces each

- 1 **cup diced yellow onion**
- ½ **cup diced red bell pepper**
- ½ **cup mayonnaise**
- 1 **tablespoon Dijon mustard**
- ¼ **tablespoon Worcestershire sauce**
- ¼ **tablespoon Old Bay seasoning**
- 1½ **teaspoons sherry**
- 2½ **cups dried bread crumbs**
- 1¼ **pounds Dungeness Crab Meat**
   olive oil

- Mix all ingredients well, except for the bread crumbs, crab and oil.
- Gently fold in the crab, taking care not to break up the delicate chunks of meat.
- Portion into 4-ounce cakes.
- Dredge lightly into dried bread crumbs to coat.
- Sauté in olive oil until crispy and golden brown on both sides.
- Serve with a side of Galiant Sauce to accompany the crab cake.

Galiant Sauce

- 5 **ounces sour cream**
- 3 **ounces mayonnaise**
- ½ **ounce horseradish**
- ½ **ounce whole grain mustard**
- ½ **ounce Spanish capers**
- ½ **teaspoon thyme**
- ½ **teaspoon basil**
- ½ **teaspoon oregano**

- Mix all ingredients well and refrigerate overnight to let all flavors blend. Stir before serving.

Chef Neil McCarley, Bodean Seafood Restaurant

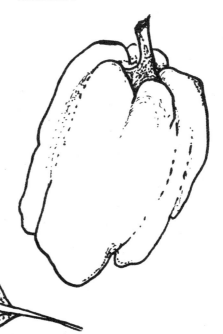

57

Tapanada

Serves 12

- 1 3 pound 7-ounce can pitted, ripe black olives
- 6 ounces Caesar salad dressing
- 4 tablespoons Dijon mustard
- ½ red or purple onion, chopped
- 4 ounces whole, tiny capers
- 1 pound button mushrooms, chopped
- 2 ounces Parmesan cheese
     juice of 2 lemons

- Dice or coarsely grind olives. Combine all ingredients in a large bowl and add olives. Mix thoroughly and chill.
- Serve on garlic rounds or French/Italian thin-cut bread. Garnish platter with sliced Roma tomatoes.

Buzz Dalesandro, Dalesandro's Restaurant

Guacamole

Serves 10

- 6 ripe avocados
- 1½ teaspoons minced or grated onion
- ½ teaspoon garlic salt
- ½ teaspoon white pepper
- ½ lemon, juiced
- ½ teaspoon salt
- 1 teaspoon vegetable oil
- 1 teaspoon sour cream
- ½ tomato, chopped

- Combine all ingredients and mash with potato-type masher.

Enrique Villanueva, Casa Laredo Mexican Restaurant

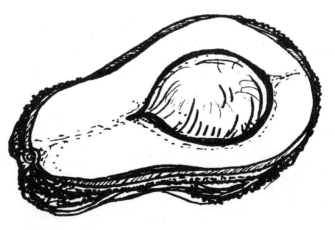

Salsa

4 quarts

- **6 cloves garlic, peeled and chopped**
- **⅛ cup cilantro, chopped**
- **3 jalapeño peppers, seeded and chopped**
- **1 bunch green onions, chopped**
- **1½ cups diced green chiles**
- **½ tablespoon crushed red pepper**
- **3 pounds plus 3 ounces canned tomatoes, crushed**
- **1 tablespoon cumin salt and pepper to taste**
- **3 pounds fresh tomatoes, chopped**

• Combine all ingredients and chill.

Laura K. Shaw, Cafe Olé

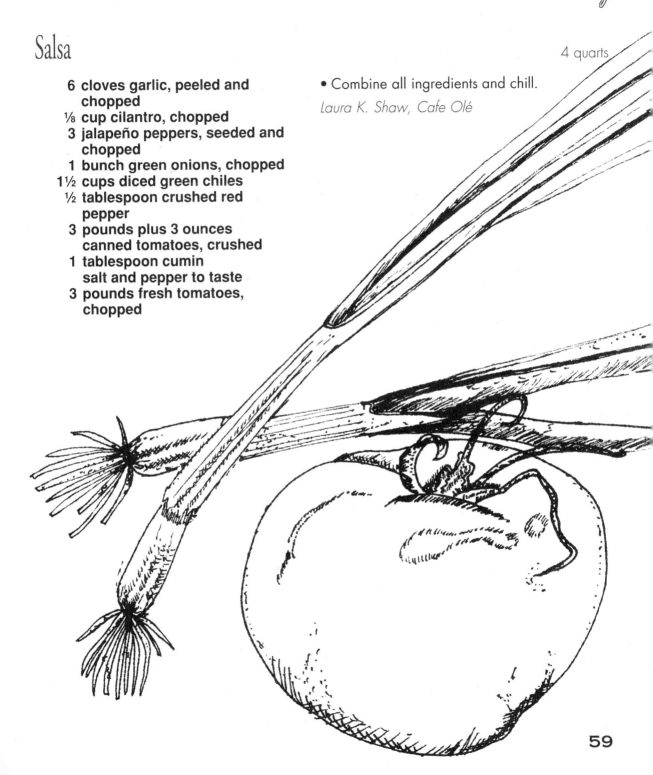

Black Gold Beginnings

Although many industries developed and prospered in Oklahoma, one has dominated the state's history since 1854 when the Chickasaw Indians discovered oil seeps on their land in Tishomingo.

Because of its use as a food preservative, salt became a prized commodity to life in Indian Territory. In 1859, a well drilled by the Chouteau Indians to enhance the harvesting of salt instead produced ten barrels of oil per day.

The Chickasaw, Choctaw and Cherokee Nations had a large part in developing the oil industry in 1865 by assigning rights for oil exploration on their land. In 1896, the Osage Nation granted one oil and gas lease for the entire reservation. Income from oil production later established the Osage as the wealthiest tribe in the United States.

The complexion of Tulsa was altered forever when Oklahoma's commercial oil well, the Nellie Johnstone Number One located 60 miles north of the city, was discovered on April 15, 1897. Drillers, investors and corporations poured into the area. Wildcatters found oil at Red Fork in 1901 setting off an oil boom. In 1905, the "fog of gas and the smell of oil" at Red Fork led a young entrepreneur to drill further south on a farm allotted to Ida Glenn, a Creek Indian. Although the selection of a site was "without benefit of geological clergy", it became the world's largest strike. The discovery caused oil prices to plummet worldwide and made Oklahoma and Indian Territories the center of oil exploration and speculation.

When Oklahoma became a state in 1907, Glenn Pool was producing more than 100,000 barrels per day. It was about this time when the term "black gold" was accepted in reference to oil which was akin to gold in value. Tulsa had a population of 7,298. By 1920, the population of Tulsa had exploded to 72,000. The men who made and lost fortunes in the oil business during this era became known as the greatest gamblers of all time.

Black Gold
Beginnings

Cold Soups

Chilled Zucchini Bisque 68
Garden Fresh Gazpacho 73
Island Cantaloupe Soup 64
Mother's Day Strawberry Orange Soup 63

Hot Soups

Almond Soup 63
Crab and Corn Chowder 71
Curried Butternut Squash Soup 67
Elegant Leek and Gruyère Soup 68
Holiday Shrimp Bisque 72
Louisiana Shrimp Gumbo 71
Perfect Chicken Stock 65
Roasted Eggplant Soup with Basil 66
Roasted Red Pepper Soup 66
Tipsy Tomato Soup 65
Viva Tomato Soup 64

Hearty Soups

Beef Barley Mushroom Soup 78
Country Vegetable Soup 69
English Pub Cheese Soup 76
Fiesta Vegetable Soup 76
Marvelous Minestrone 70
Portuguese Bean Soup 79
Pozole 77
Santa Fe Taco Soup 74
Sirloin Steak and Winter Vegetable Soup 78
Spicy Tortilla Soup 75
Time-Saver Turkey Chowder 79

Chili

Chasen's Chili 80
Howling Jalapeño Chili 81
Hunting Camp Chili 83
Turkey Picadillo Chili 82
White Chili 80
Widowmaker Chili 84

Professional Chefs

New England Clam Chowder 85
Pan Roasted Shrimp Bisque 86
St. Michael's Alley White Chili 87
Tortilla Soup 87

Mother's Day Strawberry Orange Soup

Serves 6

- **1 pint strawberries, hulled**
  juice of one orange
- **1½ tablespoons Grand Marnier**
- **3 tablespoons honey**
- **1 teaspoon powdered sugar**
- **1 cup plain yogurt or sour**
  cream
- **5½ ounces peach nectar**
- **⅓ cup half and half**
- **1 teaspoon grated orange rind**
- **1 orange, peeled and thinly**
  sliced
  mint leaves for garnish

- In food processor or blender, combine two-thirds of the strawberries and the orange juice. Blend until smooth.
- Add Grand Marnier, honey, sugar, yogurt, peach nectar, half and half and orange rind. Mix well.
- Transfer to large bowl. Chill completely.
- Slice remaining one-third of the berries, and add to the soup.
- Garnish with orange slices and mint.

  Elegant soup for a ladies' luncheon.

Almond Soup

Serves 6

- **4 tablespoons butter**
- **4 tablespoons flour**
- **1 quart chicken broth**
- **1½ cups blanched, slivered**
  almonds
- **1 shallot or 1 scallion, minced**
  juice of half a lemon
  pinch tarragon
  salt and pepper to taste
- **½ cup cream**
- **1 scant teaspoon almond**
  extract
  whipped cream
  watercress

- Melt the butter and stir in the flour, add ½ cup of broth and whisk until smooth.
- Add remaining broth, almonds, shallot, lemon juice and spices.
- Cook, stirring, for about 10 minutes. Puree, return to the stove and add the cream and the almond extract.
- Serve garnished with whipped cream and watercress.

  A great beginning for a gourmet dinner.

Island Cantaloupe Soup

Serves 6

- 2 medium cantaloupes, peeled and sliced
- ¼ cup sugar
- ⅓ cup freshly squeezed orange juice
- 1 tablespoon freshly squeezed lime juice
- 1 tablespoon freshly squeezed lemon juice
- ⅓ cup apple juice
- ¼ cup sherry
- ¼ teaspoon vanilla
- ⅛ teaspoon ground ginger
  Macadamia nuts, chopped
  lime slices

- Thoroughly combine cantaloupe, sugar, juices, sherry and seasonings in a non-metal bowl and chill.
- Process in two batches in food processor, until smooth.
- Top with nuts and lime slices.

Viva Tomato Soup

Serves 4

- 1 28-ounce can tomatoes, chopped
- 1 10-ounce can tomatoes with green chili peppers
- 1 14-ounce can chicken broth
- ½ cup chopped celery
- ½ cup chopped onion
- 1 tablespoon snipped cilantro
- 1 tablespoon sugar
- 1 tablespoon freshly squeezed lime juice
  fresh cilantro sprigs for garnish

- Combine undrained tomatoes and tomatoes with green chili peppers in a large saucepan. Add chicken broth, celery, onion, cilantro, sugar and lime juice.
- Bring to boil. Reduce heat and simmer covered, 18 to 20 minutes or until celery and onion are very tender.
- Place half of soup in blender or food processor, cover and process until smooth. Repeat with remaining soup.
- Return soup to saucepan and heat.
- Garnish with cilantro sprigs.

Tipsy Tomato Soup

Serves 6

- 5 tablespoons butter
- 1 tablespoon vegetable oil
- 1 cup chopped onion
- 2 carrots, chopped
- 2 stalks celery, chopped
- 2 cloves garlic, minced
- 3 cups diced canned tomatoes
- ½ teaspoon thyme
- 1 teaspoon basil
  grindings of black pepper
- 3 tablespoons flour
- 2 cups chicken broth
- ¼ teaspoon baking soda
- ½ teaspoon brown sugar
- ½ cup whipping cream
- ¼ cup gin
  salt to taste

- Melt butter and oil in large saucepan. Sauté onion, carrots, celery and garlic until tender, about 10 minutes. Add tomatoes and seasonings.
- Whisk flour and ½ cup broth until smooth. Slowly add to the soup, stirring constantly. Pour in remaining broth. Cover and simmer 25 minutes.
- Put soup in food processor in batches and process a few seconds. Soup should remain somewhat chunky.
- Return processed soup to pan. Add soda and stir thoroughly. Blend in the brown sugar, cream and gin. Stir and heat. Do not allow to boil. Add more pepper and salt to taste.

This can be made ahead and reheated.

Perfect Chicken Stock

10 quarts

- 1 baking hen
- 1 large onion, quartered
- 2 stalks celery, halved
  including lots of top leaves
- 2 carrots, halved
- 8 to 10 whole allspice

- Place rinsed whole hen in a 12-quart stockpot. Add remaining ingredients and cold water to within 2 inches of top. Bring to a slow simmer, never allowing stock to boil.
- Skim. Cover and let cook slowly for 1½ to 2 hours.
- Remove chicken. Cool. Remove meat from bones and reserve for another use.
- Continued cooking will further reduce stock for a richer recipe.
- Cool slightly and strain into containers. Refrigerate. After cooling, remove congealed fat and discard.

Use as the base for many soups. Substitute stock for water when preparing rice or pasta.

Roasted Red Pepper Soup

Serves 4 to 6

½ **cup butter**
1 **yellow onion, chopped**
2 **cloves garlic, minced**
4 **large red bell peppers,
   roasted and chopped**
3 **cups chicken broth**
½ **cup half and half
   salt and pepper to taste
   fresh cilantro**

- Sauté vegetables in butter until onions are transparent.
- Add chicken broth and bring to a boil; cook until tender.
- Strain vegetables. Reserve broth.
- Puree vegetables in food processor. Fold into broth and add half and half.
- Season and garnish with fresh cilantro.

Can be served hot or cold.

To roast pepper, place under broiler until skin puffs and is charred black. Turn as necessary to char entire pepper. Immediately place in plastic bag and seal for 10 minutes. Remove, peel and discard charred skin.

Roasted Eggplant Soup with Basil

Serves 6 to 8

2 **medium eggplants
   olive oil**
4 **cloves garlic, minced**
2 **medium onions, chopped**
1 **6-ounce can tomato paste**
1 **cup fresh basil leaves, or** ¼
   cup dried basil
3 **quarts chicken broth
   salt and pepper to taste
   freshly grated Parmesan
   cheese
   sun-dried tomatoes**

- Rub eggplants with olive oil. Cut in half and place skin side up on greased baking sheet. Broil until skin is crackled, dry and blackened. Cool and peel eggplant.
- Cube eggplant and sauté for 15 minutes with garlic and onion in a small amount of olive oil.
- Place mixture in food processor. Add tomato paste and basil and puree.
- Place in a saucepan. Add chicken broth and heat. When hot, season to taste.
- Serve topped with freshly grated Parmesan. Also garnish with snipped sun-dried tomatoes if desired.

May be served cold if thinned with a little more chicken stock. May be made in advance and reheated.

Curried Butternut Squash Soup

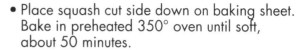

Serves 12

4 **pounds butternut squash, about 2 large, halved and seeded**
¼ **cup unsalted butter**
2 **cups chopped onion**
5 **teaspoons curry powder**
¼ **teaspoon ground allspice**
4 **cups chicken stock or canned low-salt broth**
1 **cup half and half**
 salt and pepper to taste
¼ **cup chives**

- Place squash cut side down on baking sheet. Bake in preheated 350° oven until soft, about 50 minutes.
- Scoop out squash pulp and discard skin.
- Melt butter in large, heavy skillet over medium heat.
- Add onion, curry, and allspice. Sauté until onion is tender, about 10 minutes.
- Transfer ¼ of onion mixture, ¼ of squash, and 1 cup stock to blender, puree. Pour into large, heavy saucepan.
- Puree remaining onion mixture, squash and stock in three more batches. Add to saucepan.
- Add half and half to soup.
- Bring to a boil, stirring occasionally.
- Season to taste with salt and pepper.
- Mix chives into soup.

Can be made one day ahead. Cover and refrigerate. Bring to a simmer before serving.

Chilled Zucchini Bisque

Serves 8

- 1 **medium onion, coarsely chopped**
- ½ **cup butter**
- 1½ **pounds zucchini, coarsely chopped**
- 1 **10¾-ounce can chicken broth plus 1 can water**
- 1 **teaspoon salt**
- ½ **cup fresh basil leaves**
- ½ **teaspoon nutmeg**
- ⅛ **teaspoon pepper**
- ½ **cup milk**
- ½ **cup half and half**

- In a large saucepan, sauté onions in butter until onions are transparent. Add zucchini, chicken broth and water; bring to a boil. Reduce heat and simmer, covered, for 15 minutes.
- Puree zucchini mixture in two batches in a blender or food processor, adding half the salt, basil, nutmeg and pepper to each.
- Combine batches, add milk and half and half and stir well until blended. Serve hot or chilled.

If desired, bisque may be made 2 or 3 days ahead of serving and refrigerated, covered.

Elegant Leek and Gruyère Soup

Serves 8

- 6 **cups chicken broth**
- 4 **cups sliced leeks**
- 1 **cup sliced fresh mushrooms**
- 1 **teaspoon fines herbes, crushed**
- ½ **teaspoon white pepper**
- ⅓ **cup flour**
- 6 **ounces Gruyère cheese, shredded**
- 2 **tablespoons freshly snipped parsley**
- 1 **cup whipping cream**
  extra sliced leeks for garnish

- Combine 4 cups of the broth, leeks, mushrooms, fines herbes, and pepper in a large kettle. Bring to boil and reduce heat. Cover and cook for 10 to 15 minutes or until leeks are tender. Cool slightly.
- Transfer ⅓ of the mixture at a time to a blender or food processor bowl. Cover and blend or process until smooth.
- Return all to kettle. Add 1 cup of the remaining chicken broth.
- At this time, soup may be cooled and stored in refrigerator for 1 to 2 days. Reheat and finish preparation when ready to serve.
- Mix the remaining 1 cup broth and flour until smooth. Stir into hot broth mixture along with Gruyère and parsley. Stir in whipping cream and heat. Do not boil.
- Garnish each serving with additional sliced leeks, if desired.

Very rich and well worth the effort!

Country Vegetable Soup

Serves 4 to 6

- 3 tablespoons finely chopped onion
- ½ cup finely chopped green onions
- 1 clove garlic, finely minced olive oil
- 1½ cups chopped zucchini
- 1½ cups chopped carrots
- 1½ cups chopped potatoes
- ½ cup thinly sliced celery
- 1 28-ounce can tomatoes, chopped, reserve juice
- 5 cups chicken broth
- 1 10-ounce can Great Northern beans
- ½ teaspoon salt
- ¼ teaspoon black pepper
- ½ teaspoon basil
- 1 bay leaf
- 2 sprigs parsley
- 1 10-ounce package frozen peas

- Sauté the onions and garlic in a very small amount of olive oil.
- Add zucchini, carrots, potatoes and celery. Cook for a few minutes and stir frequently.
- Add tomatoes with juice, broth, beans and seasonings. Cook 30 minutes.
- Add the frozen peas and cook 10 minutes longer.

Perfect on a winter afternoon.

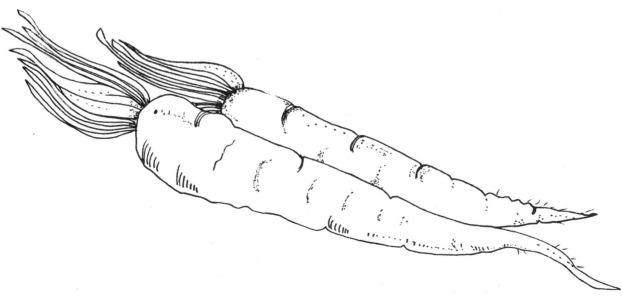

Marvelous Minestrone

Serves 8

¼ **pound bacon, diced**
2 **garlic cloves, minced**
1 **large onion, diced**
3 **leeks, diced**
2 **zucchini, diced**
1 **cup carrots, diced**
1 **large potato, peeled and diced**
½ **cup diced celery**
3 **tomatoes, peeled, seeded and diced**
5 **10-ounce cans beef broth**
1 **tablespoon chopped parsley**
1 **cup fresh peas**
½ **cup garbanzo beans**
1 **cup fresh string beans, trimmed**
1 **tablespoon Italian seasoning**
1 **cup fresh spinach, drained and chopped**
½ **cup macaroni, uncooked**
½ **cup freshly grated Parmesan cheese**

- Sauté bacon in a large soup pot.
- Add the garlic, onion, leeks, zucchini, carrots, potatoes, celery and tomatoes. Sauté until the onions and leeks are tender and translucent.
- Add broth, parsley, beans, peas and herbs. Simmer until vegetables are tender. Add spinach and macaroni. Simmer until macaroni is tender. Serve with Parmesan as garnish.

Wonderful for a Sunday night supper, Christmas Eve supper or après ski.

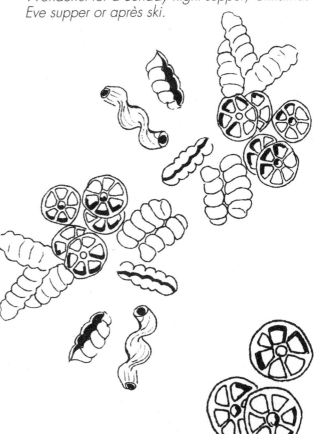

Crab and Corn Chowder

Serves 4 as main course, 6 as appetizer

 3 tablespoons butter
1½ cups finely chopped onion
1½ cups finely chopped celery
 6 medium potatoes, peeled and cubed
 2 cups clam juice or chicken stock
 1 cup whipping cream
   salt and pepper to taste
 ½ teaspoon red pepper flakes (or more if you like spicy)
 2 cups frozen corn
 2 cups crab
 ¼ cup fresh coriander or parsley

- Heat butter in large saucepan. Sauté onions and celery.
- Add potatoes and stock. Cook until potatoes are done.
- Add cream, salt, pepper, red pepper flakes, corn and crab. Simmer 6 to 8 minutes.
- To serve, garnish with coriander or parsley.

This soup can be put together in 45 minutes. A fast winter meal with bread and salad or a wonderful way to start a dinner party.

Louisiana Shrimp Gumbo

Serves 8 to 10

 4 tablespoons butter
 2 tablespoons flour
 2 large cloves garlic, chopped
 2 onions, chopped
 ½ green pepper, chopped
 2 14½-ounce cans tomatoes
 1 6-ounce can tomato paste
 3 beef bouillon cubes
 4 teaspoons Worcestershire sauce
 ½ teaspoon ground cloves
 1 teaspoon salt
 ½ teaspoon black pepper
 1 teaspoon chili powder
 1 teaspoon dry basil
 1 bay leaf
 3 cups water
 1 10-ounce package sliced frozen okra
1½ pounds raw shrimp, peeled and deveined

- Melt butter and stir in flour. Brown slightly.
- Add garlic and onions, sauté 5 minutes. Add green pepper and cook on low heat until tender.
- Add tomatoes, tomato paste, bouillon cubes, Worcestershire sauce, cloves, salt, pepper, chili powder, basil and bay leaf. Mix well.
- Add water. Simmer on low heat for 35 minutes.
- Add okra and cook 10 to 15 minutes.
- Add shrimp and simmer covered for another 10 to 15 minutes.

Serve over cooked white rice.

Holiday Shrimp Bisque

Serves 6 to 12

1 cup butter
1 cup flour
1 pound raw shrimp, any size
1 small onion, chopped
3 large garlic cloves, minced
2 to 3 tablespoons butter
¼ cup brandy
2 cups white wine
1 12-ounce can tomato paste
1 bay leaf
¾ to 1 teaspoon crushed red pepper
½ teaspoon salt
2 quarts half and half

- Melt butter. Whisk in flour to make roux. Simmer at least 10 minutes. Set aside.
- Chop shrimp finely by hand or in food processor.
- Sauté onion and garlic lightly in melted butter.
- Mix shrimp, onion and garlic in large pot and sauté slowly until shrimp is fully cooked.
- Add brandy and stir for three minutes.
- Add wine and continue cooking until hot.
- Add tomato paste and seasonings. Let simmer 10 to 15 minutes.
- Add half and half in amounts of 2 cups every three to five minutes. Stir thoroughly as you add cream and do not allow soup to get too cool by adding too much half and half too quickly.
- Thicken with roux. Add roux slowly, a spoonful at a time every 2 to 4 minutes, mixing thoroughly.
- Bring to a high heat, just under boiling.

This is a very rich soup, but a fine prelude to a holiday dinner. We like it for Christmas Eve dinner, then a small cup before an afternoon buffet on Christmas afternoon. It is not necessary to use all the half and half or all the roux. Low-fat milk in part and less roux still makes a wonderful soup. Experiment.

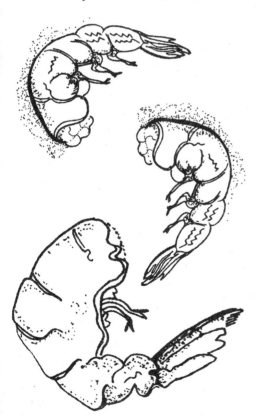

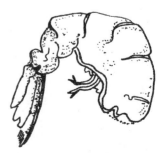

Garden Fresh Gazpacho

Serves 6 to 8

- 2 **cloves garlic**
- 1 **medium onion, sliced**
- 1 **cucumber, peeled and sliced**
- 4 **large garden-fresh tomatoes, peeled and coarsely chopped**
- 1 **green pepper, sliced**
- 2 **cups tomato juice**
- ⅛ **teaspoon salt**
- ⅛ **teaspoon cayenne pepper**
- ½ **cup wine vinegar**
- ¼ **cup olive oil**
- 1 **tablespoon Worcestershire sauce**

Garnish

- 1 **cup toasted bread cubes**
- 1 **cucumber, diced**
- 1 **tomato, diced**
- 1 **green pepper, diced fresh cilantro**

- Put all ingredients in a food processor and blend well.
- Refrigerate and serve cold with garnishes.

Some like it hot, so substitute one Anaheim chili pepper for the green pepper.

For fun: Freeze gazpacho in popsicle molds and serve as an appetizer at a backyard barbeque.

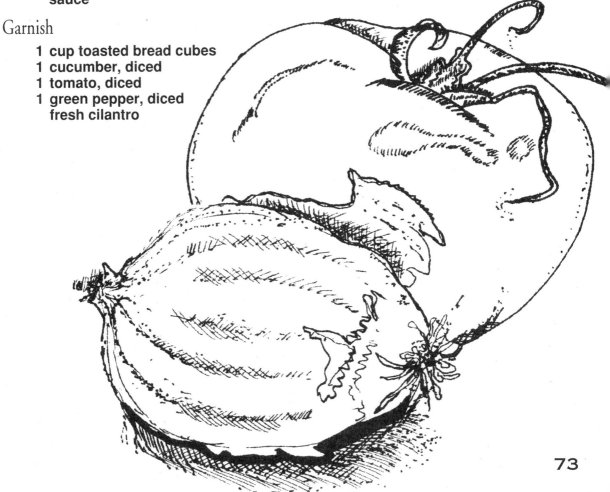

Santa Fe Taco Soup

Serves 6

- 3 **chicken breast halves**
- 2 **tablespoons oil**
- ½ **medium onion, chopped**
- 1 **clove garlic, minced**
- 1 **package taco seasoning mix**
- 1 **15-ounce can diced tomatoes**
- 1 **8 ounce jar green chili salsa**
- 1 **4-ounce can green chilies**
- 1 **can corn with peppers**
- 1 **15-ounce can ranch-style beans**
- 1 **15-ounce can black beans**
- 2 **cup chicken broth**
- 1 **cup shredded cheddar cheese**

- Cook chicken breasts. Cool and shred. Set aside.
- Sauté onion and garlic in oil. Set aside.
- In large saucepan, combine taco seasoning mix, tomatoes with juice, salsa, green chilies, corn, ranch beans, black beans, chicken broth, chicken breasts, and sautéed onions and garlic.
- Simmer 45 minutes.
- Top with shredded cheddar.

Serve with warm buttered tortillas.

Spicy Tortilla Soup

Serves 6 to 8

- 2 tablespoons vegetable oil
- 1 medium onion, chopped
- 1 jalapeño pepper, chopped
- 2 cloves garlic, minced
- 6 chicken breasts cooked, deboned and shredded
- 2 14½-ounce cans tomatoes
- 1 10½-ounce can beef broth
- 1 10½-ounce can chicken broth
- 1 10½-ounce can tomato soup
- ¾ cup water
- 1 teaspoon ground cumin
- 1 teaspoon chili powder
- 1 teaspoon salt
- ½ teaspoon lemon pepper
- 2 teaspoons Worcestershire sauce
- ⅓ cup picante sauce
- 4 corn tortillas, cut in triangles
- ½ cup cheddar cheese, grated

- Sauté onion, pepper, garlic and chicken in oil in large kettle. Add remaining ingredients and simmer 1 hour.
- Add tortillas during the last 10 minutes. Pour into mugs and garnish with cheese.

Hearty main dish soup.

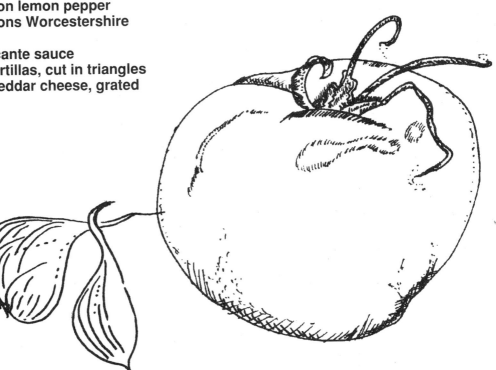

Fiesta Vegetable Soup

Serves 10

- 1 tablespoon vegetable oil
- 1 large onion, chopped
- 1 14-ounce can chicken broth
- 2 cups water
- 1 28-ounce can whole tomatoes, with green chilies
- 3 medium potatoes, scrubbed and cubed
- 2 medium zucchini, scrubbed and cubed
- 1 pound tomatillos
- 1 15-ounce can pinto beans or red kidney beans
- 1 16-ounce package frozen corn
- 1½ teaspoons ground cumin
- 1 teaspoon chili powder or to taste
- ½ teaspoon oregano
  salt and pepper to taste, cayenne pepper, if you want it HOT
  tortilla chips, crushed

- Heat vegetable oil in a large soup pot. Add onion and cook until tender, about 5 minutes. Add chicken broth, water, and liquid from tomatoes. Crush the tomatoes by hand or chop coarsely and add to the pot. Bring to a low boil.
- Add potatoes and zucchini. Remove the papery husks from the tomatillos, rinse under cold water and chop. Add to simmering soup and stir. Add beans, corn and spices, plus salt and pepper to taste.
- Cook at a steady simmer for 30 minutes to 1 hour, until potatoes are tender.
- To serve, ladle into bowls and sprinkle each portion with crushed tortilla chips.

Olé!

Tomatillos look like small green tomatoes with papery husks and can be found in produce sections of most supermarkets. Omit them if unavailable.

Extra portions can be refrigerated or frozen.

English Pub Cheese Soup

Serves 12

- 2 cloves garlic
- 1 cup chopped onion
- 1 cup chopped celery
- 1 cup chopped carrots
- 4 tablespoons butter
- ⅓ cup flour
- 3 tablespoons cornstarch
- 1 quart chicken broth
- 1 quart milk
- ½ to 1 pound Old English cheese, cubed

- Mince garlic, onion, celery and carrots finely in food processor.
- Melt butter and sauté garlic and vegetables. Slowly add flour and cornstarch, stirring until smooth.
- Add chicken broth and milk.
- Add cheese to soup and stir until melted.

Rich and tasty on a cold winter afternoon.

Pozole

Serves 8 to 10

2 tablespoons vegetable oil
1 pound boneless pork, trimmed and cut into 1-inch cubes
1 large onion, peeled and diced
3 large cloves garlic, minced
1 serrano chili pepper, seeded and minced
2 tablespoons chopped fresh oregano leaves or 1 tablespoon dried
6 cups chicken broth
3 ancho chili peppers, seeded and cut into 1-inch pieces
2 cups cooked chicken, shredded
1 30-ounce can golden hominy, well rinsed and drained
salt to taste

Garnishes

lime wedges
cilantro, chopped
radishes, sliced or julienned
tomatillos, husked and sliced

- Heat 1 tablespoon oil in a large frying pan over medium high heat. Add pork cubes, and salt to taste. Sauté until lightly browned. Set aside

- Heat 1 tablespoon oil over medium high heat, and sauté the onion until it is translucent.

- Add the garlic, serrano chili peppers, and oregano, mix well, and cook for several minutes, stirring frequently. Do not allow to burn.

- Place mixture in a large dutch oven. Add pork, chicken broth, ancho chili peppers, chicken and hominy. Bring to a boil, reduce the heat, and simmer for a few minutes.

- At the table, place small bowls of the garnishes to be added by the guests according to taste, and accompany with warmed corn or flour tortillas.

This recipe is ideal for using leftover roasted turkey but works very well with a cooked chicken.

Sirloin Steak and Winter Vegetable Soup

Serves 4

1 **pound boneless beef sirloin steak**
2 **14.5-ounce cans beef broth**
¼ **teaspoon pepper**
1 **cup Brussels sprouts, quartered**
1 **cup sliced mushrooms**
2 **carrots, sliced**
1 **large sweet potato, cubed**
1 **clove garlic, finely chopped**
1 **teaspoon chopped fresh marjoram or ½ teaspoon dried**
1 **teaspoon fresh thyme or ½ teaspoon dried**

- Trim excess fat from beef. Cut steak into 1-inch pieces. Cook beef in 3-quart saucepan over medium-high heat for 10 minutes stirring often until brown.
- Add beef broth and pepper. Reduce heat and simmer 20 to 30 minutes until beef is tender.
- Add remaining ingredients. Heat to boiling. Reduce heat. Cover and simmer about 15 minutes or until vegetables are tender.

Very colorful. Makes a great main dish. Serve with French bread.

Beef Barley Mushroom Soup

Serves 8

2 **teaspoons vegetable oil**
1 **cup chopped onion**
6 **cups beef broth**
2 **pounds meaty beef shank bones**
½ **cup uncooked barley**
  salt and pepper to taste
¾ **pound fresh mushrooms, sliced**
2 **cups peeled, diced potatoes**
1 **16-ounce can whole tomatoes, crushed**
2 **cups water**
¼ **pound fresh green beans, trimmed**
1 **tablespoon paprika**
1½ **teaspoons dill weed**

- Sauté onion in oil.
- Add beef broth, beef shank, barley, salt and pepper.
- Bring to boil. Simmer 1 hour, covered. Remove shank from soup and skim fat. Trim off meat, chop into pieces and return to soup.
- Add mushrooms, potatoes, tomatoes, water, green beans, paprika, and dill weed.
- Simmer 20 minutes or until vegetables are tender.

Time-Saver Turkey Chowder

- 1 **pound ground turkey**
- 1 **onion, chopped**
- 1 **bell pepper, chopped**
- 1 **cup chopped celery**
- 1 **cup diced carrots**
- 1 **11-ounce can corn with juice**
- 1 **14¾-ounce can creamed corn**
- 1 **16-ounce can diced tomatoes**
- 1 **6-ounce can tomato paste**
- 2 **teaspoons sugar**
- ½ **teaspoon salt**
- ½ **teaspoon pepper**
- 3 **cups chicken broth**
- 1 **chicken bouillon cube**
- 2 **large potatoes, diced**
- ⅔ **cup evaporated milk**

- Sauté ground turkey, onion and bell pepper.
- Add, in order, the remaining ingredients. Simmer on low for at least 2 hours.

Excellent! Teenagers love this!

Portuguese Bean Soup

- 1 **20-ounce can tomatoes**
- 1 **16-ounce Kielbasa sausage, sliced**
- 2 **potatoes, diced**
- 1 **onion, sliced**
- 2 **carrots, sliced**
- ½ **head cabbage, sliced**
- 2 **15-ounce cans kidney beans**

- Combine all ingredients and bring to a boil.
- Simmer for 15 minutes until vegetables are tender.

White Chili

Serves 6

- 1 cup dried navy beans
- 3 10½-ounce cans chicken broth
- 1½ cups water
- 1¼ cups chopped onion
- 1 clove garlic, minced
- ¼ teaspoon salt
- 2 cups chopped cooked chicken breasts
- 1 4-ounce can chopped green chilies
- 1 teaspoon ground cumin
- ¾ teaspoon dried whole oregano
- ¼ teaspoon ground red pepper
- ⅛ teaspoon ground cloves
- ¾ cup shredded Monterey Jack cheese

- Sort and wash beans. Cover with water and let soak 8 hours.
- Drain beans. Add broth, water, onion, garlic and salt.
- Bring to boil, cover and reduce heat. Simmer 2 hours, stirring occasionally. Add chicken, green chilies and spices. Cover and cook 30 minutes.
- Ladle into serving bowls. Top each with Monterey Jack.

Chasen's Chili

Serves 12

- 3 cups pinto beans
- 3 14½-ounce cans tomatoes
- 2½ pounds ground beef
- 1 pound ground lean pork
- 1½ pounds onions, chopped
- 1 pound green peppers, chopped
- 1 teaspoon garlic powder
- ½ cup minced parsley
- ⅓ cup chili powder
- 2 tablespoons salt
- 1½ teaspoons pepper
- 1½ teaspoons cumin seed

- Wash beans and soak overnight in water. Drain.
- Cook beans in water to cover until tender, 1 to 2 hours. Add tomatoes and simmer 5 minutes.
- Brown beef and pork. Drain and set aside. Sauté onions and peppers in skillet until onions are translucent.
- Combine meat, onion, peppers and all remaining ingredients and add to beans. Simmer 1½ hours, covered.

Serve with The Duke's Corn Bread, page 24.

Howling Jalapeño Chili

Serves 10 to 12

- **3 pounds top sirloin steak in ¼-inch cubes**
- **1 pound pork tenderloin in ¼-inch cubes**
- **4 large onions, diced**
- **20 cloves garlic**
- **¼ pound Chili Powder Mix (gourmet supplier Pendery's 1-800-533-1870)**
- **⅛ pound Jalisco Ground Chili Powder (gourmet supplier Pendery's 1-800-533-1870)**
- **3½ tablespoons freshly ground cumin seeds**
- **6 ounces beer**
- **4 to 5 tablespoons of canned pinto bean liquid as thickener salt and ground black pepper, to taste**
- **2 to 3 chipotle peppers with seeds, chopped**

- Use sirloin steak trimmings to make enough fat to sauté onions and 4 chopped garlic cloves until onions are clear.
- Add another 4 chopped garlic cloves.
- Set aside sautéed onions and garlic mix.
- Brown meat in the pot with 8 more chopped garlic cloves
- Add onion and garlic mix and simmer for 20 minutes.
- Add chili powders, 2½ tablespoons of cumin and beer to cover the meat.
- Simmer for 40 minutes.
- Add remaining chopped garlic cloves and cumin seeds.
- Simmer another 40 minutes.
- Add pinto bean liquid, chipotle peppers, salt and pepper. Simmer until all ingredients are melded together.

Winner of 1994 Tulsa Chili Contest.

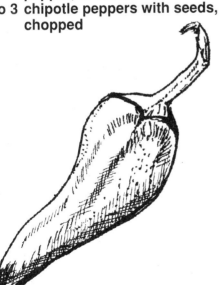

81

Turkey Picadillo Chili

Serves 4 to 6

vegetable cooking spray
1 **pound freshly ground turkey breast**
½ **cup sliced green onions**
1 **4-ounce can chopped green chiles, undrained**
1 **clove garlic, minced**
½ **cup raisins**
3 **tablespoons slivered almonds**
1 **teaspoon chili powder**
½ **teaspoon ground cumin**
½ **teaspoon ground cinnamon**
¼ **teaspoon ground cloves**
¼ **teaspoon ground red pepper**
¼ **teaspoon black pepper**
1 **8-ounce can tomato sauce**
1 **14½-ounce can whole tomatoes, undrained and chopped**
8 **pimiento-stuffed olives, halved**

- Coat a large saucepan with cooking spray, and place over medium to high heat until hot. Add ground turkey breast and cook until browned, stirring to crumble.
- Add green onions, chilies, and garlic. Cook 3 minutes. Add raisins and remaining ingredients. Cover, reduce heat, and simmer 20 to 30 minutes.

Hunting Camp Chili

Serves 4

- **1 pound ground meat, deer meat is especially good**
- **1 large yellow onion, chopped**
- **1 large bell pepper, chopped**
- **2 10-ounce cans Rotel tomatoes**
- **1 teaspoon white vinegar**
- **1½ teaspoons salt**
- **½ teaspoon ground cumin**
- **½ teaspoon oregano**
- **3 whole cloves**
- **1 bay leaf**
- **2 tablespoons chili powder**
- **1 dash paprika**
- **1 dash parsley flakes**
- **1 dash celery salt**

- Sauté ground meat and drain. Add onion, bell pepper and remaining ingredients.
- Slowly simmer covered for 2 hours. Canned, drained beans can be added if desired.

This recipe doubles easily and freezes well.

83

Widowmaker Chili

Serves 6

2 **pounds round steak**
2 **tablespoons olive oil**
1½ **medium white onions**
1 **serrano chili pepper, chopped**
1 **jalapeño chili pepper, chopped**
1 **14½-ounce can diced tomatoes**
1 **14½-ounce can chicken broth**
1 **teaspoon Worcestershire sauce**
1 **teaspoon salt**
1 **teaspoon cayenne pepper**
2 **tablespoons ground cumin**
4 to 6 **tablespoons chili powder**
1 **can coke**
½ **cup tequila**
1 **teaspoon instant coffee**
1 **teaspoon sugar**
masa harina to thicken
1 **teaspoon fresh lime juice**

- Cut round steak into ¼-inch cubes and sauté in oil until brown. Add onions and peppers.
- Sauté until onions are translucent.
- Add remaining ingredients except masa harina and lime juice. Cook covered over medium low heat approximately 2 hours.
- Before serving, thicken if necessary with masa harina and add lime juice.

A meal in itself.

New England Clam Chowder

Serves 10 to 12

12 **large chowder clams**
2 **quarts of water**
¾ **cup butter**
1 **cup coarsely chopped onions**
1 **cup coarsely chopped celery**
½ **teaspoon thyme**
¾ **cup flour**
2 **cups diced cooked potatoes**
2 **cups cream or milk**
salt and white pepper to taste

- Boil clams in water till they open, approximately 7 minutes. Reserve the liquid and discard the shells and any closed clams. Chop the meat to a medium dice and strain the liquid removing the particles.
- Melt butter in heavy pot that holds one gallon.
- Sauté onions and celery until translucent, add thyme.
- Add flour slowly to incorporate the butter stirring constantly.
- Cook mixture on medium heat for 5 minutes.
- Add clam stock and bring to boil stirring occasionally.
- When thick turn down to low heat and stir not to burn.
- Add potatoes and clams. Stir while adding cream and do not boil.
- Add salt and white pepper to taste. Mix salt and pepper to avoid clumping.

Remember not to boil the chowder once the cream has been added. Taste for seasoning, clam juice can be added to adjust flavor and consistency

Chef Michael Fusco

Pan Roasted Shrimp Bisque

Serves 10

4 ounces extra virgin olive oil
1 large carrot, diced
1 large red onion, diced
3 stalks celery, diced
1 pound shrimp shells (from approximately 3 pounds shrimp)
3 tablespoons minced garlic
1 cup brandy
1 cup dry vermouth
32 ounces light fish or shrimp fumet
   salt and pepper to taste
6 Roma tomatoes, Concasse
2 quarts whipping cream
4 ounces roux (made from 6 tablespoons butter and 5 tablespoons flour

- Sauté carrots, onion and celery in olive oil and caramelize to rich brown color. Add shrimp shells and roast in 350° oven for 15 minutes. After first 5 minutes, add garlic and roast until soft. Remove from oven and deglaze with brandy and vermouth. Reduce until most of the liquid is gone and add Fish Fumet. Simmer for 30 minutes, strain through a fine mesh and season with kosher salt and freshly ground pepper. Add tomatoes to broth and blend adding cream slowly. Bring to light boil and reduce to ⅔rd's. Add roux to adjust consistency and simmer. Strain through a cheesecloth.

- Garnish with fresh chopped chives and a dollop of crème fraîche mixed with lemon pepper to give a tangy smoothness to this rich soup. Top with a shrimp halved lengthwise.

Fish Fumet (Stock)

1 pound fish bones (sole or any white fish bones)
4 ounces parsnips
4 ounces leeks
4 ounces celery
1 whole lemon, halved
2 bay leaves
12 crushed peppercorns
1 cup dry white wine
2 quarts water

- Add all ingredients to pot and bring to simmer for 15 minutes, strain.

Crème Fraîche

2 ounces buttermilk
1 pint warm whipping cream

- Fold together and let sit out on counter overnight then refrigerate.

Chef Curt Herrmann, Montrachet Restaurant, owned by David Sheehan, Cascia Alumnus

St. Michael's Alley White Chili

Serves 10 to 12

- 2 **yellow onions, chopped**
- 5 **cloves garlic, finely chopped**
- 2 **pounds cooked chicken, chopped**
- 6 **1-pound cans Great Northern beans**
- 1 **4-ounce can chopped green chilies**
- 3 **cups chicken broth**
- ⅓ **cup chopped jalapeños**
- 2 **teaspoons chili powder**
- 1 **tablespoon cayenne pepper**
- 1 **tablespoon cumin**
- 1 **tablespoon Tabasco Sauce**
- 1 **tablespoon Worcestershire sauce**
- 1 **16-ounce can chopped tomatoes, drained**
  salt and pepper to taste
- 2 **teaspoons oregano**

- Sauté onions and garlic until onions are clear. Add remaining ingredients and cook on medium heat, stirring every 10 minutes or so until mixture is hot and well blended, about 45 minutes.

St. Michael's Alley Restaurant

Tortilla Soup

Serves 20

- 1 **cup butter**
- 2½ **cups flour**
- 1 **gallon chicken broth**
- 1 **teaspoon white pepper**
- 2 **cups Monterey Jack/cheddar cheese mix**
- 2 **pints half and half**
- 3 **teaspoons jalapeños**
- 1 **15-ounce can diced tomatoes**
- 6 **ounces green chilies**
- 2 **cups chicken meat, marinated in fajita seasonings**

- Melt butter and stir in flour to make a roux. Cook over low heat, stirring constantly until mixture is smooth and thickened.
- In separate pan, combine chicken broth and white pepper and bring to boil. Stir roux into chicken broth.
- Add cheese to stock and stir until melted. Add remaining ingredients to stock and heat. To hold, place soup in top of double broiler over hot water.

Peppers Restaurant

Deco Delights

Propelled to world prominence by the unprecedented nearby oil discoveries, Tulsa quickly changed from a hardscrabble Western depot to an elegant, forward-looking city, worthy of its unofficial status as "oil capital of the world".

With profits from the seemingly inexhaustible flow of black gold, Tulsans built elaborate office buildings, churches, homes and theatres mimicking traditional European styles. In 1918, Josh Cosden, known as the "Prince of Petroleum," built a fifteen-story headquarters for his oil empire in downtown Tulsa. An oil field supply company later had that original building duplicated next door and then suspended a cantilevered office tower over the existing buildings, a rare architectural feat.

An English Gothic building once known as the queen of the Tulsa skyline, the Philtower features gargoyles and Waite Phillips' initials at the entrance. Another of Tulsa's historically interesting buildings located at 320 South Boston featured lights atop its 27th floor which changed color to indicate expected weather.

The excitement and the energy of the oil boom in Tulsa produced some of the country's finest examples of Art Deco architecture. The Pythian and Philcade buildings, and The Union Depot illustrate the ornate, flamboyant Art Deco style embraced in the 1920's. Completed in 1929, Boston Avenue United Methodist Church was the first church in the world to be built on cathedral scale using Art Deco architectural style. It has been cited as one of the world's outstanding examples of ecclesiastical architecture.

When oil industry giants and visiting dignitaries came to Tulsa, they invariably stayed at the opulent Mayo Hotel, which was patterned after the Plaza Hotel in New York City. The Mayo became the hub of the young city's social and business communities, with the marbled first floor, elegant chandeliered ballroom and luxurious suites complete with ice water on tap.

Once home to successful wildcatters and oil company founders, the older neighborhoods feature tree-lined avenues of mansions reflecting the oil rich legacy. Tulsa's eclectic style from the simple to the impressive includes the Frank Lloyd Wright designed home, Westhope.

Each year thousands of visitors tour the Oral Roberts University campus to view its unique space age architecture, its crown of thorns styled prayer tower and its huge praying hands sculpture.

In the 1960's, Tulsa began an ambitious downtown revitalization. The Main Mall now offers respite where Tulsa's first citizens gathered. The Performing Arts Center, a 52 story office building and a luxury hotel combine to reposition Tulsa to face the future. Its brash, oil boom days may have passed, but neither time nor experience will deplete Tulsa's exuberant optimism.

Deco
Delights

Entrée Salads

Bayside Crab Louis Salad 94
Cantonese Chicken Salad 96
Chicken Primavera Pasta Salad 98
Chicken Salad with Cranberry Dressing 97
Chicken Waldorf Salad 95
Chutney Chicken Salad Supreme 95
Classic Niçoise Salad 93
Crunchy Oriental Chicken Salad 96
Curry Fettuccine Salad 100
Hearts of Palm Chicken Salad 94
Mediterranean Shrimp and Pasta Salad 99
Royal Roast Beef Salad 92
Shanghai Shrimp and Pasta Salad 99
Sirloin Salad in Mustard Vinaigrette 91

Vegetable Salads

Elegant Wild Rice Salad 102
Garden Bean and Potato Salad with Balsamic
   Vinaigrette 103
Helen of Troy Salad 101
Picnic Potato Salad 104
Salad Olé with Chile Vinaigrette 101
Scrumptious Salad 103
Snappy Tomato Aspic 109
Stolen Broccoli Salad 104
Summer Tomato Salad with Brie 100
Sunshine Confetti Salad 105

Green Salads

Greens with Jícama, Almonds and Oranges 107
Spinach, Strawberry and Bleu Cheese Salad 105
Very Caesar Salad 106

Fruit Salads

Bridal Shower Fruit 107
Cranberry Fluff 109
Fruit Salad with Orange Sherbet Dressing 108
Green and Gold Salad 106
Portofino Mold 108

Dressings

Balsamic Vinaigrette 103
Basic Vinaigrette 92
Bleu Cheese Dressing 94
Chile Vinaigrette 101
Chutney Dressing 106
Cranberry Dressing 97
Dressing of the Sea 110
Garlic Vinaigrette 98
Green Goddess Dressing 110
Honey-Lime Cilantro Vinaigrette 109
Mustard Vinaigrette 91
Orange Dressing 107
Orange Sherbet Dressing 108
Original Spinach Salad Dressing 111
Sesame Dressing 115
Special Caesar Dressing 110
Thai Noodle Salad Dressing 111

Professional Chefs

Alysann's Tuna Salad 114
Asian Chicken, Cashew and Spinach Salad with
   Sesame Dressing 115
"Dillicious" Chicken Pasta Salad 112
Jícama Orange Ginger Slaw 112
Shrimp, Baby Corn and Avocado 113
Smoked Turkey Pasta Salad 114
Tabouli 113

Sirloin Salad in Mustard Vinaigrette

Serves 8 to 10

2 **pounds boneless sirloin, 2
inches thick
salt and freshly ground
pepper to taste**
¾ **pound mushrooms, sliced**
6 **scallions, sliced**
1 **14-ounce can artichokes
hearts, drained and quartered**
1 **pint cherry tomatoes, halved**
½ **pound fresh sugar snap peas**
2 **tablespoons chopped chives**
2 **tablespoons chopped parsley**
2 **tablespoons chopped fresh
dill
romaine lettuce**

- Season steak with salt and pepper. Broil to rare or medium rare. Cool and cube. Combine steak, mushrooms, scallions, artichokes, tomatoes, snap peas and herbs. Toss gently.
- Pour dressing over salad and refrigerate overnight.
- Serve over romaine lettuce.

Mustard Vinaigrette

1 **egg, beaten**
⅓ **cup extra-virgin olive oil**
2 **teaspoons country-style
Dijon mustard**
1½ **teaspoons freshly squeezed
lemon juice**
3 **tablespoons tarragon vinegar**
1 **teaspoon Worcestershire
sauce**
1 **teaspoon salt**
¼ **teaspoon freshly ground
black pepper
dash Tabasco Sauce**

- Combine dressing ingredients and blend well.

Great to prepare in advance for that weekend at the cabin or for a gourmet picnic.

Royal Roast Beef Salad

Serves 8

2 **pounds rare roast beef, cut into 2-inch strips**

1 **8-ounce can whole beets, drained and cut into julienne strips**

4 **large shallots, minced**

¾ **pound fresh snow peas or two 6-ounce packages frozen snow peas**
salt
freshly ground pepper

¼ **cup freshly snipped parsley**

- Combine roast beef, beets and shallots in large bowl. Add vinaigrette. Toss to coat. Refrigerate covered 2 hours or overnight.
- Pour boiling salted water over peas. Drain and rinse under cold running water. Refrigerate.
- Just before serving, add snow peas to roast beef mixture and toss. Place in serving bowl and season to taste with salt and pepper.
- Sprinkle with parsley and serve cold.

Basic Vinaigrette

¼ **cup freshly squeezed lemon juice**

1 **teaspoon red wine vinegar**

¾ **teaspoon Dijon mustard**

1 **small clove garlic, minced**

¼ **teaspoon salt**

½ **cup vegetable oil**
freshly ground pepper

- Combine lemon juice, vinegar, mustard, garlic and salt in small bowl. Whisk in oil in slow steady stream. Season to taste with pepper.

Classic Niçoise Salad

Serves 6 to 10

2 **pounds green beans, blanched to tender crisp**
2 **green peppers, cored and sliced into thin rounds**
2 **cups sliced celery**
1 **pint cherry tomatoes, halved**
5 **medium, red potatoes, cooked, peeled, and sliced**
3 **7-ounce cans albacore tuna**
1 **2-ounce can flat anchovies, drained**
2 **small or 1 large red onion or Bermuda onion, thinly sliced**
10 **stuffed olives**
10 **black olives**
2 **tablespoons chopped fresh basil or 1 teaspoon dried basil**
⅓ **cup finely chopped fresh parsley**
¼ **cup finely chopped green onions**
6 **hard-cooked eggs, quartered**

- In large salad bowl, make a symmetrical pattern of the green beans, peppers, celery, tomatoes and potatoes. Flake the tuna and add. Arrange the anchovies and onions on top. Scatter olives over all.
- Sprinkle with basil, parsley and green onions. Garnish with hard cooked eggs.
- Toss with salad dressing after presenting.

Dressing

2 **teaspoons Dijon mustard**
2 **tablespoons wine vinegar**
6 **tablespoons vegetable oil**
6 **tablespoons olive oil**
1½ **teaspoons salt**
1 to 2 **cloves garlic, minced freshly ground pepper**
1 **teaspoon chopped fresh thyme or ½ teaspoon dried thyme**

- Combine mustard, vinegar, oils and seasonings. Beat until well blended.

A flavorful luncheon salad.

Bayside Crab Louis Salad

Serves 4

½ **cup mayonnaise**
½ **cup sour cream**
2 **tablespoons chili sauce**
2 **tablespoons vegetable oil**
1 **tablespoon vinegar**
1 **tablespoon prepared horseradish**
1 **tablespoon freshly squeezed lemon juice**
1 **tablespoon snipped parsley**
2 **teaspoons grated onion**
½ **teaspoon salt**
4 **drops Tabasco Sauce iceberg lettuce**
1 **pound fresh crab**

- Blend dressing ingredients.
- Shave iceberg lettuce and place on 4 plates. Divide crab evenly over lettuce. Pour dressing over crab.

Garnish with lemon and watercress.

Hearts of Palm Chicken Salad

Serves 6

½ **pound bacon, cooked and crumbled**
4 **cups cooked and cubed chicken breasts**
1 **14-ounce can hearts of palm, drained and sliced lettuce leaves**
4 **tomatoes, cut in 6 wedges each**
24 **pitted black olives**

- Combine bacon, chicken and hearts of palm. Add dressing and mix well. Cover and refrigerate several hours. Serve on lettuce leaves and garnish with tomatoes and olives.

Bleu Cheese Dressing

½ **cup mayonnaise**
½ **cup sour cream**
3 **tablespoons milk**
2 **tablespoons freshly squeezed lemon juice**
½ **teaspoon seasoned salt**
⅔ **cup bleu cheese, crumbled**

- Whisk mayonnaise, sour cream, milk, lemon juice, and salt together. Stir in bleu cheese. Chill overnight.

Chicken Waldorf Salad

Serves 6

- 1½ **cups instant brown rice**
- 1 **cup mayonnaise, may be reduced calorie**
- 1 **large red apple, diced**
- 1 **tablespoon freshly squeezed lemon juice**
- 2 **cups cooked and cubed chicken**
- 1 **cup diced celery**
- 1 **cup seedless green grapes**

- Prepare rice as directed on package.
- Mix in mayonnaise.
- Mix apple with lemon juice. Stir into rice mixture with remaining ingredients. Chill.

Chutney Chicken Salad Supreme

Serves 8

- 4 **cups cooked and cubed chicken breasts**
- 2 **cups diagonally sliced celery**
- 4 **scallions with tops, sliced**
- 5 **ounces canned sliced water chestnuts, drained lettuce, personal preference**
- 8 **slices bacon, cooked and crumbled**
- ½ **cup slivered almonds, toasted**
- 2 **large avocados, sliced in wedges**

Dressing

- 1 **cup mayonnaise**
- ¼ **cup chopped mango chutney**
- ¼ **cup freshly squeezed lime juice**
- 2 **teaspoons grated lime peel**
- 1 **teaspoon curry powder**
- ½ **teaspoon salt**

- In large bowl, combine chicken, celery, scallions, and water chestnuts.
- Line bowl or individual plates with lettuce. Mound salad onto lettuce. Sprinkle with bacon and almonds. Surround with avocado slices.
- Pour dressing over salad. Toss to coat well.

- In jar with tight-fitting lid, combine all dressing ingredients. Shake to blend thoroughly.

An unusual main dish salad.

Crunchy Oriental Chicken Salad

Serves 8

- 6 **chicken breast halves, skinned and boned**
- 3 **slices ginger**
- 1 **teaspoon salt**
- 2 **heads greens, preferably 1 spinach and 1 red-leaf**
- 1 **large can Chinese noodles**
- 6 **green onions, chopped**
- ½ **cup sliced almonds, toasted**
- ¼ **cup sesame seeds, toasted**

Dressing

- ½ **cup sugar**
- 2 **teaspoons seasoned salt**
- ½ **cup white wine vinegar**
- 1 **teaspoon pepper**
- 1 **cup vegetable oil**

- The day before serving, simmer chicken covered in water with ginger and salt 20 minutes. Tear into large pieces.
- Marinate chicken overnight in half the dressing, reserving the rest to toss with salad.
- When ready to serve, combine lettuce with marinated chicken, noodles, onions, almonds and seeds. Toss with reserved dressing and serve immediately.

- Make dressing by combining all ingredients except oil. Bring to a boil, cool, add oil and refrigerate.

There may be extra dressing.

Cantonese Chicken Salad

Serves 6

- ½ **cup cream-style peanut butter**
- ½ **cup water**
- 3 **tablespoons soy sauce**
- 3 **tablespoons cider vinegar**
- 1 **tablespoon sugar**
- 1 **tablespoon vegetable oil**
- 8 **ounces linguine, cooked, drained and rinsed**
- 1½ **pounds cooked chicken breasts, skinned and boned**
- 4 **cups coarsely shredded cabbage**
- 6 **scallions, including tops, thinly sliced**
- 1 **scallion, including top, coarsely chopped**
- 2 **tablespoons coarsely-chopped, dry-roasted peanuts**

- Blend peanut butter, water, soy sauce, vinegar, sugar and oil in a food processor 30 seconds or until smooth. Transfer to a large bowl. Add linguine.
- Tear the chicken into shreds and add to the bowl along with the cabbage and sliced scallions. Toss well and garnish with scallion and peanuts.

An impressive noodle dish.

Chicken Salad with Cranberry Dressing

Serves 4

4 cups cooked and cubed chicken
1 cup chopped celery
2 cups seedless green or red grapes
½ teaspoon salt
½ teaspoon pepper
½ cup mayonnaise
½ cup sour cream
½ cup sliced almonds, toasted

• Combine salad ingredients.

Cranberry Dressing

½ cup jellied cranberry sauce
¾ cup vegetable oil
¼ cup wine vinegar
1 teaspoon salt
1 teaspoon sugar
½ teaspoon paprika
¼ teaspoon dry mustard
dash pepper

• Whip cranberry sauce and add other ingredients. Pour over salad.

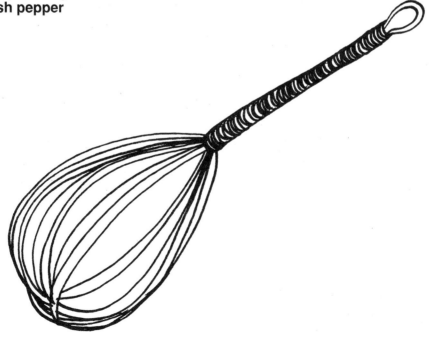

Chicken Primavera Pasta Salad

Serves 4 to 6

½ **pound vermicelli**
1 **cup frozen peas, thawed**
1 **cup broccoli florets,
    blanched**
1 **pint cherry tomatoes**
6 **fresh mushrooms, sliced**
⅓ **cup fresh basil, chopped
    or 1 tablespoon dried basil**
⅓ **cup pine nuts, toasted**
2 **cups cooked and cubed
    chicken breasts**
5 **slices bacon, cooked and
    minced**
1 **cup Garlic Vinaigrette
    dressing**

- Cook pasta al dente. Transfer to large bowl. Add ⅓ of dressing to pasta. Toss and let cool. Chill 3 hours.

- In another bowl, place remainder of dressing, add vegetables, basil and pine nuts. Stir to coat thoroughly.

- When ready to serve, add chicken to pasta, then add all vegetables. Toss. Sprinkle bacon on top.

Garlic Vinaigrette

4 **large cloves garlic, minced**
½ **teaspoon salt**
2 **tablespoons Dijon mustard**
⅓ **cup red wine vinegar**
1 **cup extra virgin olive oil
    ground black pepper, to taste**

- Blend garlic, salt, mustard and vinegar together to form paste. Add olive oil, whisking constantly. Add ground black pepper to taste.

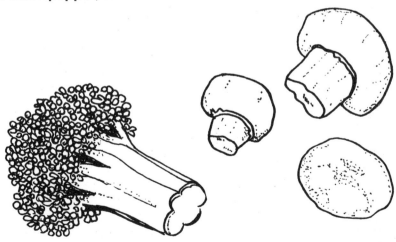

Mediterranean Shrimp and Pasta Salad

Serves 8

2 zucchini, chopped
2 carrots, peeled and curled
1 small can sliced olives
½ pound mushrooms, sliced
1 can artichoke hearts, drained
1 cucumber, thinly sliced
1 pound small shrimp, cooked
½ cup Garlic Vinaigrette
1 pound vermicelli noodles
  feta cheese
  cherry tomatoes
  parsley

- Marinate the vegetables and shrimp in vinaigrette for 24 hours prior to serving.
- Day of serving, cook vermicelli noodles and use some of marinade to coat noodles after cooking. Chill.
- Put vegetable and shrimp mixture on noodles and top with crumbled feta cheese.
- Garnish with cherry tomatoes and parsley.

See Garlic Vinaigrette, page 98.

Shanghai Shrimp and Pasta Salad

Serves 6 to 8

½ pound linguini
¼ cup sesame oil, divided
¼ cup peanut oil, divided
1 pound fresh mushrooms, sliced
2 tablespoons grated fresh ginger
2 cloves garlic, minced
1½ pounds shrimp, cooked and peeled
1 pound snow peas, steamed one minute (until just crisp and bright green)
⅓ cup soy sauce
¼ cup sesame seed, toasted

- Cook linguini in boiling salted water until al dente. Drain and rinse under cold water. Transfer noodles to a large bowl.
- Toss noodles with ½ teaspoon of the sesame oil and ½ teaspoon of the peanut oil.
- Sauté mushrooms, ginger and garlic in remaining sesame and peanut oils. Let cool and add to linguini.
- Add shrimp, snow peas, soy sauce and toasted sesame seeds. Toss to mix well.
- Cover and chill.

If you plan to chill longer than two hours, store the snow peas separately and add shortly before serving to retain their bright green color and crispness.

Curry Fettuccine Salad

Serves 8

12 ounces curry-flavored fettuccine
10 ounces frozen peas, thawed
1 cup toasted sliced almonds
⅓ cup raisins

Dressing

½ cup olive oil
2 tablespoons mango chutney (or substitute peach preserves)
1 teaspoon minced garlic
1 tablespoon Dijon mustard
salt to taste
dash cayenne pepper

- Cook fettuccine according to package directions. Rinse with cold water and drain.
- Toss pasta with peas, almonds and raisins
- Add dressing and toss again. Serve at room temperature.

- Combine all dressing ingredients and blend until smooth.

Wonderful summer salad to serve along side Lemon Grilled Halibut, page 209.

Summer Tomato Salad with Brie

Serves 6 to 8

5 medium garden fresh tomatoes, cut into chunks, save juice
½ pound Brie cheese, rind removed, torn into pieces
½ cup fresh basil, snipped into strips with scissors
3 large garlic cloves, minced
⅓ cup olive oil
½ teaspoon salt
½ pound fresh pasta, linguini, shells, etc.
½ cup freshly grated Parmesan cheese

- Combine tomatoes and juices, Brie, basil, garlic, olive oil and salt. Leave at room temperature at least 2 hours.
- Cook pasta as directed on package. Drain and immediately toss with tomato mixture. Brie should melt. Mix. Sprinkle with Parmesan. Add more salt to taste. Serve at room temperature.

Freeze Brie for 20 minutes to remove the rind easily.

Helen of Troy Salad

Serves 4 to 6

- 1 **pound mushrooms, sliced**
- ½ **pound Swiss or Monterey Jack cheese, grated**
- ½ **cup chopped green onions**
- 1 **pound fresh spinach, cleaned and stemmed**

Dressing

- ¼ **cup oil**
- ¼ **cup vinegar**
- ¼ **teaspoon sugar**
- 2 **tablespoons Cavender's Greek seasoning**

- Toss mushrooms, cheese, onions and spinach together. Add dressing no more than 2 hours before serving, or mushrooms will turn brown.

- Blend together oil, vinegar, sugar and seasoning.

For a main dish, add grilled chicken pieces and julienned red bell pepper.

Salad Olé with Chile Vinaigrette

Serves 8 to 10

- 2 **cups converted rice**
- 3 **teaspoons salt**
- 2 **cans pinto beans, rinsed and drained**
- 1 **can corn, drained or 3 cups cooked fresh corn kernels**
- 1 **bunch scallions, chopped**
- ½ **cup chopped red bell pepper**
- ⅔ **cup canola oil**
- ¼ **cup freshly squeezed lime juice**
- 2 **tablespoons cider vinegar**
- 2 **tablespoons brown sugar, packed**
- 4 **pickled jalapeño peppers, stemmed, seeded and quartered**
- 2 **teaspoons chili powder**
- 1 **teaspoon cumin**
  fresh cilantro

- Cook the rice as directed on the package, using 5 cups water and 1 teaspoon of salt. The rice can be made ahead.
- In a large bowl, combine the rice, beans, corn, scallions and red pepper. Toss lightly to mix.
- In a food processor, combine the oil, lime juice, vinegar, brown sugar, jalapeño peppers, chili powder, cumin and remaining 2 teaspoons salt. Process until the peppers are finely minced.
- Pour the dressing over the salad and toss to coat. Let stand at room temperature for up to 4 hours tossing occasionally. May cover and refrigerate for up to 2 days. Bring back to room temperature to serve.

Low-fat and great on a Mexican menu.

Elegant Wild Rice Salad

Serves 8 to 10

2 quarts plus 1 cup water
2 cups wild rice
2 6-ounce jars marinated
  artichoke hearts
1 10-ounce package frozen
  peas
1 green pepper, chopped
1 bunch green onions,
  chopped
1 pint cherry tomatoes, halved
  toasted slivered almonds

- In large saucepan, heat water and rice to boiling. Reduce heat to low, cover and simmer 45 minutes. Drain excess liquid from rice.
- Drain artichoke hearts, reserving marinade. Halve artichoke hearts and add to rice with peas, green peppers, green onions, tomatoes, reserved marinade and half the dressing. Toss well. Cover and chill.
- Just before serving, toss again and taste. Add some remaining dressing, if desired. Sprinkle with almonds and serve.

Dressing

1⅓ cups vegetable oil
½ cup white wine vinegar
¼ cup freshly grated Parmesan
  cheese
1 tablespoon sugar
2 teaspoons salt
1 teaspoon celery salt
½ teaspoon ground white
  pepper
½ teaspoon dry mustard
¼ teaspoon paprika
1 clove garlic, minced

- Combine all dressing ingredients in jar with lid and shake well. Refrigerate until ready to use.

May use 5-minute wild rice to reduce preparation time. Seasoned long grain and wild rice mix is also good. The seasoning gives the salad additional punch. Delicious served with grilled meats or seafood.

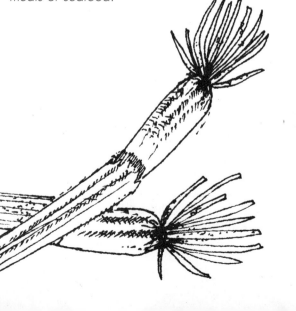

Scrumptious Salad

Serves 8

1 **large red onion**
1 **large garden-fresh tomato**
1 **green pepper**
1 **large can hearts of palm lettuce**
1 **large can pickled artichoke hearts**
1 **small jar capers**
3 to 4 **ounces bleu cheese**
⅔ **cup Italian dressing**
1 **tablespoon fresh dill**

- Thinly slice onion, tomato, and green pepper into rings. Slice hearts of palm in ½-inch lengths.
- Place lettuce on a platter or individual salad plates. Next, place onion rings, then bell pepper rings, then slices of tomato; surround with "coins" of hearts of palm. Place artichoke hearts on top and sprinkle with capers.
- Crumble bleu cheese into a cup. Add Italian dressing and dill. Mix and pour over salad.

Garden Bean and Potato Salad with Balsamic Vinaigrette

Serves 6

1½ **pounds small red-skinned potatoes, steamed, cooled and quartered**
¾ **pounds green beans, blanched to tender crisp and halved**
1 **small red onion, chopped**
¼ **cup chopped fresh basil**

- Combine potatoes, beans, onion and basil in serving dish. Add dressing to coat.

May be served cool or may be warmed in microwave.

Balsamic Vinaigrette

¼ **cup balsamic vinegar**
2 **tablespoons Dijon mustard**
2 **tablespoons freshly squeezed lemon juice**
1 **clove garlic, minced dash Worcestershire sauce**
½ **cup extra-virgin olive oil salt and pepper to taste**

- Whisk together vinegar, mustard, lemon juice, garlic and Worcestershire. Slowly add oil. Season to taste with salt and pepper. If refrigerated, return to room temperature and rewhisk before using.

A great picnic salad to take to Symphony at Sunset.

Picnic Potato Salad

Serves 6

- ½ **pound bacon**
- 10 **new potatoes, unpeeled and cubed**
- ¼ **cup vinegar**
- 1 **large bunch green onions, sliced**
- ¼ **cup sliced green olives**
- 1 **cup sliced celery**
- 1 **bottle ranch dressing**
- 2 **eggs, hard-boiled and sliced**

- Cook bacon and crumble. Reserve 2 tablespoons bacon drippings.
- Cook potatoes in salted water and drain. While hot, pour vinegar and bacon fat over potatoes.
- Add onions, olives and celery.
- Toss with ranch dressing until moist and top with bacon and eggs.

Stolen Broccoli Salad

Serves 6 to 8

- 1 **3-ounce package cream cheese**
- 1 **egg**
- 1 **tablespoon vinegar**
- 2 **tablespoons sugar**
- 2 **tablespoons vegetable oil**
- 1 **tablespoon mustard**
- ¼ **teaspoon salt**
- ¼ **teaspoon pepper**
- ⅛ **teaspoon garlic salt**
- 6 **cups chopped broccoli (about 2 bunches)**
- 2 **tablespoons chopped onion**
- ½ **cup raisins**
- ½ **pound bacon, cooked and crumbled**

- Combine dressing ingredients in jar or blender. Pour over broccoli and onion. Sprinkle with raisins and bacon.

Different and great for a buffet.

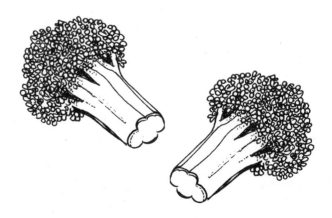

Sunshine Confetti Salad

Serves 8 to 10

4 tomatoes, chopped
4 cucumbers, chopped
2 yellow squash, chopped
1 sweet onion, chopped
croutons
freshly grated Parmesan cheese
pitted black olives

- Pour dressing over vegetables and toss. Cover and refrigerate at least 2 hours before serving. Garnish with croutons, Parmesan and olives.

Dressing

¼ cup chopped fresh basil
2 tablespoons chopped fresh parsley
½ cup olive oil
¼ cup red wine vinegar
2 tablespoons freshly squeezed lemon juice
1 clove garlic, finely minced

- Combine dressing ingredients and shake well.

Spinach, Strawberry and Bleu Cheese Salad

Serves 8

1 large bunch fresh spinach, washed and stemmed
1 pint strawberries, washed, trimmed and sliced
½ cup walnuts, toasted and chopped
½ cup crumbled bleu cheese

- Place salad ingredients in a large bowl in the order listed. Top with dressing.

For a very special presentation, serve on individual plates.

Dressing

½ cup sugar
1 tablespoon sesame seeds
1 tablespoon poppy seeds
1½ teaspoons minced onions
¼ teaspoon Worcestershire sauce
¼ teaspoon paprika
½ cup white wine vinegar
½ cup vegetable oil

- Blend dressing ingredients in a jar, blender or food processor. The sugar should dissolve.

Spinach and strawberries at their best!

Green and Gold Salad

Serves 8

- 1 cucumber, thinly sliced
- 1 11-ounce can mandarin oranges, drained
- 3 bananas, peeled and sliced
- 3 avocados, peeled and sliced leaf lettuce freshly squeezed lemon juice

Chutney Dressing

- ½ cup mayonnaise
- ½ cup sour cream
- ⅓ cup chutney, including syrup
- ¼ teaspoon curry powder
- ½ teaspoon salt
- ⅛ teaspoon Tabasco Sauce
- 2 tablespoons vegetable oil
- 1 tablespoon white wine vinegar

- Arrange cucumber and fruits on a large, lettuce-lined platter or eight individual salad plates. Brush bananas and avocados lightly with lemon juice if salad is to stand for a few minutes before serving. Drizzle about ½ cup Chutney Dressing over all. Serve with remaining dressing.

- Place in blender container the mayonnaise, sour cream, chutney with syrup, curry powder, salt, Tabasco, oil, and vinegar. Blend until smooth.

This has great eye appeal on a buffet table. The dressing is great for other salads including chicken salad.

Very Caesar Salad

Serves 6 to 8

- 1 egg, coddled, hold on slotted spoon in boiling water for exactly one minute
- ¾ cup light olive oil juice of 1 lemon
- ½ teaspoon salt
- ¼ teaspoon freshly ground pepper
- 2 teaspoons Worcestershire sauce
- 1 teaspoon anchovy paste
- 1 large clove garlic, minced
- 1 clove garlic, halved romaine lettuce
- ¼ cup freshly grated Parmesan cheese
- ½ cup garlic croutons

- Break egg in a small bowl. Beat until light and lemon colored.
- Add oil slowly, beating continuously. Beat in lemon juice, salt, pepper, Worcestershire, anchovy paste, and garlic. Refrigerate in covered glass jar until well chilled.
- Rub large wooden bowl with a split garlic clove, add lettuce and dressing. Toss until leaves are well coated with dressing.
- Sprinkle cheese and croutons over salad and toss lightly.
- Serve on well-chilled plates or in shallow bowls.

Dressing will keep for several days.

Greens with Jícama, Almonds and Oranges

Serves 8

- **1 large head red leaf lettuce, washed, torn and chilled**
- **1 medium red or Bermuda onion, sliced into rings**
- **2 oranges, peeled and thinly sliced, or one 11-ounce can mandarin oranges, drained**
- **1 small jícama, peeled and cut into julienne strips**
- **3 tablespoons sugar**
- **¼ cup sliced almonds**

- Place lettuce, onion, orange and jícama in salad bowl and chill.
- In small skillet, sprinkle sugar over almonds and cook over medium heat until almonds are coated and sugar has dissolved. They brown quickly, so do not burn. Place in small bowl and allow to cool
- Pour salad dressing over chilled salad and top with sugared almonds. Toss and serve.

Orange Dressing

- **½ teaspoon grated orange peel**
- **⅓ cup fresh orange juice**
- **2 tablespoons red wine vinegar**
- **½ cup vegetable oil**
- **2 tablespoons sugar**
- **1 tablespoon dry Italian dressing mix**

- Mix all dressing ingredients in a shaker jar and chill.

Jícama is a lovely Mexican vegetable with a clean, crisp flavor.

Bridal Shower Fruit

Serves 4 to 6

- **1 cup blueberries**
- **1 cup raspberries**
- **2 cups small cantaloupe balls or in season melon**
- **⅓ cup shredded coconut**
- **3 tablespoons coconut liqueur**

- Combine fruit, coconut and coconut liqueur. Mix well. Refrigerate for several hours before serving.

Fruit Salad with Orange Sherbet Dressing

**your favorite mixture of fresh
fruit: strawberries, grapes,
kiwi, oranges, bananas,
pears**

Orange Sherbet Dressing

1 quart

- ¼ **cup powdered sugar**
- 1 **pint orange sherbet, softened**
- 1 **3-ounce package cream cheese**
- 1 **cup crushed pineapple, drained**
- 2 **tablespoons chopped maraschino cherries**
- 1 **tablespoon maraschino cherry juice**
- 1 **pint whipping cream**
- ¼ **teaspoon vanilla**

- Blend all but cream and vanilla in food processor Whip cream with vanilla. Fold into dressing. Serve immediately or you may make ahead and freeze. Soften to serve.
- Toss with fresh fruit using enough dressing to coat generously.

Keeps 3 to 6 months in freezer. May be used as a fruit dip.

Portofino Mold

Serves 12

- 1 **6-ounce package raspberry jello**
- ¾ **cup boiling water**
- 1 **20-ounce can crushed pineapple, chilled**
- 1 **16-ounce can whole cranberry sauce, chilled**
- ¾ **cup dry red wine**
- 1 **cup chopped pecans**
- 1 **8-ounce package cream cheese**
- 1 **cup sour cream**

- Dissolve jello in boiling water. Stir in pineapple with juice, cranberry sauce and wine. Chill until mixture thickens slightly.
- Fold in pecans and turn into 9 x 13-inch glass baking dish and chill until firm.
- Soften cream cheese and gradually beat in sour cream until smooth. Spread over gelatin and sprinkle with pecans.

Can substitute white wine for red wine.

Cranberry Fluff

Serves 8 to 10

- 2 **cups ground raw cranberries**
- 3 **cups miniature marshmallows**
- ¾ **cup sugar**
- 2 **cups diced apples**
- ½ **cup chopped pecans**
- 1 **cup frozen whipped topping**

- Combine cranberries, marshmallows and sugar. Cover and chill.
- Add apples and pecans. Fold in whipped topping. Pour into serving bowl and chill.

Snappy Tomato Aspic

Serves 8

- 1 **cup chopped celery**
- 1 **cup sliced green olives**
- 4 **hard-boiled eggs, chopped, or cooked popcorn shrimp**
- 1 **12-ounce can V-8 juice**
- 1 **12-ounce can tomato juice**
- 2½ **packages powdered gelatin juice of 1 lemon**
- 1 **teaspoon horseradish**
- ½ **teaspoon salt**
- 3 **dashes Tabasco Sauce**
- 1 **tablespoon Worcestershire sauce**

- Place celery, olives, and eggs in 7 x 12-inch glass baking dish.
- Heat juices and add gelatin that has been dissolved in cold water. Add lemon juice, horseradish, salt, Tabasco and Worcestershire. Pour over celery, eggs and olives.
- Refrigerate until congealed. Cut into squares and serve on bed of lettuce or topped with mayonnaise.

Try with sliced avocados on top.

Honey-Lime Cilantro Vinaigrette

1½ cups

- 1 **clove garlic**
- 1 **small shallot**
- 1 **bunch cilantro, washed and trimmed, leaves only**
- 1 **tablespoon cider vinegar**
- 3 **tablespoons honey**
- ½ **teaspoon salt and pepper or to taste**
- 2 to 3 **large limes, juiced**
- 1 **cup walnut oil or other light oil**

- In a food processor chop garlic and shallot with quick on/off. Add cilantro, vinegar, honey, salt, pepper and lime juice. Process. With processor on, slowly add oil.

This is outstanding on a bed of mixed greens.

Green Goddess Dressing

1½ cups

1 cup mayonnaise
1 to 2 cloves garlic, minced
1 tablespoon anchovy paste
6 green onion tops
¼ cup fresh parsley, chopped
1 tablespoon freshly squeezed
  lemon juice
1 tablespoon tarragon vinegar
½ teaspoon salt
½ teaspoon freshly ground
  pepper
  sour cream, to taste

• Combine in blender. Add as much sour cream as suits your taste.

Dressing of the Sea

1¼ pints

2 cups mayonnaise
1 tube anchovy paste
1 tablespoon horseradish
  chives, snipped

• Mix and set aside in refrigerator for a few hours to let flavors marry.

Zippy, zesty and simple! Try to be modest!

Special Caesar Dressing

1 cup

1 egg
10 shakes garlic powder
2 teaspoons salt
½ teaspoon coarse ground
  pepper
2 teaspoons dry onion
3 shakes Worcestershire sauce
1 tablespoon basil
1 tablespoon oregano leaves
⅓ cup olive oil
¼ cup freshly squeezed lemon
  juice
⅛ cup vinegar

• Beat egg until it has a thickened quality, herein lies the secret of success. Add spices. Slowly add oil while whisking constantly.
• Whisk lemon juice and vinegar into egg mixture. More oil may be added for a thicker dressing.

A tablespoon of anchovy paste may be added if desired.

A Caesar dressing to please the gods. Compliments will be forthcoming.

Original Spinach Salad Dressing

2 cups

1 cup vegetable oil
⅔ cup red wine vinegar
2 cloves garlic, minced
1 teaspoon sugar
1 teaspoon dry mustard
2 dashes Worcestershire sauce
3 tablespoons catsup
⅔ cup brown sugar

• Combine all ingredients and chill.

Garnish spinach salad with crumbled bacon, chopped hard-boiled eggs and red onion slices.

Thai Noodle Salad Dressing

1 pint

½ cup creamy peanut butter
6 ounces Hoisin sauce
1 tablespoon sesame oil
1 tablespoon hot oil
⅓ cup soy sauce
½ cup safflower oil
2 tablespoons minced garlic
1 tablespoon minced fresh ginger

• Mix ingredients and store in refrigerator. Use as needed.

Use as a dressing for cooked angel hair pasta.

Garnish pasta with any or all of the following: freshly trimmed pea pods, fresh bean sprouts, fresh cilantro, shrimp or crab.

Chef Harry Schwartz, original owner of Back Bay Gourmet.

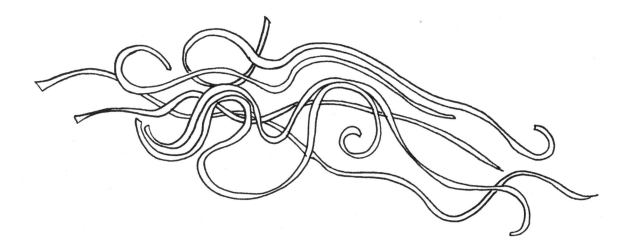

"Dillicious" Chicken Pasta Salad

Serves 4 to 6

8 ounces medium-size pasta shells, cooked and drained
2 cups cooked chicken breasts, shredded
1 bunch green onions, cut diagonally
2 medium-size cucumbers, peeled, seeded and chopped
½ cup sliced black olives

- Combine pasta, chicken and vegetable.

Dressing

1 cup sour cream
½ cup mayonnaise
⅓ cup fresh dill, chopped
¼ teaspoon salt
white pepper to taste

- Whisk sour cream and mayonnaise. Add finely chopped dill and seasonings. Toss with chicken-pasta mixture.
- Adjust seasoning to taste.

Ruth Young, Queenie's Restaurant.

Jicama Orange Ginger Slaw

Serves 4 to 6

1½ cups jícama, peeled and julienned
1 orange, peeled and cut into segments
1 ounce red pickled ginger, julienned
2 teaspoons rice vinegar
1 ounce sugar
4 ounces of mayonnaise radicchio

- Combine jícama, orange segments, red ginger and set aside.
- Mix vinegar and sugar first to dissolve sugar crystals.
- Add mayonnaise.
- Combine everything and refrigerate to intensify flavors.
- Serve in radicchio cup.

This can be served as salad or as accompaniment to an entrée of grilled shellfish, salmon, beef, pork or chicken.

Chef Robert Kennedy, Southern Hills Country Club

Shrimp, Baby Corn and Avocado

Serves 4

1 large avocado, peeled, pitted, ½-inch cubes
2 tablespoons freshly squeezed lemon juice
⅓ cup chili sauce
1 tablespoon olive oil
1 tablespoon horseradish
salt and freshly ground black pepper to taste
½ teaspoon Tabasco Sauce
8 ounces orzo (rice-shaped pasta), cooked, rinsed and cooled
1 pound medium shrimp, peeled, deveined, cooked
1 can baby corn on the cob, drained
1 cup slivered radishes
2 serrano chili peppers, chopped finely
3 green onions, chopped
1 tablespoon chopped cilantro
lettuce

- Toss avocado in 1 tablespoon lemon juice and set aside.
- In a large bowl combine chili sauce, oil, horseradish, salt, pepper and Tabasco. Blend well. Add the pasta, shrimp, corn, radishes, peppers, green onions and cilantro and toss. Add the avocado and gently combine.
- Serve on a bed of lettuce.

Chef Keith Lindenberg, Cooking School of Tulsa

Tabouli

Serves 10 to 12

2½ cups fine bulgur wheat
1 cup olive oil
1½ cups freshly squeezed lemon juice
1½ tablespoons salt
½ teaspoon red pepper
3 to 4 bunches parsley, finely chopped
3 bunches green onions, finely chopped
6 tomatoes, finely diced

- In large mixing bowl, wash wheat 3 to 4 times. Drain well.
- Add oil, lemon juice, salt and pepper. Mix well. Set aside and let soak 2 hours.
- Add parsley, onions and tomatoes to wheat mixture.
- Toss and refrigerate 2 hours before serving.

Chef Chuck Gawey, Albert G's Bar-B-Q

Smoked Turkey Pasta Salad

Serves 12

1½ pounds broccoli
1 pound fusilli (corkscrew) pasta, cooked and drained
2 carrots, grated
2 celery stalks, diced
6 green onions, thinly sliced
1 sweet red pepper, sliced into thin strips
1 cup freshly grated Parmesan cheese
4 cups cooked and cubed smoked turkey
1 6-ounce can small ripe olives, drained

- Cook broccoli heads in boiling water for 3 minutes. Cool in ice water. Cut into florets. Combine pasta, broccoli and remaining ingredients. Toss gently with dressing. Refrigerate.
- Remove from refrigerator 1 hour before serving.

Dressing

¼ cup balsamic vinegar
1 tablespoon Dijon mustard
2 to 3 cloves garlic, minced
1 teaspoon sugar
½ teaspoon dried basil
¾ teaspoon salt
½ teaspoon freshly ground pepper
½ cup vegetable oil

- Whisk together all ingredients except oil. Gradually add oil, whisking continually.

Barbara Lander and Jean Paulsen, Cornucopia Catering

Alysann's Tuna Salad

Serves 4

1 12½-ounce can albacore tuna in water, drained
¼ cup finely chopped celery
⅛ teaspoon ground cumin
¼ teaspoon cayenne pepper
⅓ cup mayonnaise
⅛ cup slivered almonds

- Mix tuna, celery, cumin, pepper and mayonnaise. Add almonds.

May adjust seasonings to taste.

Chef Vikki Martinus, Felini's Bakery and Deli

Asian Chicken, Cashew and Spinach Salad with Sesame Dressing

Serves 6 to 8

2 tablespoons peanut oil
1 teaspoon salt
1 teaspoon black pepper
1 teaspoon leaf oregano
1 teaspoon leaf thyme
1 teaspoon paprika
1 teaspoon fresh ground garlic
¼ teaspoon cayenne pepper
4 chicken breasts, skinned and boned

- Combine oil and seasonings. Marinate chicken at least four hours or overnight. Heat non-stick skillet and sear chicken breasts. Finish in 350° oven until chicken is completely done, approximately 10 minutes. Cool and slice into thin strips.

Salad

2 bags fresh-picked and washed spinach leaves
1 head napa cabbage, thinly sliced
1 red pepper, seeded and sliced into thin strips
1 cup shiitake mushrooms, sliced
½ cup carrots, julienne
½ cup whole cashew nuts
¼ cup diced green onions
fried wontons
toasted sesame seeds

- Toss all ingredients together and add chicken. Top with dressing, toss and serve in large salad bowl or on individual dinner plates. Garnish with crispy fried wontons and toasted sesame seeds.

Sesame Dressing

¼ cup rice vinegar
¼ cup soy sauce
¼ sesame oil
¼ cup vegetable oil
2 teaspoons dry mustard
2 teaspoons sesame seeds, toasted
2 teaspoons freshly grated ginger

- Whisk all dressing ingredients until smooth.

Chef Devin Levine, Southern Hills Country Club

Green Country Gatherings

Like moths drawn to a candle's flickering light, people gravitate toward home and the kitchen for special times in their lives. Whether their homecomings occur after long or brief absences, they usually include favorite foods, family and friends - ingredients for happy occasions.

Living in Oklahoma's verdant Green Country region, Tulsa families have created traditions surrounding a variety of civic activities. They picnic before the Greenwood Jazz Festival, Reggaefest, the Fourth of July fireworks at River Parks and the Tulsa Philharmonic Symphony at Sunset. At the Bluegrass Chili Festival and at the Tulsa State Fair, they sample regional foods. Favorite pancake recipes are enjoyed after finishing the Tulsa Run or the Corporate Challenge and picnic crumbs become favorite treats for the ducks and rare trumpeter swans at historic Swan Lake.

Tulsans enjoy the taste of foods from many cultures when visiting Oktoberfest's Biergarten for German fare and Glendi for Greek delicacies. The Tulsa Indian Powwow and the Hispanic Fiesta feature authentic costumes and dances along with tastefully prepared dishes. The International Mayfest, an outdoor art and craft fair presents food for the eye in a timely downtown festival of the arts.

Throughout life each family fashions its celebrations to reflect its personalities and preferences. When family and friends gather to eat, they share more than the food consumed, they celebrate life! The arts of cooking and conversation combine to provide comfort, security and continuity. Recollections of the occasion give us fond memories that sustain long after the tables have been cleared.

Memories as simple as the aroma of freshly baked bread nourish the senses and connect us to our shared beginnings - the family.

Green Country Gatherings

VEGETABLES
Our Way

Vegetables

Basil Tomato Tart 119
Broccoli with Cashew Butter 121
Cheesy Rice and Spinach 124
Company Spinach with Artichokes 124
Easter Carrot Tarts 122
Mediterranean Green Beans 120
Picnic Carrots 122
Pretty Summer Squash 123
Ratatouille 125
Rice Stuffed Tomatoes 119
Savory Green Beans and Mushrooms 120
Springtime Asparagus 121
Sugar Snaps 121
Zippy Carrots 122
Zucchini Potato Pie 125

Potatoes

Apricot Glazed Sweet Potatoes 126
Chili Pepper Cheese Fries 130
Garlic Parsley Potatoes 127
Orange Baked Sweet Potatoes 127
Parmesan Scalloped Potatoes 129
Potato, Anaheim Chili and Sweet Corn Hash 126
Rosemary Potatoes 128
Snowy Mashed Potatoes 129
Teriyaki New Potatoes 128

Rice and Beans

Almost Wild Rice 130
Arroz con Tomato 131
Basque Black Beans and Garbanzos 134
Black Bean Enchilada Pie 133
Carrot Mushroom Pilaf 132
Cattle Trail Beans 136
Ginger Rice 130
Red Beans and Rice 134
Southern Baked Rice 132
Spicy Black Beans and Rice 133
Thai Fried Rice 131
Tulsa Baked Beans 135

Seasoned Butters and Relish

Baked Cranberry Relish 123
Cheese Butter 136
Jalapeño Pepper Butter 136

Professional Chefs

Bacon Horseradish Potato Quiche 137

Basil Tomato Tart

Serves 6

1 unbaked 9-inch pie crust
1½ cups shredded mozzarella cheese
6 Roma or 4 medium tomatoes
1 cup loosely packed fresh basil leaves
4 cloves garlic, minced
½ cup mayonnaise
¼ cup freshly grated Parmesan cheese
⅛ teaspoon ground white pepper
fresh basil leaves

- Place pie crust in quiche dish or glass pie plate. Flute edges and prick bottom and sides. Bake in preheated 475° oven 8 to 10 minutes until light brown. Sprinkle with ½ cup of the mozzarella cheese. Cool on a wire rack.
- Cut tomatoes into wedges; drain on paper towels. Arrange tomato wedges atop melted cheese in the baked pie shell.
- In a food processor combine basil and garlic and chop coarsely. Sprinkle over tomatoes.
- In a medium mixing bowl combine remaining mozzarella cheese, mayonnaise, Parmesan and pepper. Spoon cheese mixture over basil mixture, spreading to evenly cover the top.
- Bake in 375° oven 35 to 40 minutes or until golden and bubbly. Serve warm. If desired, sprinkle with basil leaves.

Great to serve when your garden is bountiful with fresh tomatoes and basil.

Rice Stuffed Tomatoes

Serves 6

6 tomatoes
4 tablespoons oil
6 tablespoons rice
2 tablespoons chopped parsley
2 garlic cloves
salt and black pepper to taste
1 tablespoon tomato paste
1 cup chicken broth

- Slice the tops off the tomatoes and remove pulp. Cook pulp on low heat with 1 tablespoon oil, rice, parsley and garlic.
- Add salt and pepper and cook for a few minutes. Remove garlic before stuffing tomatoes with the mixture.
- Place tomatoes in a baking dish. Cover with remaining oil and the paste which has been diluted with broth.
- Bake at 300° for 1 hour.

Savory Green Beans and Mushrooms

Serves 6

1½ **pounds fresh green beans, washed and trimmed**
8 **ounces fresh mushrooms, sliced**
1 **tablespoon thinly sliced green onions**
3 **tablespoons butter**
⅓ **cup vegetable oil**
1 **tablespoon wine vinegar**
1 **tablespoon freshly squeezed lemon juice**
1 **tablespoon snipped parsley**
2 **tablespoons snipped fresh savory or 1 teaspoon dried savory**
1 **teaspoon sugar**
1 **teaspoon salt**
⅛ **teaspoon pepper**
4 **slices bacon, cooked and crumbled**

• In large saucepan cook beans uncovered in boiling salted water until tender crisp. Drain.
• Sauté mushrooms and green onions in melted butter over medium heat until tender, about 5 minutes. Toss with beans.
• Heat oil, vinegar, lemon juice, herbs and seasonings in small saucepan to boiling. Pour over bean mixture. Stir to coat evenly. Sprinkle with bacon and serve immediately.

Mediterranean Green Beans

Serves 6 to 8

2 **large garlic cloves, minced**
1 **large onion, chopped**
¼ **cup olive oil**
2 **pounds fresh green beans, washed and trimmed**
1 **28-ounce can tomatoes with the juice (chopped)**
salt to taste

• Sauté garlic and onions in oil until soft. Add green beans and tomatoes with juice. Cover and cook, stirring occasionally 10 to 15 minutes, or until tender.

Sugar Snaps

Serves 4 to 6

> 1 **pound sugar snap peas**
> 1 **tablespoon freshly squeezed lemon juice**
> 1 **tablespoon red wine vinegar**
> 2 to 3 **cloves garlic, minced**
> 1 **teaspoon Dijon mustard**
> ¼ **teaspoon each salt and pepper**
> 2 **tablespoons olive oil**
> 1½ **teaspoons sesame oil**
> ½ **cup sesame seeds, toasted**

- Blanche peas in boiling water.
- Whisk together lemon juice, vinegar, garlic, mustard, salt, pepper and oils. Pour over peas. Garnish with seeds and serve.

Vinaigrette is also tasty on fresh asparagus.

Springtime Asparagus

Serves 4

> 1 **pound fresh asparagus**
> 3 **tablespoons virgin olive oil**
> 1 **teaspoon freshly squeezed lemon juice**
> ¼ **teaspoon salt**
> **dash ground nutmeg**
> **dash fresh ground black pepper**
> 1 **tablespoon freshly grated Parmesan cheese**

- Wash and snap off hard ends of asparagus, tie in a bundle and steam to desired doneness.
- Whisk together olive oil, lemon juice and salt. Pour over the steamed asparagus.
- Sprinkle nutmeg over the dressing, followed by the black pepper and Parmesan.

Broccoli with Cashew Butter

Serves 10

> 3 **pounds fresh broccoli**
> ½ **cup butter**
> 6 **teaspoons freshly squeezed lemon juice**
> ½ **teaspoon marjoram**
> ½ **cup salted cashews, coarsely chopped**

- Cook broccoli until tender; drain and arrange spears on serving platter.
- Melt butter; add lemon juice, marjoram and cashew nuts. Simmer together over low heat about 3 minutes.
- Pour over broccoli and serve.

Easter Carrot Tarts

Serves 8

3 **pounds carrots, peeled and sliced**
½ **cup water**
¼ **cup sugar**
½ **cup butter**
½ **cup whipping cream**
   salt and pepper to taste
8 **tart shells**
1 **tablespoon sugar**

- Cook 1 cup sliced carrots in salted water until crisp tender, drain and reserve.
- Cook remaining carrots in ½ cup water until tender. Add ¼ cup sugar and 3 tablespoons butter. Puree in blender.
- Blend in remaining butter, cream, salt and pepper. Fill tart shells with puree, arrange sliced carrots on top. Dust with sugar
- Bake in 450° oven 10 to 15 minutes.

Save one for the Easter Bunny!

Zippy Carrots

Serves 3 to 4

6 **carrots, peeled and cut into sticks or slices**
2 **tablespoons grated onion**
2 **tablespoons horseradish**
½ **cup mayonnaise**
   salt and freshly ground pepper to taste
   bread crumbs
   paprika

- Cook carrots until tender. Drain, reserving ¼ cup carrot juice. Mix juice with onion, horseradish, mayonnaise, salt and pepper.
- Place carrots in baking dish. Pour sauce over carrots. Sprinkle with bread crumbs and paprika. Bake in 375° oven 15 minutes.

Picnic Carrots

Serves 8 to 10

3 **pounds carrots, peeled and sliced at angle**
¼ **teaspoon garlic powder**
1 **teaspoon pepper**
1 **teaspoon salt**
3 **tablespoons sugar**
½ **cup oil**
½ **cup vinegar**
1 **teaspoon onion salt**
1 **teaspoon prepared mustard**

- Cook carrots in unseasoned water until just crispy, 10 minutes. Drain. Add seasonings and marinate overnight.

Easy! Perfect for a picnic.

Baked Cranberry Relish

Serves 8

- 1 **cup chopped pecans**
- 1 **package fresh whole cranberries**
- 1¾ **cups sugar**
- ½ **teaspoon cinnamon**
- 1 **cup orange marmalade**
- 3 **tablespoons freshly squeezed lemon juice**

- Spread pecans in 9 x 13-inch baking dish. Bake in preheated 350° oven 10 to 12 minutes. Do not let pecans burn.
- Mix cranberries, sugar and cinnamon. Combine with toasted pecans. Cover with foil and bake 45 minutes.
- When baked, carefully remove foil and stir in marmalade and lemon juice. Chill.

Great holiday gift.

Pretty Summer Squash

Serves 6

- 1 **pound very small zucchini, scrubbed, left whole**
- 1 **pound small yellow crookneck squash, scrubbed, left whole**
- 1 **tablespoon butter**
  salt and pepper
- ⅓ **cup freshly grated Parmesan cheese**

- Steam squash until tender when pierced with a fork, approximately 12 to 15 minutes. The yellow squash sometimes takes longer, so may have to remove zucchini first.
- Rinse with cold water. Slice into ⅛-inch slices. Drain for a few minutes in a colander or on paper towels.
- Butter shallow baking dish with half the butter. Arrange overlapping slices of zucchini and yellow squash in rows. Sprinkle with salt and pepper. Dot with remaining butter and cover with Parmesan.
- This can be done several hours in advance.
- When ready to serve, place in 450° oven 7 minutes or until cheese is bubbly.

This is pretty, easy and a nice accompaniment to grilled meats.

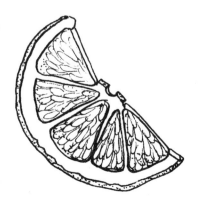

Company Spinach with Artichokes

Serves 6

1½ **pounds fresh spinach,
    cleaned
    salt and pepper to taste**
 11 **ounces cream cheese**
  8 **ounces sour cream**
  3 **tablespoons butter, melted**
 ¼ **cup milk**
  2 **14-ounce cans artichoke
    hearts, drained**
 ½ **cup freshly grated Parmesan
    cheese**

- Cook spinach with salt and pepper until wilted. Drain well.
- Add cheese, sour cream, butter and milk.
- Cut artichokes in fourths and mix with spinach. Place in buttered baking dish.
- Cover with Parmesan and bake in 350° oven until bubbly.

Cheesy Rice and Spinach

Serves 8

  1 **cup long grain rice**
  1 **small onion, chopped**
 ¼ **cup butter, melted**
 ¼ **cup flour**
2½ **cups milk**
  8 **ounces grated cheddar
    cheese**
  1 **package frozen chopped
    spinach, thawed and drained**
  1 **teaspoon salt**
 ½ **teaspoon pepper**

- Cook rice according to package directions, until half done. Rinse in cold water and drain.
- Sauté onion in butter. Whisk in flour, add milk and cook until thickened. Add cheese and spinach. Season with salt and pepper.
- Combine with rice in baking dish.
- Bake at 350° one hour and 10 minutes.

Ratatouille

Serves 6 to 8

- 1 **large eggplant**
- ¼ **cup olive oil**
- 2 **green peppers, seeded and cut into strips**
- 1 **large onion, chopped**
- 2 **cloves garlic, minced**
- 1 **medium zucchini, sliced and quartered**
- 1 **medium butternut squash, peeled and chunked**
- 1 **28-ounce can Italian tomatoes, drained**
- 2 **tablespoons minced fresh basil or 1 teaspoon dried**
- ½ **teaspoon salt or to taste freshly ground black pepper to taste**
- ¼ **cup chopped parsley**

- Peel eggplant, slice it into rounds. Salt both sides and stand the slices in a colander to drain for 30 minutes. Rinse, pat dry and quarter the eggplant.
- Combine oil, green peppers, onion and garlic in a large glass baking dish. Bake in 400° oven 10 minutes or until vegetables are sizzling but not brown. Add eggplant and bake until it is softened, about 10 minutes.
- Layer the zucchini on top and bake 10 minutes more.
- Add butternut squash, tomatoes, basil, salt and pepper. Stir well, and continue to bake, uncovered, for 30 to 40 minutes.
- The vegetables should be very well cooked but still retain their shape, and the pan juices should be reduced.
- Remove from oven and stir in parsley.

This dish can be made ahead, refrigerated, and reheated in a skillet.

Zucchini Potato Pie

Serves 6

- 1 **pound potatoes, 3 medium**
- 1 **tablespoon butter, divided**
- 2 **eggs**
- 3 **ounces mozzarella cheese, shredded**
- ½ **cup freshly grated Parmesan cheese**
- 1 **large zucchini, grated**
- ¼ **cup minced onion salt and pepper to taste**
- 2 **tablespoons fine dry bread crumbs, divided**

- Cook potatoes. Drain, peel and mash. Add ½ tablespoon butter, eggs, cheeses, zucchini, onion and spices. Stir until blended.
- Sprinkle well buttered 9-inch pie plate with 1 tablespoon bread crumbs.
- Pour mixture into pie plate and smooth top with spatula. Sprinkle remaining crumbs on top.
- Dot with remaining butter.
- Bake in 400° oven 30 minutes.

Potato, Anaheim Chili and Sweet Corn Hash

Serves 4

½ **pound baking potatoes, russets**
½ **cup fresh corn kernels**
1 **Anaheim chili, diced,**
1 **red bell pepper, diced**
¼ **cup scallions, sliced thinly**
1 **tablespoon salt**
½ **teaspoon freshly ground pepper**
3 **tablespoons butter**

- Wash and julienne the potatoes, leaving skins on. Wrap in a towel and squeeze out all the excess moisture.
- In a bowl, toss the potato with the corn, chili, red pepper, scallions, salt and pepper.
- Melt butter in a skillet over moderate heat. Place small piles of potato in the pan as if making pancakes, taking care not to compress the mixture so hash will remain light.
- Cook until the hash reaches a rich golden brown, about 2 minutes per side. Remove from pan, drain on a paper towel and serve.

A different taste for the potato. Serve with grilled meats.

Apricot Glazed Sweet Potatoes

Serves 8

3 **pounds sweet potatoes**
1 **cup brown sugar**
1 **tablespoon plus 1½ teaspoons cornstarch**
¼ **teaspoon salt**
⅛ **teaspoon cinnamon**
1 **cup apricot nectar**
½ **cup hot water**
2 **tablespoons butter**
½ **cup pecans, chopped**

- Bake sweet potatoes wrapped in foil until done. Cool, peel, and cut into ½ inch slices. Arrange in 2-quart casserole.
- Combine brown sugar, cornstarch, salt and cinnamon. Mix together. Add nectar and water. Cook, stirring constantly until thickened. Stir in butter and pecans. Pour sauce over sweet potatoes.
- Bake in 350° oven 25 minutes or until bubbly.

Great for the holidays, a change from the traditional sweet potatoes with marshmallows.

Orange Baked Sweet Potatoes

Serves 8

- **8 small oranges**
- **6 sweet potatoes**
- **½ cup butter, softened**
- **¾ cup brown sugar**
- **1 8-ounce can crushed pineapple, drained**
- **¼ teaspoon cinnamon**
- **⅛ cup orange juice**
- **¼ cup sliced almonds**

- Cut oranges in half, scoop out pulp and flute edges. Set aside to be used for baking.
- Cook and mash sweet potatoes.
- Combine potatoes, butter, brown sugar, pineapple, cinnamon, and orange juice.
- Fill orange cups with potato mixture and top with almonds.
- Bake in 350° oven 20 minutes.

A great addition to your meat platter.

Garlic Parsley Potatoes

Serves 8

- **3 pounds medium-size red potatoes, unpeeled and sliced**
- **¼ cup olive oil**
- **6 cloves garlic, minced**
- **1 teaspoon salt**
- **½ teaspoon freshly ground pepper**
- **2 tablespoons chopped parsley, divided**

- Combine potatoes, oil, garlic and spices in a large bowl and toss to coat well.
- Layer half of potato mixture in a lightly buttered 12 x 8-inch baking dish. Sprinkle half the parsley over potatoes. Layer remaining potato mixture.
- Cover and bake in 350° oven 45 minutes or until tender.
- Uncover and sprinkle remaining parsley over potatoes.

Great with grilled meats.

Rosemary Potatoes

Serves 8 to 10

- **8 medium potatoes**
- **⅓ cup and 1 tablespoon butter, melted**
- **1 cup minced onion**
- **1½ cups grated cheddar cheese**
- **¾ cup hot milk**
  salt
  freshly ground black pepper
- **1 teaspoon fresh rosemary or ½ teaspoon dried**
- **2 eggs, well beaten**

- Peel the potatoes and cook in salted water. Drain and mash.
- Sauté onions in 1 tablespoon butter until transparent.
- Combine mashed potatoes, onions, remaining butter, cheese, milk, salt, pepper to taste and rosemary.
- Fold in beaten eggs and pour mixture into a lightly buttered casserole.
- Bake in 350° oven 45 minutes until puffy and brown.

Teriyaki New Potatoes

Serves 4 to 6

- **1½ pounds tiny new potatoes or medium red potatoes**
- **1 tablespoon butter, cut into pieces**
- **1 tablespoon teriyaki sauce**
- **¼ teaspoon garlic salt**
- **¼ teaspoon Italian seasoning, crushed**
  dash ground black pepper
  dash ground red pepper
  fresh snipped rosemary
  sour cream

- Cut tiny new potatoes into quarters or the medium potatoes into 1-inch pieces. Place potatoes in 1½ quart microwave-safe casserole.
- Add butter, teriyaki sauce, garlic salt, Italian seasoning, black pepper, and red pepper. Toss to combine.
- Cover and microwave on high power 15 to 20 minutes or until potatoes are tender. Stir twice during cooking.
- Stir before serving. Garnish with snipped rosemary and sour cream.

Serve with pork tenderloin for a great middle of the week dinner.

Parmesan Scalloped Potatoes

Serves 6 to 8

⅔ **cup freshly grated Parmesan cheese**
1 **tablespoon dried marjoram**
1 **teaspoon salt**
½ **teaspoon garlic powder**
¼ **teaspoon grated nutmeg**
¼ **teaspoon coarsely ground pepper**
4 **large baking potatoes, peeled and thinly sliced**
2 **cups whipping cream**
½ **cup water**
2 **tablespoons freshly grated Parmesan cheese**
   fresh parsley

- Combine ⅔ cup Parmesan and herbs in a small bowl. Set seasoning mixture aside.
- Layer one-third potatoes in lightly greased 11 x 7-inch baking dish. Sprinkle half of the seasoning mixture over the potatoes. Repeat layers with remaining potatoes and seasoning mixture, ending with potatoes.
- Combine whipping cream and water; pour over potatoes. Sprinkle evenly with Parmesan.
- Cover with foil.
- Bake in 350° oven 1½ hours; uncover and bake for 30 minutes or until lightly browned. Let stand 10 minutes before serving. Garnish with fresh parsley sprigs.

Serve with Roast Lamb with Herbs.

Snowy Mashed Potatoes

Serves 8 to 10

4 **pounds potatoes, peeled and quartered**
1 **8-ounce package cream cheese, softened**
1 **cup sour cream**
2 **teaspoons salt**
⅛ **teaspoon pepper**
⅛ **teaspoon minced garlic**
¼ **cup chopped chives**
½ **teaspoon paprika**
1 **tablespoon butter**

- Cook potatoes in boiling water until tender. Drain. Beat with mixer until light.
- Add cream cheese, sour cream, salt, pepper and garlic. Beat at high speed until smooth. Stir in chopped chives. Spoon into lightly buttered casserole dish and sprinkle with paprika. Dot with butter.
- Bake uncovered in 350° oven until top is golden brown, about 30 minutes.

Excellent with Pork Roast with Peppercorn-Mustard Crust and Cider Gravy.

Chili Pepper Cheese Fries

Serves 6 to 8

8 **potatoes**
1 to 2 **tablespoons vegetable oil**
½ **teaspoon dried red chili pepper**
½ **cup Parmesan cheese, shredded**
3 to 4 **tablespoons fresh basil, chopped fine**

- Slice potatoes. Toss with oil. Place in large baking pan. Sprinkle with chili pepper.
- Bake in 350° oven 45 minutes, or until lightly browned.
- In large mixing bowl, combine Parmesan and basil. Add warm potatoes, toss and serve.

Also good without chili pepper.

Ginger Rice

Serves 4

2 **cups chicken broth**
1 **tablespoon butter**
1 **cup rice**
2 **teaspoons vegetable oil**
¼ **cup carrots, diced**
¼ **cup green onion, diced**
2 **garlic cloves, minced**
1 **tablespoon minced ginger**
2 **tablespoons soy sauce**
1 **teaspoon coriander**

- In a saucepan, boil the broth and butter. Stir in rice, cover and simmer 20 to 25 minutes.
- Heat oil in a skillet. Sauté carrots 2 minutes. Add green onion, garlic and ginger. Sauté 3 minutes.
- When rice is cooked, stir in carrot mixture, soy sauce and coriander.

Almost Wild Rice

Serves 6 to 8

½ **cup butter**
4 **ounces vermicelli**
1½ **cups long grain rice**
3 **cups chicken broth**
1 **cup sliced fresh mushrooms**
½ **medium onion, finely chopped**
½ **teaspoon salt**
½ **teaspoon fresh ground pepper**
½ **cup sliced almonds, toasted**

- Melt butter in saucepan. Break vermicelli into very small pieces. Add to butter and sauté over medium heat, stirring often, until golden brown.
- Add rice, broth, mushrooms, onion, salt and pepper. Bring to boil. Reduce heat and simmer, covered, about 20 minutes. Serve topped with almonds.
- If made ahead, place in a covered glass baking dish in oven in 300° oven 15 to 20 minutes to reheat.

May be made with beef broth to accompany beef or lamb.

Arroz con Tomato

Serves 6

½ **cup finely chopped green pepper**
2 **jalapeño peppers, chopped**
¼ **cup chopped onion**
1 **clove garlic, minced**
½ **teaspoon dried basil, crushed**
½ **teaspoon dried rosemary, crushed**
2 **tablespoons vegetable oil**
1 **16-ounce can chopped tomatoes**
1 **cup long grain rice**
1 **teaspoon salt**
⅛ **teaspoon pepper**

• In skillet, cook green pepper, jalapeño pepper, onion, garlic, basil and rosemary in hot oil until vegetables are tender.
• Drain tomatoes thoroughly, reserving liquid. Add enough water to make 2 cups of liquid. Stir tomatoes, rice, salt, pepper and liquid into vegetables.
• Bring to boil. Cover and cook over low heat for 35 minutes until rice is done.

Thai Fried Rice

Serves 12 to 16

3 **tablespoons olive oil**
1½ **teaspoons finely chopped garlic**
1 **cup small broccoli florets**
¾ **cup sliced onions**
⅔ **cup sliced snow peas**
⅔ **cup diced tomatoes**
¼ **cup diced mushrooms**
¼ **cup julienned carrots**
¼ **cup diced celery**
½ **cup diced red bell pepper**
4 **cups cooked white or brown rice**
2 **tablespoons oyster sauce**
1½ **tablespoons Thai fish sauce**
1 **teaspoon black pepper**
1½ **tablespoons diced scallions**
¼ **cup thinly sliced leeks**

• Heat olive oil in a large skillet over high heat. Add garlic and sauté until lightly browned, about one minute.
• Add broccoli, onions, snow peas, tomatoes, mushrooms, carrots, celery and bell pepper and stir fry one minute.
• Add rice, oyster sauce, fish sauce and black pepper. Cook, stirring constantly for 3 minutes.
• Transfer to platter and top with scallions and leeks.

Add chicken or shrimp and serve as a main dish to a large gathering.

Carrot Mushroom Pilaf

Serves 4

1⅓ **cups water**
1 **teaspoon reduced sodium chicken bouillon granules**
½ **cup long grain rice**
1½ **cups sliced fresh mushrooms**
1¼ **cups shredded carrots**
½ **cup water**
¼ **cup chopped fresh parsley**
¼ **teaspoon pepper**
⅓ **cup sliced green onions**
¼ **cup chopped pecans**

- Combine 1⅓ cups water and bouillon in saucepan. Bring to a boil and add rice. Cover, reduce heat, and simmer 20 minutes or until liquid is absorbed and rice is tender.
- Add mushrooms, carrots, ½ cup water, parsley and pepper. Cover, cook over low heat 5 minutes. Stir in onions and pecans.

Healthy, delicious and different!

Southern Baked Rice

Serves 8 to 10

2 **cups long grain rice**
4 **tablespoons butter**
2½ **teaspoons salt**
2 **14½-ounce cans beef broth plus ½ can of water**
½ **cup chopped almonds**

- Sauté rice in butter and salt, stirring constantly until golden brown.
- Add liquids and nuts.
- Place in greased casserole and bake in 325° oven 1 hour.

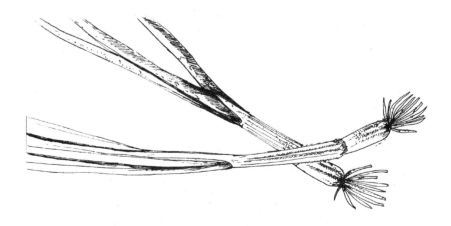

Spicy Black Beans and Rice

Serves 4

- 1 tablespoon olive oil
- 1 small onion, chopped
- 3 serrano chilies, halved, seeded and chopped
- 2 15-ounce cans black beans
- ¼ teaspoon ground cumin
- ⅛ teaspoon cayenne pepper
- 1 cup uncooked long grain rice
- 1¾ cups chicken broth
- 3 cloves garlic, minced

- Heat olive oil in skillet over medium heat. Add onion and chilies. Sauté 6 to 8 minutes or until tender.
- Drain beans, reserving ½ cup liquid. Add beans and liquid to onions and chilies. Cook uncovered, 20 to 30 minutes or until half the liquid is absorbed.
- Season with cumin and cayenne pepper.
- Rinse rice until water runs clear and drain. Combine rice, chicken broth and garlic. Bring to a boil and stir. Reduce heat, cover and simmer 20 to 30 minutes or until broth is absorbed and rice is tender.
- Ladle black beans over rice.

Good and Healthy!

Black Bean Enchilada Pie

Serves 6 to 8

- 2 cups chopped onion
- 1½ cups chopped green bell pepper
- 1 14½-ounce can tomatoes, diced
- ¾ cup picante sauce
- 2 cloves garlic, minced
- 2 teaspoons ground cumin
- 2 15-ounce cans black beans, drained
- 12 6-inch corn tortillas
- 2 cups shredded Monterey Jack cheese
- 2 medium tomatoes, chopped
- 2 cups shredded lettuce
- ½ cup sliced green onions
- 1 cup sliced ripe olives
  sour cream
  picante sauce

- In large skillet combine onion, bell pepper, tomatoes, picante sauce, garlic and cumin. Bring to boil then reduce heat. Simmer uncovered for 10 minutes. Add beans.
- In a 9 x 13-inch baking dish, spread one-third of the bean mixture over bottom. Top with one-half of the tortillas, overlapping as necessary, and one-half of the cheese. Add another one-third of the bean mixture, then remaining tortillas and bean mixture.
- Cover and bake in 350° oven 30 to 35 minutes or until heated through. Sprinkle with remaining cheese. Cover and let stand 10 minutes until cheese melts.
- Cut into squares. Garnish with tomatoes, lettuce, onions and olives. Top with additional sour cream and picante sauce.

The bean mixture makes a great warm dip with chips!

Basque Black Beans and Garbanzos

Serves 4 to 6

1 16-ounce can garbanzo
  beans, drained
2 15-ounce cans black beans,
  drained
  salt and pepper to taste
3 large tomatoes, chopped
1 large onion, chopped
5 cloves garlic, chopped
1 teaspoon rosemary
½ cup olive oil
  chopped parsley

- Place black beans and garbanzos in a baking dish and season with salt and pepper.
- Combine remaining ingredients and toss with beans.
- Bake in 375° oven 45 to 60 minutes. Garnish with parsley and serve warm.

Serve with grilled meats or fish on your patio.

Red Beans and Rice

Serves 4 to 6

6 cups water
1 pound dried small red beans
  or dried red kidney beans
4 tablespoons butter
1 cup finely chopped scallions,
  including 3 inches of green
  tops
½ cup finely chopped onions
1 teaspoon finely minced garlic
2 1-pound smoked ham hocks
1 teaspoon salt
½ teaspoon freshly ground
  black pepper
2 cups long-grain rice

- In a heavy saucepan, bring water to boil. Add beans and boil briskly, uncovered 2 minutes. Turn off heat and let the beans soak 1 hour. Drain beans and reserve 4 cups of soaking liquid, add water if necessary.
- In large bean pot, melt butter and sauté ½ cup of the scallions, onions and garlic until tender.
- Stir in the beans and liquid, ham hocks, salt and pepper. Bring to boil. Reduce heat and simmer partially covered for 3 hours. Check periodically for liquid and smash soft beans for a thick sauce.
- Remove ham hocks and cut the meat away from the bones. Cut the meat into ¼-inch pieces and return meat to the beans. Taste for additional seasonings.
- Prepare rice according to package directions.
- Serve beans over rice and top with remaining scallions.

A real crowd pleaser.

Tulsa Baked Beans

Serves 8

1	**pound Navy beans**
2 to 3	**teaspoons brown sugar**
1	**teaspoon salt**
¼	**teaspoon cayenne pepper**
1	**green banana pepper, minced**
½	**teaspoon freshly ground black pepper**
½	**cup molasses**
1	**teaspoon dry mustard**
2 to 3	**cloves garlic, minced**
1	**medium onion, quartered**
1	**4-inch square salt pork, cut in ½-inch squares down to rind but not through**

- Cover beans with water and boil hard for 2 minutes. Let stand in liquid for 1 hour. Boil for 50 minutes until the beans are done yet firm. Drain and reserve 3 cups of the bean liquid.

- Combine sugar, salt, peppers, molasses, mustard and garlic with drained beans and 2 cups of bean liquid. Place in bean pot. Sink onions in middle and spread salt pork, rind side up on beans.

- Cover and bake in 300° oven 4 hours. The remaining bean liquid may be added if the beans get too dry.

The beans may be served as a side dish, or as a main entrée with your favorite cornbread. This has a totally different taste from regular baked beans and it will become a favorite with your family.

Serve with The Duke's Corn Bread, page 24.

Cattle Trail Beans

Serves 16

2 **pounds pinto beans**
2 **quarts water**
½ **pound salt pork**
2 **cups chopped onion**
½ **cup chopped green onion**
½ **cup chopped green pepper**
1½ **tablespoons chopped garlic**
2 **tablespoons chopped parsley**
1 to 2 **ham hocks**
1 **tablespoon salt**
½ **teaspoon pepper**
⅛ **teaspoon cayenne**
½ **teaspoon crushed red pepper**
2 **bay leaves**
½ **teaspoon thyme**
⅛ **teaspoon basil**

- Wash beans and soak in water overnight. Drain. Add beans to water.
- Sauté salt pork with onions, peppers, garlic and parsley. Add to beans along with ham hocks.
- Add all remaining spices and bring to boil. Simmer 1 to 2 hours until tender.

Even better the next day.

Jalapeño Pepper Butter

½ **cup butter, softened**
2 **jalapeño peppers, seeded and finely minced**
½ **teaspoon cumin**

- Beat butter with electric mixer until light. Add peppers and cumin.
- Cover and refrigerate until ready to use.

Adds a new twist to corn on the cob.

Cheese Butter

1 pound

1 **pound butter**
½ **pound sharp cheddar cheese, grated**
¼ **pound Romano cheese, grated**
1 **teaspoon Worcestershire sauce**
¼ **teaspoon garlic powder**
½ **teaspoon paprika**

- Have all ingredients at room temperature. Whip slowly with mixer until fluffy. Spread on sour dough bread. Broil until topping is brown.

This makes 1 pound of spread at a time and can be frozen.

Try on baked potatoes or fresh steamed vegetables.

Bacon Horseradish Potato Quiche

Serves 12

3½ **pounds baking potatoes, peeled and sliced ⅜-inch thick**
6 **large fresh eggs**
2 **cups whipping cream**
½ **cup cooked crisp bacon, chopped**
2 **tablespoons prepared horseradish, not creamy-style salt and white pepper to taste parchment paper non-stick spray**

This quiche will reheat in a microwave quite nicely. Place 1 wedge on microwave safe plate and microwave 2 minutes. Quiche also keeps well in the refrigerator, covered for several days. At the Bistro this side dish is served with grilled filets. It will also go well with lamb, venison, buffalo and elk.

- Steam or boil sliced potatoes until barely done. Drain and then plunge into ice water bath to stop cooking.
- Beat eggs until completely blended. Add cream, bacon and horseradish.
- Cut parchment paper to fit bottom of 10 x 2-inch round cake pan. Spray bottom and sides of pan with non-stick cooking spray. Press parchment paper round in bottom of pan and spray lightly with non-stick spray.
- Ladle a thin layer of quiche batter into bottom of pan. Next arrange half of the sliced potatoes on top of batter. Season with salt and white pepper. Repeat ending with layer of batter.
- Put potato quiche in a slightly larger pan with at least 1-inch sides. Place both in preheated 350° oven. Add enough hot water to larger pan to reach half way up sides of quiche pan.
- Bake until quiche is set and potatoes are done. Top should be lightly browned. Remove from oven and cool. Refrigerate quiche at least 2 hours or overnight.
- When quiche is cold, run a knife around edge to loosen edges. Set pan directly on stove burner with flame for a few seconds to loosen bottom. Place a cookie sheet over top and carefully invert quiche onto cookie sheet.
- With a thin-bladed, sharp knife, slice quiche into 10 to 12 wedges. With a spatula, lift each wedge and turn browned side up onto a fresh cookie sheet. Arrange each wedge closely to the other wedges but not quite touching. This will prevent the edges from drying during the reheating.
- Reheat in a 350° oven until hot all the way through. Use a spatula to serve.

Sherry Swanson, The Bistro at Brookside

Seasonal Fare

Each Oklahoma season attracts sports and nature enthusiasts to hit a trail, jogging path or playing field, or to simply step outdoors to enjoy the fine weather. With relatively mild winters, Tulsans pursue favorite sports and pastimes such as fishing, hunting, tennis, golf, horseback riding, gardening or boating year round.

The path along the banks of the Arkansas River in Tulsa afford walkers, runners, bikers and skaters serene beauty and the possibility of viewing a majestic bald eagle in flight. Free Wheel, a cross-state family oriented annual bicycle tour, attracts hundreds of cycling enthusiasts to experience the state's diverse scenery.

The Tulsa Zoo and Oxley Nature Center, located in 2,800-acre Mohawk Park, present native animals and their habitats. Visitors to the Oklahoma Tall Grass Prairie Preserve or to Woolaroc, a museum and game preserve, can relive the Wild West when they observe buffalo herds grazing as they have for centuries on Oklahoma's plains. At the Redbud Valley Nature Preserve hikers can view native wildlife and plants. In the spring there is a profusion of blooming redbuds, Oklahoma's state tree.

A drive through Woodward Park to view the dogwoods and azaleas in spring, a walk through the Tulsa Rose Garden and the horticultural areas around the Tulsa Garden Center, allow spectacular views of nature's flower shows.

Oklahoma's beautiful woodlands, prairies and abundant water resources offer opportunities for game hunting and sport fishing.

Numerous horse shows, rodeos and polo matches feature outstanding examples of Oklahoma's perennial leadership in raising championship horses of all breeds.

Many equate Oklahoma with football and in the fall football fever does prevail. On Friday nights, alumni, student and family fans pack high school stadiums in Tulsa. High school and college football teams enjoy tremendous local support, and many college and professional football players have begun their careers to the cheers of friends and neighbors in their Oklahoma home towns.

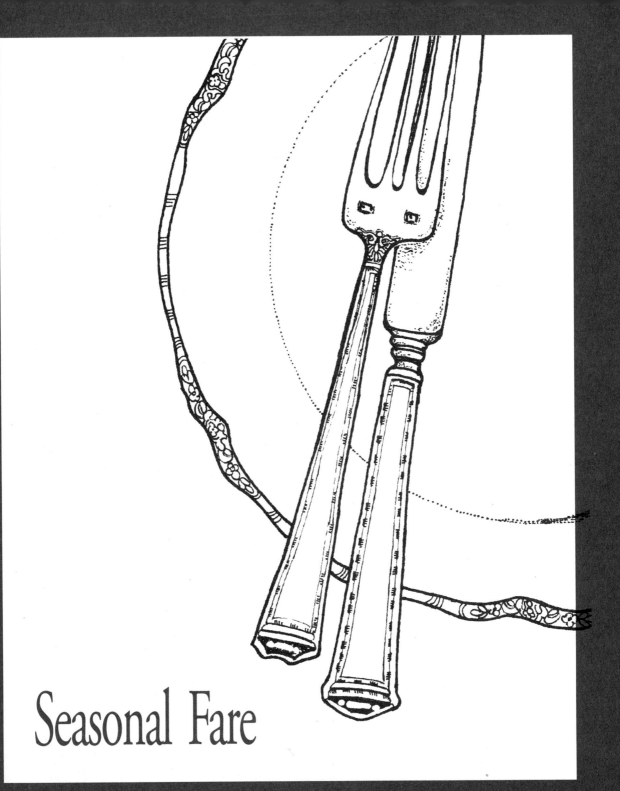

Seasonal Fare

POULTRY, MEAT & GAME
Our Way

Poultry

Breast of Chicken Dijon 150
Cheddar Chicken Lasagna 153
Chicken and Ham
  Wrapsodies 144
Chicken and Italian Sausage 153
Chicken Breasts Stuffed with
  Cilantro, Pesto and Goat
  Cheesed 142
Chicken Cordon Bleu 151
Chicken Curry with Peanuts and
  Noodles 147
Chicken Florentine 143
Chicken in Fresh Mushroom Wine
  Sauce 143
Chicken in Orange Sauce 149
Chicken Roma 146
Chinese Sweet and Sour 148
Classic Turkey Tetrazzini 152
Cranberry-Orange Glazed
  Cornish Hens 173
Curried Turkey with Almonds 151
Green Country Chicken 146
Honey-Mustard Chicken 148
Lemon Chicken with Thyme 145
Marinated Seared Chicken with
  Tropical Salsa 141
Picante Chicken and Rice 149
Sherried Chicken with Artichoke
  Hearts 147
Tasty Yogurt Parmesan
  Chicken 150

Pork

Apple-Stuffed Crown Roast of Pork
  Flambé 157
Chalupa 163
Chinese Sweet and Sour 148
Classic New Mexico Green Chile
  Stew 163
Coach's Favorite Pork Roast 155
Country-Style Pork Ribs 159
Crown Roast of Pork with Sausage
  and Raisin Stuffing 154
Grilled Hoisin Pork 159
Pork Roast with Peppercorn-
  Mustard Crust and Cider
  Gravy 156
Pork Tenderloin à la Orange 158

Beef and Game

Beef Brisket with Gruyère 161
Beef Carnavon 160
Company Quail 171
Fruited Pot Roast 161
Game Night Beef Burgundy 162
Gingered Orange Beef 164
Patio Kabobs 165
Red Wine Drip Beef 162
Roast Pheasant with Wild Rice
  Stuffing and Creamed Pan
  Sauce 172
South of the Border Lasagna 166
Southwestern-Style Brisket 162
Stir-Fry Broccoli Beef 164
Stuffed Aubergine 165

Lamb and Veal

Herb Crusted Lamb in Wine 168
Roast Lamb with Herbs and
  Pistachios 167
Saltimbocca 169
Veal Chops in Fruited Rosemary
  Sauce 169
Veal Marengo 170
Veal Scaloppine au Vin 171

Sauces and Marinades

Carolina Barbeque Sauce 175
Fresh Mango Chutney 180
Fresh Mango Salsa 175
Green Peppercorn Sauce 183
Homemade Barbeque Sauce 174
Pineapple Teriyaki
  Marinade 174
"Sizzling" Steak Marinade 173
Tomatoes Provençal 182
Tropical Salsa 141

Professional Chefs

Artichoke and Asparagus Stuffed
  Chicken Breast 179
Beef and Pasta Strudel 182
Chicken Alfresco 178
Chicken Margarita 178
Chicken Piccata 179
Curried Breast of Chicken with
  Mango Chutney 180
Grilled Venison Backstrap 183
Hanover's Brisket 183
Medallions of Veal with Wild
  Mushroom Sauce and Sun-Dried
  Tomato Cream 176
Pork Savoyard 181
Sesame Chicken Breast with
  Scallion Dipping Sauce 177
Stuffed Pork Tenderloin 181

Marinated Seared Chicken with Tropical Salsa

Serves 4

- ½ cup pineapple juice
- ¼ cup vegetable oil
- 2 tablespoons soy sauce
- 2 tablespoons Dijon mustard
- 1 tablespoon minced ginger
- 1 tablespoon honey
- 1½ teaspoons sesame oil
- 1½ teaspoons Chinese 5-spice powder
- 4 chicken breast halves, skinned and boned
- ½ cup chopped, toasted macadamia nuts

- Combine marinade ingredients. Add the chicken and turn to coat. Cover and refrigerate overnight.
- Remove from marinade and pat dry. Grill or broil until done. Thinly slice the chicken and fan around salsa on plates. Sprinkle with nuts.

Tropical Salsa

- ¼ cup diced pineapple
- ¼ cup diced papaya
- ¼ cup diced mango
- ¼ cup diced red onion
- 1 tablespoon minced mint
- 1 serrano or jalapeño pepper, minced

- Mix the salsa ingredients together.

Nectarines, peaches or cantaloupe could be substituted.

Summer-time favorite.

Chicken Breasts Stuffed with Cilantro, Pesto and Goat Cheese   Serves 4 to 6

- 8 **boneless chicken breast halves with skin**
- 1 **cup grapefruit juice**
- ½ **cup orange juice**
- ½ **cup olive oil**
- ½ **cup rice wine vinegar**
- 2 **bay leaves**
- 2 **chopped jalapeño peppers**
- 4 **large cloves garlic, minced**
- ⅛ **cup Tabasco Sauce**
- ½ **cup chopped cilantro leaves**
- 1 **onion, chopped**

• Marinate chicken in remaining ingredients 4 to 6 hours or overnight in refrigerator.

Stuffing

- 1 **cup cilantro leaves**
- 5 **ounces goat cheese**
- 5 **tablespoons freshly grated Parmesan cheese**
- ½ **cup ricotta cheese**
- 4 **cloves garlic**
- 2 **tablespoons olive oil**
- 3 to 4 **jalapeño peppers**

• Place all ingredients in food processor and blend until smooth.
• Pipe stuffing under skin.
• Place breasts in baking dish with marinade and bake in preheated 375° oven for 25 to 30 minutes.

A taste of the Mediterranean.

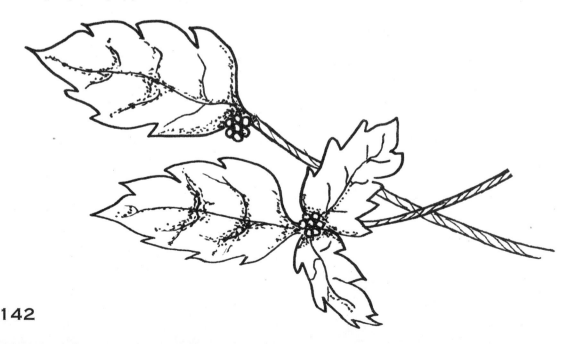

Chicken in Fresh Mushroom Wine Sauce

Serves 4

3 tablespoons flour
1½ tablespoons Italian-style
    bread crumbs
1 teaspoon dried parsley flakes
1 teaspoon garlic salt
¼ cup freshly grated Parmesan
    cheese
1½ pounds boneless chicken
    breast, pounded to ⅛-inch
    thickness
½ cup unsalted butter
¾ pound fresh mushrooms,
    sliced
1 cup white wine
    juice of 1 lemon

- Combine flour, bread crumbs, parsley flakes, garlic salt and Parmesan cheese. Lightly dredge each chicken "fillet" in flour mixture.
- Sauté about 2 or 3 pieces of chicken in 2 tablespoons of butter. Remove chicken to platter as you finish. Repeat process with remaining chicken, adding butter as needed.
- After chicken is sautéed, return pieces to skillet. Add mushrooms.
- Pour wine over mushrooms and chicken. Cover and simmer for 10 minutes, rotating bottom and top pieces.
- Squeeze lemon over chicken.

Chicken Florentine

Serves 6 to 8

8 chicken breast halves,
    skinned and boned
    flour and salt
2 beaten eggs
    vegetable oil
1½ pounds fresh spinach
    butter
    freshly grated Parmesan
    cheese
6 ounces mozzarella cheese,
    sliced
¾ cup dry white wine
    juice of ½ lemon
1 cup chicken broth

- Dredge chicken in salted flour. Dip in eggs and sauté in a small amount of vegetable oil for about 8 minutes per side in oven proof pan.
- Cook fresh spinach just until wilted, drain, chop and add butter to taste. Top chicken with spinach. Sprinkle liberally with Parmesan. Top with mozzarella.
- Bake in preheated 350° oven 10 to 12 minutes.
- Remove chicken to a platter in warm oven. Add wine and lemon juice to pan. Simmer until reduced to half. Add chicken broth and simmer another 2 minutes.
- Pour sauce over chicken.

Great served with a light pasta and Caesar salad.

143

Chicken and Ham Wrapsodies

Serves 6

6 8-ounce chicken breast
  halves
½ cup dry sherry
3 chicken bouillon cubes
3 cups hot water
6 tablespoons prepared
  mustard
¾ teaspoon garlic powder
1 tablespoon fines herbes
6 4 x 6-inch slices Monterey
  Jack cheese
6 4 x 6-inch slices cooked ham
1 10-ounce package frozen
  puffed pastry shells
1 egg white, beaten
  poppy or sesame seeds

- In large pan combine chicken, sherry, and bouillon dissolved in hot water. Bring to boil. Reduce heat and cover. Simmer 20 minutes or until tender.
- Cool in broth 30 minutes. Remove chicken from broth; skin and bone. Refrigerate until thoroughly cooled.
- Combine mustard, garlic powder and fines herbes. Mix well. Spread 1 tablespoon of mixture over each chicken piece, coating thoroughly. Wrap 1 slice cheese followed by 1 slice ham around each piece.
- On lightly floured board, roll each pastry shell into 8-inch circle. Place 1 chicken piece seam side down in center of each pastry circle. Bring up sides of pastry to overlap in center. Moisten and pinch to seal.
- Place bundles, seam side down, at least 2 inches apart on large baking sheet lightly sprayed with cooking oil. Brush with egg white and sprinkle with poppy or sesame seeds. Chill 30 minutes.
- Bake in preheated 425° oven 30 minutes or until brown and crisp. Cool 20 minutes on rack.
- May be served warm or cold.

Symphony at Sunset First Prize Winner!

Lemon Chicken with Thyme

Serves 4

- 3 **tablespoons flour**
- ½ **teaspoon salt**
- ¼ **teaspoon pepper**
- 4 **chicken breast halves, skinned and boned**
- 2 **tablespoons olive oil**
- 1 **medium onion, chopped**
- 1 **tablespoon butter**
- 1 **cup chicken broth**
- 3 **tablespoons freshly squeezed lemon juice**
- ½ **teaspoon thyme lemon wedges**
- 2 **tablespoons freshly chopped parsley**

- In a plastic bag, combine flour, salt and pepper and shake to mix. Add chicken and shake to coat lightly. Remove the chicken and reserve the excess seasoned flour.

- In a large skillet, warm 1 tablespoon of the oil over medium heat. Add the chicken and brown on one side, about 5 minutes. Add the remaining tablespoon of oil, turn the chicken and brown well on the second side, about 5 minutes longer. Remove chicken and set aside.

- Sauté onion in butter. Stir in the reserved seasoned flour and cook, stirring, until the flour is completely blended, about 1 minute. Add broth, 2 tablespoons of lemon juice and thyme and bring to a boil, stirring constantly.

- Return the chicken to the skillet, reduce the heat and cover. Cook until the chicken is tender, about 5 minutes.

- Remove chicken to serving platter. Add remaining 1 tablespoon lemon juice to the sauce and pour over chicken. Serve the chicken with lemon wedges and a sprinkling of parsley.

Serve with steamed broccoli and lightly buttered pasta.

Green Country Chicken

Serves 4 to 6

- 6 **large chicken breast halves, skinned and boned**
- 4 **tablespoons butter**
- 1 **onion, sliced**
- 1 **clove garlic, minced**
- 2 **tablespoons flour**
- ½ **teaspoon salt**
- ¼ **teaspoon pepper**
- 1 **chicken bouillon cube**
- 1 **cup hot water**
- ¼ **cup dry red wine**
- 6 to 10 **small new potatoes**
- ½ **cup green peas snipped parsley**

- Sauté chicken breasts in butter until browned. Add onion and garlic and cook for 5 minutes.
- Combine flour, salt and pepper in bowl.
- Dissolve bouillon cube in water and add wine. Pour slowly into flour and mix well.
- Pour over chicken and add potatoes and peas.
- Cook covered for 25 minutes. Garnish with parsley.

A great recipe for the family during the school week.

Chicken Roma

Serves 4

- 4 **chicken breast halves, skinned and boned**
- 2 **tablespoons olive oil**
- 2 **tablespoons butter**
- 1 **onion, sliced**
- 2 **cloves garlic, minced**
- ½ **cup sliced green olives**
- ¼ **cup capers**
- 1 **14-ounce can Italian stewed tomatoes**
- 1 **cup chicken broth**

- Brown chicken in oil and butter and remove from pan.
- Add onions and garlic. Sauté until onion is translucent. Do not burn garlic.
- Place chicken in pan with remaining ingredients.
- Cover and simmer 35 minutes or until chicken is tender.

Great served over rice.

Sherried Chicken with Artichoke Hearts

Serves 6

6 chicken breast halves,
   skinned and boned
   salt and pepper
¼ cup butter
1 13½-ounce can artichoke
   hearts, drained and cut in
   halves
¾ pound fresh mushrooms,
   sliced
½ cup sherry
1 tablespoon freshly squeezed
   lemon juice
1 cup whipping cream
1½ teaspoons chopped chives
¼ cup sour cream

- Salt and pepper chicken and brown in butter. Add artichokes and mushrooms.
- Stir in sherry and lemon juice. Cover and cook on low to medium heat 15 minutes.
- Stir in whipping cream and chives. Cook on low heat for 5 minutes. Remove chicken to platter. Whip sour cream until light and stir into rest of sauce.
- Serve chicken on bed of rice and cover with sauce.

Gourmet dining in 30 minutes.

Chicken Curry with Peanuts and Noodles

Serves 4

6 chicken breasts, skinned,
   boned and cubed
½ teaspoon salt
½ teaspoon pepper
2 tablespoons curry powder
3 bay leaves, broken in
   quarters
4 tablespoons vegetable oil
4 cloves garlic, minced
1 large onion, coarsely
   chopped
1 can coconut milk
½ package bean thread
   noodles, soaked, drained and
   cut in pieces
½ cup crushed unsalted
   peanuts

- Toss chicken in salt, pepper, curry powder and bay leaves. Refrigerate 2 hours.
- Heat oil in large wok. Add garlic and onions. Stir-fry until softened. Add chicken and fry until golden brown.
- Pour coconut milk over chicken, stir well and cover. Cook over low heat until chicken is almost done.
- Add noodles, salt and pepper to taste. Simmer 5 minutes.
- Remove from heat. Add crushed peanuts.
- Serve with steamed rice.

Coconut milk is the secret ingredient.

Chinese Sweet and Sour

Serves 4

- 1 **pound chicken or lean pork, cut in 1-inch pieces**
- 1 **tablespoon wine**
- 2 **tablespoons soy sauce**
- 1 **carrot, cut in pieces**
- 1 **large onion, cut in pieces**
- 1 **bell pepper, cut in pieces cooking oil**
- 2 **slices canned pineapple, cut in pieces**
- 1 **egg**
- 2 **tablespoons flour**
- 1 **tablespoon cornstarch**

- Marinate meat in wine and soy sauce for 15 minutes.
- Parboil carrot for 10 minutes. Stir-fry onion and pepper for 5 minutes over high heat. Add carrot and pineapple, set aside.
- Beat egg lightly with flour and cornstarch. Dip meat in mixture, heat oil and deep fry until golden brown. Set aside.

Sauce

- ½ **cup water**
- 3 **tablespoons sugar**
- 3 **tablespoons soy sauce**
- 2 **tablespoons vinegar**
- ½ **cup pineapple juice**
- 3 **tablespoons tomato paste**
- 1 **tablespoon cornstarch**

- Heat water, sugar, soy sauce, vinegar and pineapple juice, bring to a boil.
- Add tomato paste and stir constantly; add cornstarch. Stir until it thickens. Add cooked vegetables, mix well and pour over meat.
- Serve hot over steamed rice.

A family favorite.

Honey-Mustard Chicken

Serves 4 to 6

- ¼ **cup butter**
- ½ **cup honey**
- ¼ **cup prepared mustard**
- 1 **teaspoon dry mustard**
- 1 **teaspoon salt**
- 1 **teaspoon curry powder**
- 4 to 6 **chicken breast halves, skinned and boned**

- Melt butter in shallow baking dish and stir in remaining ingredients.
- Roll chicken in butter mixture. Arrange in single layer with remaining sauce.
- Bake in 375° oven 1 hour basting occasionally until chicken is tender and richly glazed.

Easy and good for beginner cooks.

Picante Chicken and Rice

Serves 6

- 2 **garlic cloves, minced**
- ¾ **cup onion, chopped**
- 1 **tablespoon olive oil**
- 1½ **cups chicken broth**
- 1 **cup mild picante sauce**
- 1 **cup long grain rice**
- 6 **chicken breast halves, skinned and boned**
- 1 **tomato, chopped**
- ½ **cup Monterey Jack cheese, shredded**

- In large skillet sauté garlic and onion in oil until onions are clear. Add chicken broth and picante sauce. Bring to a boil. Stir in rice.
- Arrange chicken breasts over rice. Cover tightly and simmer 20 minutes.
- Remove from heat and let stand covered for 5 minutes until liquid is absorbed.
- Serve with tomatoes and cheese sprinkled on top.

Chicken with a spicy flavor the whole family will enjoy!

Chicken in Orange Sauce

Serves 6

- 6 **chicken breast halves, skinned and boned**
- ½ **cup unsalted butter**
- ¼ **cup flour**
- 2 **tablespoons brown sugar**
- 1 **teaspoon salt**
- ½ **teaspoon ginger**
- ⅛ **teaspoon pepper**
- 1¾ **cups orange juice**
- ½ **cup water**
- 1 **can of mandarin oranges, drained**

- Brown chicken in butter; remove from pan.
- Blend flour, brown sugar and spices. Stir into pan drippings. Add orange juice and water. Stir until boiling; boil one minute.
- Return chicken breasts to pan. Cover and cook 40 minutes. Garnish with mandarin oranges.
- Serve with couscous or rice.

Orange Rice

- Prepare rice as usual except substitute orange juice for the required liquid. Add ⅓ cup currants or raisins.

Tasty Yogurt Parmesan Chicken

Serves 6

- **6 chicken breast halves, skinned and boned**
- **2 tablespoons freshly squeezed lemon juice**
- **cayenne pepper to taste**
- **½ cup plain low-fat yogurt**
- **2 tablespoons low-fat mayonnaise**
- **1 tablespoon Dijon mustard**
- **1 teaspoon Worcestershire sauce**
- **½ teaspoon thyme**
- **¼ cup thinly sliced green onions**
- **¼ cup freshly grated Parmesan cheese**

- Arrange chicken in a lightly oiled baking dish. Drizzle with lemon juice. Sprinkle with cayenne pepper to taste.
- Combine yogurt, mayonnaise, mustard, Worcestershire, thyme and green onions. Spread over the chicken.
- Bake in a preheated 350° oven uncovered 1 hour or until fork tender.
- Drain off the pan juices and sprinkle the chicken with Parmesan. Broil until the cheese is slightly browned.

This dish goes quite well with Southern Baked Rice, page 132, and Sugar Snaps, page 121.

Breast of Chicken Dijon

Serves 4

- **3 tablespoons butter**
- **4 chicken breast halves, skinned and boned**
- **2 tablespoons flour**
- **1 cup chicken broth**
- **1 cup light cream or milk (can use skim)**
- **4 tablespoons Dijon mustard**

- Melt butter. Add chicken breasts and cook until done and lightly browned, about 15 to 20 minutes.
- Remove chicken to a warm serving platter.
- Stir flour into drippings in the skillet and cook for 1 minute. Add chicken broth and light cream. Stir and cook until sauce thickens and bubbles.
- Stir in mustard and return chicken to the skillet. Cover and heat for 10 minutes.
- May garnish with cherry tomatoes and parsley.

Chicken Cordon Bleu

Serves 6

- 6 chicken breast halves, skinned and boned
- 6 slices provolone cheese
- 6 thin ham slices
- 6 slices of bacon, uncooked
- 1 box long grain and wild rice, cooked
- 1½ cans cream of mushroom soup
- 8 ounces sour cream
- ⅓ pound fresh mushrooms, sliced

- Wrap each chicken breast in a slice of cheese then a slice of ham. Secure with one slice of bacon.
- Place cooked rice on bottom of baking dish. Arrange chicken on top of rice.
- Combine soup and sour cream and spread over chicken.
- Bake in 350° oven 45 minutes.
- Sauté mushrooms in butter, drain and put on chicken. Bake an additional 15 minutes.

Classic that continues to be popular.

Curried Turkey with Almonds

Serves 4 to 6

- ¼ cup butter
- ½ cup almonds, sliced
- 1 cup fresh mushrooms, sliced
- 1 teaspoon curry powder
- 1 tablespoon grated onion
- 1 can cream of mushroom soup
- ⅔ cup milk
- 2 tablespoons sherry
- 1½ cups cooked turkey, diced

- Lightly brown almonds in butter.
- Remove almonds and sauté mushrooms, remove.
- Add curry powder and onion to remaining butter and blend.
- Stir in soup, milk, sherry. Cook over low heat.
- Add mushrooms, almonds, and turkey.
- Simmer 10 minutes. Serve over rice.

Leftover Thanksgiving turkey never tasted so good.

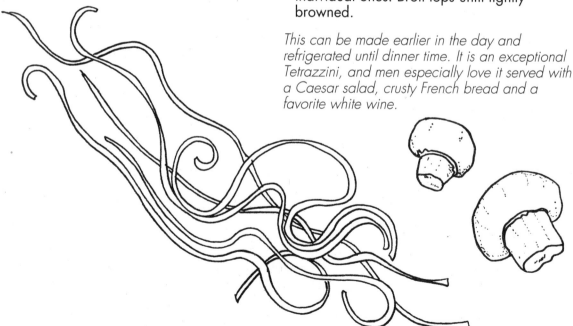

Classic Turkey Tetrazzini

Serves 6 to 8

- 6 **tablespoons butter**
- 5 **tablespoons flour**
- 2½ **cups chicken broth**
- 1¼ **cups half and half**
- ½ **cup dry white wine**
- ¾ **cup freshly shredded Parmesan cheese**
- ¾ **pound fresh mushrooms, sliced but reserve a few for garnish**
- 8 **ounces pasta, spaghetti or fettuccine, cooked and drained**
- 3 to 4 **cups cooked turkey salt**

- Melt 2 tablespoons butter, whisk in flour and gradually blend in the chicken broth, cream and wine. Cook, stirring, for about 3 minutes after mixture starts to simmer. Stir in ½ cup of Parmesan. Remove 1 cup of the sauce and blend in remaining cheese.

- Melt the remaining 4 tablespoons butter in a pan, add mushrooms, and cook quickly, stirring, until lightly brown.

- Combine the large portion of sauce, mushrooms, pasta, and turkey. Salt to taste. Turn into a large, shallow casserole or individual casseroles. Spoon the 1 cup of sauce evenly over the surface and top with reserved mushroom slices.

- Bake in 375° oven until bubbling; allow 15 minutes for large casserole and 8 minutes for individual ones. Broil tops until lightly browned.

This can be made earlier in the day and refrigerated until dinner time. It is an exceptional Tetrazzini, and men especially love it served with a Caesar salad, crusty French bread and a favorite white wine.

Chicken and Italian Sausage

Serves 6 to 8

1 pound Italian sausage, cubed
1 large onion, minced
6 to 8 chicken breast halves, skinned, boned and cubed
2 tablespoons oil
4 tablespoons butter
1 28-ounce can of tomatoes, diced
2½ cups chicken broth
½ teaspoon pepper
½ teaspoon basil
¼ teaspoon oregano
2 tablespoons parsley flakes
1 cup long grain rice
¼ cup freshly grated Parmesan cheese
salt to taste

- Brown sausage and onion for 5 minutes and drain. Set aside.
- In same pan brown chicken in oil and butter.
- Add sausage, onion, tomatoes and broth. Add pepper, basil, oregano and parsley. Stir in rice.
- Cover and simmer 15 minutes.
- Stir again, recover and simmer an additional 50 minutes.
- Stir in Parmesan before serving. Salt to taste.

Cheddar Chicken Lasagna

Serves 8 to 10

1 8-ounce package lasagna noodles
1 can cream of chicken soup
1 can cream of mushroom soup
1 cup freshly grated Parmesan cheese
1 cup sour cream
1 cup finely chopped onion
1 cup sliced ripe olives
¼ cup chopped pimentos
½ teaspoon garlic salt
3 cups cooked and cubed chicken
2 cups shredded cheddar cheese

- Cook and drain noodles.
- Combine soups, Parmesan, sour cream, onion, olives, pimentos and garlic salt. Add chicken.
- Layer in 9 x 13-inch pan: ⅓ chicken mixture, ⅓ cheddar, ½ noodles, ⅓ chicken mixture, ⅓ cheddar, ½ noodles and ⅓ chicken mixture. Reserve ⅓ cheddar.
- Cover and bake 20 minutes at 350°.
- Uncover and add remaining ⅓ cheddar, bake 10 minutes more.

Excellent choice for pre-game dinner.

Crown Roast of Pork with Sausage and Raisin Stuffing

Serves 8 to 10

crown roast of pork (about 16 chops, leaving 3-inch cavity)
salt, pepper and thyme
1 empty tin can with top and bottom lids removed

- Have butcher prepare crown roast of pork. Sprinkle pork well with salt, pepper and thyme.

- Fit an empty tin can into roast and cover the ends of the chops with foil. Place into a pan just large enough to hold it and roast the pork in a preheated 400° oven 20 minutes. Reduce the heat to 325° and roast the pork for 40 minutes.

- Remove the pork from the oven and remove the tin can. Fill the cavity of the roast with Sausage and Raisin Stuffing, doming it.

- Return the pork to the oven and roast it 1 hour and 10 minutes more, or until a meat thermometer inserted in the thickest part of the chop registers 175°.

- Transfer the roast to a warm round serving platter. Remove the foil from the ends of chops and replace with paper frills. Keep roast warm. Serve with Mustard Sauce.

Sausage and Raisin Stuffing

4 cups

2 cups fresh bread crumbs
⅓ cup milk
½ cup minced onion
2 tablespoons butter
½ pound pork sausage
¾ cup chopped celery
¼ cup raisins
¼ cup chopped raw cranberries
2 tart apples, peeled and diced
salt, pepper, sage and thyme to taste

- Moisten bread crumbs with milk. Set aside.

- Sauté onion in butter until softened. Add sausage and sauté lightly. Add celery, raisins, cranberries and apples and cook mixture for 5 minutes.

- Add the bread crumbs to mixture. Season the stuffing with salt, pepper, sage and thyme to taste.

Continued on next page

Mustard Sauce
- **2 tablespoons of drippings**
- **2 tablespoons flour**
- **½ cup dry white wine**
- **½ cup hot chicken broth**
- **1 cup whipping cream**
- **1 tablespoon Dijon mustard**
  salt and pepper

• Pour off all but the 2 tablespoons of fat from the roasting pan and sprinkle in 2 tablespoons flour. Cook the roux over low heat, stirring for 2 minutes.

• Pour in wine and scrape up all the brown bits clinging to the bottom and sides of the pan. Reduce the sauce over high heat to 2 tablespoons and add chicken broth and cream.

• Cook sauce 5 minutes until thickened. Thin 1 tablespoon mustard with 2 tablespoons sauce and add to the sauce.

• Season with salt and pepper to taste and pour into sauceboat.

An elegant autumn dinner!

Coach's Favorite Pork Roast

Serves 6 to 8

- **4 pound pork roast (loin)**
- **1 package dried onion soup mix**
- **1 quart glass jar sauerkraut**

• Place roast in crockpot. Cover with soup mix and sauerkraut. Cook on low all day. Leave in the morning, and it will be done for dinner.

May bake in 300° oven in covered casserole 6 to 8 hours.

Pork Roast with Peppercorn-Mustard Crust and Cider Gravy

Serves 6

¼ cup plus 1 tablespoon
**unsalted butter at room
temperature**
4 to 5 pound **boneless pork
loin roast, rolled and tied**
2 tablespoons **flour**
2 tablespoons plus 1 teaspoon
Dijon mustard
1 tablespoon **dry mustard**
1 tablespoon **cracked black
peppercorns**
1 tablespoon **cracked dried
green peppercorns**
1 tablespoon **cracked white
peppercorns**
1 tablespoon **whole mustard
seeds**
2 teaspoons **golden brown
sugar**
2 teaspoons **dried thyme,
crumbled**
1½ cups **apple cider**
3 tablespoons **Calvados**
2 tablespoons **flour**
¾ cup **chicken broth**
1 tablespoon **cider vinegar
salt and pepper**

- Melt 1 tablespoon butter in heavy, large skillet over medium-high heat. Add roast and cook until brown, about 4 minutes per side. Remove from skillet. Cool 10 minutes, transfer to roasting pan.

- Combine remaining ¼ cup butter with flour, mustards, peppercorns, mustard seeds, sugar, and thyme in bowl. Spread paste over top and sides of roast. Roast in preheated 475° oven 30 minutes, with rack in lowest third of oven. Reduce heat to 325°. Continue cooking about 1 hour and 20 minutes for medium doneness.

- Transfer roast to cutting board and tent with foil. Transfer 2 tablespoons drippings from pan to heavy saucepan. Discard remaining drippings.

- Heat roasting pan over medium-low heat. Add cider and boil until liquid is reduced to ¾ cup, scraping up any browned bits, about 8 minutes. Stir in Calvados and boil 1 minute.

- Heat drippings in saucepan over medium-heat. Add flour and stir until golden brown, about 2 minutes. Whisk in cider mixture and broth. Simmer until thickened, stirring occasionally, about 2 minutes. Remove from heat. Mix in vinegar and remaining teaspoon Dijon mustard. Season with salt and pepper.

- Carve roast and serve with gravy.

Dinner party favorite.

Apple-Stuffed Crown Roast of Pork Flambé

Serves 6

- **5 pound crown roast of pork**
  vegetable oil
  salt and pepper
- **4 tablespoons butter**
- **3 whole green onions, sliced**
- **4 large fresh mushrooms,**
  sliced
- **2 tart apples, diced**
- **3 cups packaged stuffing mix**
- **½ cup applesauce**
- **3 tablespoons plus ½ cup apple**
  brandy
- **1 10-ounce jar apricot**
  preserves

- Rub meat with vegetable oil and salt and pepper
- Place meat on triple thickness aluminum foil in roasting pan. Cover bone tips with small pieces of foil. Insert meat thermometer.
- Heat butter in large skillet until bubbly. Sauté onions until tender. Add mushrooms, cook until tender. Add apples and stir one minute.
- Blend in stuffing mix, applesauce and 3 tablespoons brandy. Add more applesauce if stuffing seems dry. Pack in prepared roast, mounding high. Cover stuffing with foil cap.
- Bake in 325° oven 2½ hours. Remove foil cap and continue roasting.
- Reserving ¼ cup of preserves, heat the rest with ¼ cup of the brandy in small saucepan. Brush remaining preserves mixture on meat every 10 minutes. Roast until meat thermometer registers 170°, an additional 30 minutes.
- Remove roast from oven. Let stand 15 minutes. Put foil or paper tips on rib tips. Heat reserved ¼ cup preserves and float remaining ¼ cup brandy on top. Ignite and pour over roast.

Your guests will be de-lighted!

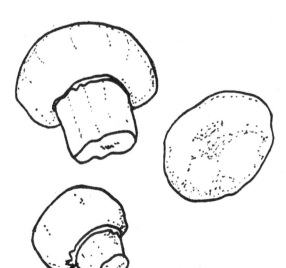

Pork Tenderloin à la Orange

Serves 4 to 6

1½ **pound pork tenderloin**
1 **tablespoon Dijon mustard**
1 **orange rind, finely grated**
¼ **cup sugar**
1 **tablespoon flour**
¼ **teaspoon cayenne pepper**
   salt and pepper to taste
1 **tablespoon olive oil**
¾ **cup freshly squeezed orange juice**

- Dry the tenderloin and rub with mustard.
- Combine orange rind, sugar, flour, cayenne, salt, and pepper to taste and spread the mixture on a plate.
- Heat a 10 or 12-inch nonstick skillet over medium high heat for 3 to 5 minutes, add oil and swirl.
- Roll pork in sugar mixture and immediately transfer to the hot oil. Brown the pork on all sides, regulating the heat to keep the coating from burning. The pork will brown nicely over medium high heat in less than 10 minutes.
- Add orange juice, bring to a boil, cover and lower heat to simmer gently until the pork reaches an internal temperature of 155°, about 12 to 18 minutes.
- Transfer the pork to serving platter and keep warm.
- Over high heat quickly reduce the remaining sauce in the skillet until it is thick and almost syrupy.
- To serve, slice pork into medallions. Top with sauce and serve with rice.

This is a great dish to serve to company and is very low-fat.

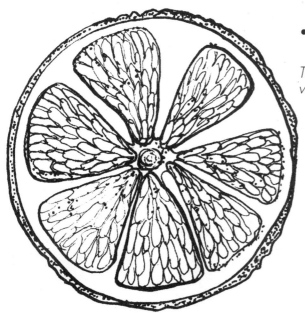

Grilled Hoisin Pork

Serves 4 to 6

- 2 **tablespoons soy sauce**
- 2 **tablespoons Hoisin sauce**
- 1 **tablespoon brown sugar**
- 1 **tablespoon peanut oil**
- 1½ **teaspoons honey**
- ½ **teaspoon garlic salt**
- ½ **teaspoon ground cinnamon**
- 2 **tablespoons dry sherry**
- 1½ **pound pork tenderloin**

- Combine marinade ingredients, stir well.
- Add pork tenderloin, cover and chill 8 hours.
- Remove from marinade and grill until done, turning often.

Country-Style Pork Ribs

Serves 4

- 1 **medium onion, diced**
- ½ **teaspoon garlic powder**
- 3 **pounds country-style pork ribs**
- 3 **teaspoons vinegar**
- 3 **tablespoons Worcestershire sauce**
- ⅓ **cup soy sauce**
- ½ **teaspoon salt**
- ½ **teaspoon black pepper**
- ¼ **teaspoon ginger powder**
- ½ **teaspoon thyme**
- ¾ **cup water**
- 3 **tablespoons olive oil**

- Sprinkle onion and garlic over pork.
- Combine vinegar, Worcestershire sauce, soy sauce, salt, pepper, ginger and thyme with water.
- Add olive oil and pour mixture over meat. Bake in 350° oven 1 hour.

Beef Carnavon

Serves 8

Pastry
1 box frozen puff pastry, thawed

Beef
4 pound whole filet of beef, trimmed
3 tablespoons butter, room temperature
freshly ground pepper
⅓ cup Cognac

Duxelles
½ cup butter
2 shallots, finely chopped
1 pound mushrooms, finely chopped

Assembly
1 egg white, lightly beaten
1 egg yolk
1 teaspoon cream
parsley for garnish
salt to taste

- Preheat oven to 450°. Rub meat with butter and pepper. Place meat thermometer in the filet. Roast on rack until thermometer reads 120° for rare center and 140° for medium. Remove from the oven and flame with Cognac. Cool on rack and then refrigerate.

- Melt butter and sauté shallots until translucent. Add mushrooms and cook slowly until moisture is evaporated. Chill.

- Roll pastry and cut large enough to cover beef. Spread pastry with duxelles.
- Place filet on the duxelles and salt to taste. Bring the edges of the pastry together and seal with a few drops of water. Invert, placing the seam side down on a lightly greased baking sheet.
- Cut small pieces of the left over pastry into the shape of leaves and fasten to the top of the filet with egg white. Mix egg yolk and cream and brush over entire pastry surface. Chill 30 minutes.
- Preheat oven to 425°. Bake 10 minutes. Reduce heat to 375° and bake 20 to 25 minutes.
- Remove from oven and let stand 10 minutes before carving in thick slices. Garnish with parsley.

Not as difficult as it appears! Plan ahead and take it in steps. It makes a wonderful centerpiece for a holiday table. The presentation is elegant!

Beef Brisket with Gruyère

Serves 4

- **2 pounds beef brisket, trimmed and cubed**
- **3 tablespoons Dijon mustard**
- **2 cloves garlic, minced**
- **2 tablespoons vegetable oil**
- **2 bunches green onions or 1 bunch leeks, cut into 1-inch lengths**
- **1 teaspoon sugar**
- **2 tablespoons Worcestershire sauce**
- **8 ounces beef broth (may include dash of sherry)**
- **8 ounces finely grated Gruyère cheese**

- Place meat, mustard and garlic in large bowl. Stir together until meat is coated.
- In large flameproof baking dish, heat oil and fry meat, stirring constantly until lightly browned, about 6 to 8 minutes.
- Add leeks, sugar, Worcestershire and broth.
- Cook uncovered in preheated 350° oven 2 hours, stirring occasionally.
- Sprinkle cheese over top and return to oven for 10 to 15 minutes until cheese is bubbly and brown.

Tastes delicious and rich, but is easy to prepare.

Fruited Pot Roast

Serves 6 to 8

3 to 4 pound pot roast
vegetable oil or butter

Marinade
- **12 ounces mixed dried fruit (apricots, pitted prunes, pears, etc.)**
- **16 ounces beer**
- **½ cup water**
- **1 clove garlic, minced**
- **¼ cup brown sugar**
- **1 bay leaf**
- **2 onions, sliced**
- **1 teaspoon parsley**
- **¼ teaspoon cinnamon**
- **1½ teaspoons salt**
- **¼ teaspoon freshly ground black pepper**

- Brown pot roast in oil or butter. Combine marinade ingredients. Pour over roast. Cover and bake in 275° oven 4 hours.

Marinade is also good with pork tenderloin.

Game Night Beef Burgundy

Serves 4 to 6

3 pounds beef tips
1½ cups red wine
3 10½-ounce cans consommé
2 onions, sliced
1 pound small fresh mushrooms
2 14½-ounce cans beef broth
½ cup flour
½ cup bread crumbs
1½ teaspoons Kitchen Bouquet

- Combine beef, wine, consommé, onions, mushrooms and broth. Place in large ovenproof pot.
- Combine flour and bread crumbs. Stir into beef mixture. Add Kitchen Bouquet.
- Bake in 300° oven about 3 hours. Stir occasionally. Salt and pepper to taste.

Serve over wide noodles.

Red Wine Drip Beef

Serves 6 to 8

3-pound boneless beef roast, trimmed
1 tablespoon garlic salt
½ teaspoon oregano
½ teaspoon rosemary
3 beef bouillon cubes
1 cup red wine
water to cover

- Combine beef with herbs, bouillon, wine and water. Simmer 8 or more hours in stock pot until tender. Remove meat and shred. Return to au jus.

Serve with Homemade Barbeque Sauce, page 174.

Southwestern-Style Brisket

Serves 6

4 pound brisket, trimmed
1 onion, sliced
salt and pepper to season
2 bay leaves
1 teaspoon instant coffee
2 teaspoons brown sugar
1 tablespoon Worcestershire sauce
½ cup catsup

- Cover brisket with water and boil with onion, salt, pepper and bay leaves. Boil 3½ hours or until tender.
- Remove brisket from water and place in baking dish.
- Combine coffee, sugar, Worcestershire and catsup. Pour over brisket and bake in 350° oven 15 minutes.

Chalupa

Serves 10

4 pound boneless pork roast
16 ounces dry pinto beans
1 tablespoon garlic salt
2 tablespoons chili powder
2 teaspoons salt
1 teaspoon oregano

- Place all ingredients in large stock pot.
- Fill with water to cover meat and cook on low covered 8 to 10 hours or until tender.
- Remove meat and shred. Put meat back in pot. Stir. May add chicken broth if mixture is too dry.
- Serve over tortilla chips or corn tortillas with the following: chopped tomatoes, chopped green onion, chopped lettuce, grated cheese, sour cream, picante sauce, black olives and guacamole.

This is a great recipe for a crowd. Guests can prepare their Chalupas to their taste, and the hostess can enjoy her guests.

Classic New Mexico Green Chile Stew

Serves 8

2 pounds round steak, cubed
vegetable oil
3 large onions, chopped
1 clove garlic, minced
5 10-ounce cans Rotel tomatoes
4 to 6 10-ounce cans whole green chilies, coarsely chopped
2 cups water
2 beef bouillon cubes

- Brown cubed steak slowly in small amount of oil; add chopped onion and garlic. Simmer for 5 minutes.
- Add remaining ingredients and simmer, covered for 3 hours or until meat is fork tender.

There are many variations on this recipe such as adding potatoes, carrots, and celery. This is the classic.

Gingered Orange Beef

Serves 4 to 6

⅔ cup freshly squeezed orange or tangerine juice
1 large orange or tangerine, peeled and sectioned
3 tablespoons teriyaki sauce
1½ teaspoons cornstarch
3 tablespoons sesame oil fresh ginger, about 2 x 3-inches, grated
2 cloves garlic, minced
3 large carrots, sliced diagonally
1 pound fresh parboiled green beans, raw asparagus or ½ pound peas
¼ teaspoon dried red pepper
1 pound flank steak, sliced in 2-inch strips
2 tablespoons sherry

- Mix juice, teriyaki sauce and cornstarch until thoroughly combined; set aside.
- Heat oil in medium skillet or wok over medium-high heat. Add ginger and garlic; stir-fry for 2 to 3 minutes. Add vegetables and hot pepper. Cook 2 to 3 minutes. Remove vegetables.
- Stir-fry beef until slightly pink, adding sherry.
- Return vegetables to skillet with steak. Stir in orange-cornstarch mixture until smooth. Bring to a boil and cook 2 minutes, or until slightly thickened. Gently stir in orange sections. If using tangerines, toss in a few bits of cleaned peel.
- Serve over steamed rice.

The orange and ginger flavors make this dish delightfully different.

Stir-Fry Broccoli Beef

Serves 6

2 tablespoons oil
1½ pound sirloin steak, sliced in ½-inch wide strips
3 tablespoons finely grated fresh ginger
1 tablespoon minced fresh garlic
3 carrots, sliced diagonally
¼ cup rice wine vinegar
¼ cup soy sauce
1 medium onion, sliced
¾ cup chopped broccoli

- Heat oil in wok. Add steak, ginger and garlic. Stir fry 3 to 5 minutes or until meat is brown. Add carrots and stir fry additional 1 to 2 minutes.
- Mix vinegar and soy together and add. Mixture will steam if wok is hot enough. Then quickly add onion and broccoli.
- Stir-fry entire mixture another 1 to 2 minutes, or until onions become slightly limp.
- Serve over rice.

A complete meal that is low in fat. Great for do-ahead dinners.

Patio Kabobs

Serves 8

- ½ **cup vegetable oil**
- ¼ **cup freshly squeezed lemon juice**
- 2 **tablespoons prepared mustard**
- 1 **teaspoon black pepper**
- 6 **tablespoons soy sauce**
- 2 **tablespoons Worcestershire sauce**
- 3 to 4 **pounds sirloin steak, cut for kabobs**
- 1 **pound mushrooms**
- 2 **onions, quartered**
- 1 **green pepper, cut in large pieces**
- 1 **yellow pepper, cut in large pieces**
- 1 **pint cherry tomatoes**

- Combine oil, lemon juice and seasonings. Pour over steak and marinate overnight.
- Thread skewers with beef, mushrooms, quartered onions, green and yellow peppers and cherry tomatoes. Grill to desired doneness, basting with marinade.

A favorite summer meal, excellent with rice and spinach salad.

Stuffed Aubergine

Serves 2

- 1 **large eggplant**
- 1 **cup chopped onion**
- 1 **cup chopped fresh mushrooms**
- 1¼ **teaspoons sweet basil or oregano**
- 1 **teaspoon salt**
- ¼ **teaspoon freshly ground black pepper**
- 2 **tablespoons butter**
- 1 **cup cooked ground beef**
- ½ **cup dry bread crumbs**
  fresh parsley
  freshly grated Parmesan cheese

- Wash eggplant, wrap in aluminum foil and bake in 350° oven 50 minutes or until partly done. Cut in half, remove pulp to within ⅓-inch of outer skin. Chop pulp.
- Sauté onions, mushrooms, and seasonings in butter and add eggplant pulp. Add meat and bread crumbs, mix well. Spoon mixture into eggplant shells and place in baking dish.
- Bake long enough to heat through, 15 to 20 minutes. Garnish with parsley and Parmesan

A meal in itself.

South of the Border Lasagna

Serves 8

- 2 pounds lean ground beef
- 1 onion, chopped
- 1 clove garlic, minced
- 2 tablespoons chili powder
- 3 cups tomato sauce
- 1 teaspoon sugar
- 1 tablespoon salt
- ½ cup sliced black olives
- 1 4-ounce can chopped green chilies
- 12 corn tortillas
     vegetable oil
- 2 cups small curd cottage cheese
- 1 egg, beaten
- 8 ounces Monterey Jack cheese, grated
- 4 ounces cheddar cheese, grated

- Brown meat. Drain. Add onion and garlic and cook until soft. Sprinkle chili powder over meat and mix well. Add tomato sauce, sugar, salt, black olives and green chilies. Simmer 15 minutes.
- Soften tortillas in hot oil and drain on paper towels while meat simmers.
- Beat cottage cheese and egg together and set aside.
- Layer in a 9 x 13-inch casserole, ⅓ meat sauce, followed by ½ Jack cheese, ½ cottage cheese, ½ tortillas. Repeat layering one more time, topping with last ⅓ meat sauce.
- Cover with grated cheddar cheese and bake in 350° oven 30 minutes.

Easy and can be prepared ahead for casual entertaining. A Christmas Walk favorite.

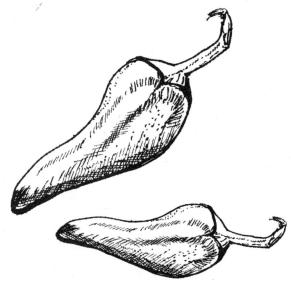

Roast Lamb with Herbs and Pistachios

Serves 6

6 **slices of bread with crust removed**

3 **tablespoons chopped fresh parsley**

2 **teaspoons chopped fresh chives**

1 **teaspoon thyme**

1 **teaspoon rosemary**

2 **cloves garlic, minced**
salt and pepper

¼ **cup whole shelled pistachio nuts**
boneless leg of lamb, butterflied

- Place 2 slices of bread, the herbs and salt and pepper into food processor. Blend until bread and herbs are finely chopped. Add nuts and process briefly.

- Spread mixture onto the inner surface of the lamb. Roll the lamb and tie at 2-inch intervals.

- Put the remainder of the bread into the blender for bread crumbs. Roll the tied lamb in the bread crumbs covering the outer surface completely.

- Place the lamb on a rack in a roasting pan. Bake in center of preheated 425° oven and roast uncovered for 30 minutes. Reduce the temperature to 350° and continue cooking, allowing 30 minutes to the pound.

- The total cooking time for the leg of lamb will be approximately 2 hours. Allow 20 minutes for the roast to rest.

Makes Easter Dinner even more special.

Herb Crusted Lamb in Wine

Serves 6

5 pound whole leg of lamb, well trimmed

Marinade

**2 onions, sliced
6 to 8 cloves garlic crushed
6 to 8 sprigs fresh thyme
6 to 8 sprigs fresh oregano
1 bottle white wine
1 cup virgin olive oil**

Baking lamb

**1½ teaspoons salt
2 teaspoons coarsely ground black pepper**

- Combine onions and garlic in bowl. Add bruised herbs, wine and oil.
- Place lamb in dish and pour marinade over lamb.
- Marinate in a cool place 6 to 8 hours or overnight and turn the lamb frequently.

- Remove lamb from marinade. Pat the lamb dry and set aside.
- Remove thyme and oregano leaves and mince them finely with the garlic from the marinade. Add salt and pepper to the herbs and make a rather stiff paste with a little of the marinade.
- Rub the paste on the lamb and place it on a rack in a shallow pan.
- Bake in preheated 450° oven 15 minutes. Reduce heat to 350°. Continue to bake 1 hour and 15 minutes turning lamb every 30 minutes. Remove the lamb from the oven and let it rest 15 minutes.

Exceptional lamb for special occasions.

Bruised herbs are herbs that are rubbed between fingers to release full flavors before adding to recipe.

Saltimbocca

- 8 **4-ounce slices of boneless veal**
  salt and freshly ground pepper to taste
- 8 **sage leaves or dried sage to taste**
- 12 **thin slices of prosciutto**
- 4 **tablespoons butter**
- 1 **clove garlic, minced**
- ¼ **cup Marsala wine or sweet Vermouth**

- Place veal slices between pieces of wax paper and pound slices thin. Sprinkle slices on both sides with salt and pepper. Top each slice with a leaf of fresh sage or sprinkle with dried sage. Cover with a slice of prosciutto. Roll and secure with toothpicks.
- Melt butter and sauté garlic. Brown meat quickly. Add wine to skillet, cook rapidly to reduce slightly, and serve hot with sauce.

Saltimbocca is a whimsically named dish, the exact translation is "jump in the mouth". No one can offer a satisfactory explanation of how it got its name, but it is one of the best-known and best-tasting veal dishes in Italian cookery.

Veal Chops in Fruited Rosemary Sauce

- 2 **veal chops cut 1½-inch thick**
  olive oil
  paprika
  ground white pepper
- 1 **teaspoon flour**
- 2 **teaspoons olive oil**
- 2 **cups chicken broth**
- 2 **bay leaves**
- 1 **tablespoon rosemary leaves**
- ½ **cup chopped dried mixed fruit (apples, raisins, apricots)**

- Brush veal chops with olive oil and sprinkle lightly with paprika and white pepper. Grill over medium heat approximately 10 minutes per inch of thickness.
- With flour and oil, make a light roux in a saucepan. Add chicken broth and bay leaf and bring to light boil. Crush rosemary leaves and add to liquid. Add dried fruit, increase heat and reduce by half.
- Spoon sauce over chops and serve.

Veal Marengo

Serves 8 to 10

- ½ **cup vegetable oil**
- 4 **pounds veal, cut in 1-inch cubes**
- 1 **cup chopped onion**
- 1 **cup chopped celery**
- 1 **clove garlic, minced**
- 1 **cup dry white wine**
- 2 **8-ounce cans tomato sauce**
- 2 **bay leaves**
- 1 **teaspoon dried oregano**
- ½ **teaspoon dried rosemary**
- 2 **teaspoons salt**
- ½ **teaspoon pepper**
- 2 **sprigs of parsley**
- 1 **pound sliced mushrooms**
- 2 **tablespoons freshly squeezed lemon juice**
- ¼ **cup butter**
- 1 **tablespoon flour**
- 2 **tablespoons water**
  fresh chopped parsley

- Heat oil in 6-quart Dutch oven.
- Add veal cubes and sauté until evenly browned. Remove veal as it browns.
- Add onion, celery and garlic, sauté until onion is translucent, about 5 minutes.
- Stir in ½ cup wine, tomato sauce, bay leaves, oregano, rosemary, salt, pepper, parsley and veal.
- Bring to boil and reduce heat; simmer, covered 1½ hours until veal is tender. Remove bay leaves.
- Toss mushrooms with lemon juice and sauté in butter until tender.
- Add remaining wine and mushrooms to veal mixture, along with flour dissolved in 2 tablespoons of water. Simmer covered 15 minutes.
- Place veal on heated serving dish and garnish with chopped parsley.

May be made the day before and reheated.

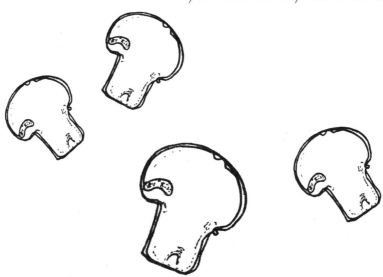

Veal Scaloppine au Vin

Serves 6

- ¼ **cup flour**
- ½ **cup freshly grated Parmesan cheese**
- 1 **teaspoon salt**
- ⅛ **teaspoon pepper**
- 1½ **pounds veal cutlets, sliced ¼-inch thick and cut into 2-inch strips**
- 2 **tablespoons olive oil**
- 1 **clove garlic**
- ½ **cup dry white wine**
- ½ **cup beef broth**
- 1 **tablespoon freshly squeezed lemon juice**
  parsley

- Mix flour, cheese, salt and pepper together.
- Wipe meat dry and sprinkle with flour mixture. Pound flour into meat with meat tenderizer mallet.
- Heat olive oil with garlic and brown meat lightly on both sides. Remove garlic, add wine, broth and lemon juice.
- Cover and simmer slowly for about 30 minutes.
- Sprinkle with chopped parsley.

This recipe can be made with boneless chicken breasts. Pound chicken to tenderize.

Company Quail

Serves 4

- 8 **quail (if frozen, thaw in milk)**
- 1 **cup flour**
- 1 **tablespoon seasoned salt**
- 1 **teaspoon pepper**
- ¼ **cup butter**
- 1½ **cups chicken broth**
- 1 **cup fresh mushrooms, sliced**
- 4 **tablespoons dry white wine**

- Wipe quail and dry with a cloth. Sprinkle liberally with flour mixed with seasoned salt and pepper. Melt butter in skillet and sauté birds on both sides.
- Add broth and mushrooms to pan.
- Simmer, slowly, covered for 45 minutes. Add wine and cook 10 minutes uncovered.

Hunter's favorite dish.

Roast Pheasant with Wild Rice Stuffing and Creamed Pan Sauce Serves 8

4 **2½ to 3 pound pheasants**
salt and pepper
softened butter
24 slices of bacon

- Season the cavities of the pheasants with salt and pepper and coat each with softened butter. Fill the cavities with the Wild Rice Stuffing, skewer the openings. Rub the skin with softened butter. Cover each breast with 4 to 6 bacon strips and secure with string.
- Roast the pheasant in a 425° oven 15 to 20 minutes per side. Remove the bacon and roast them breast side up for 15 minutes more or until they are cooked.

Wild Rice Stuffing

1½ cups wild rice
5 tablespoons butter
½ cup finely chopped onion
4 pheasant livers, chopped
½ pound mushrooms, chopped
¼ cup chopped celery
½ cup coarsely chopped pecans
¼ cup chopped parsley
½ teaspoon of thyme
½ teaspoon marjoram

- Rinse rice well in cold water. Pour the rice into boiling water and boil uncovered for 20 minutes. Drain the rice in a sieve and set the sieve over 1 inch of boiling water. Cover the rice with the lid of a saucepan and steam it for 20 to 25 minutes, or until it is dry. Transfer the rice to a shallow dish, add 2 tablespoons butter and fluff rice.
- Sauté onion and liver in 3 tablespoons butter over low heat for 2 minutes. Add mushrooms and celery. Sauté until mushrooms are cooked. Combine the mushroom mixture with the rice.
- Add pecans, parsley, thyme and marjoram. Salt and pepper to taste. Let mixture cool.

Creamed Pan Sauce

¼ cup carrot, minced
¼ cup onion, minced
3 tablespoons flour
½ teaspoon thyme
2¼ cups chicken broth
½ cup whipping cream
¼ cup dry sherry

- Skim off all but 3 tablespoons of fat and heat the remaining juices over low heat. Add the carrot and onion and sauté for 1 minute. Add the flour and thyme and cook for 2 minutes.
- Remove the pan and stir in broth, cream and sherry. Bring the sauce to a boil and then simmer for 5 minutes until it thickens. Season with salt and pepper to taste.

This Christmas Eve Dinner will bring lots of compliments.

Cranberry-Orange Glazed Cornish Hens

Serves 4

4 Cornish hens
½ cup butter, melted
   salt and pepper to taste
½ cup whole berry cranberry
   sauce
½ cup orange marmalade
⅓ cup mandarin oranges
3 tablespoons lemon juice
1 tablespoon instant minced
   onion

- Rinse hens and pat dry. Coat inside and out with butter. Salt and pepper as desired.
- Place hens on rack in shallow roasting pan. Roast in preheated 425° oven 15 minutes.
- Reduce oven to 375° and roast 45 minutes to 1 hour, basting often with pan juices.
- Combine cranberry sauce and remaining ingredients. During the last 20 minutes brush hens with glaze and glaze again before serving.

Easy but elegant!

"Sizzling" Steak Marinade

Serves 4

2 tablespoons prepared
   mustard
   seasoned salt
   lemon pepper
   garlic powder
3 tablespoons freshly squeezed
   lemon juice
¼ cup ketchup
¼ cup water
3 tablespoons Worcestershire
   sauce
¼ cup olive oil
2 tablespoons wine vinegar
2 tablespoons soy sauce
2 tablespoons plum or cherry
   jam
3 tablespoons brown sugar
2 drops Tabasco Sauce

- Spread mustard on each side of meat and sprinkle with the salt, pepper and garlic powder. Place steaks in a glass dish. Pour lemon juice over the meat. Set aside for 1 hour, turning often.
- Combine remaining ingredients in a small saucepan. Heat until ingredients are dissolved. Cool 5 to 10 minutes and pour over the meat in the glass dish. Marinate in refrigerator 2 to 3 hours (even overnight is better).
- When ready to grill, remove the meat from the marinade, but keep the marinade in the glass dish.
- Grill to desired degree of doneness. Baste with marinade while grilling.

Use this on a thick sirloin roast, strip steaks, even tenderloin.

Pineapple Teriyaki Marinade

1 ¼ cups

- **6 ounces pineapple juice**
- **3 ounces soy sauce**
- **1 to 2 cloves garlic, minced**
  chopped cilantro or chives, to
  taste
- **½ teaspoon ground ginger**
- **½ teaspoon seasoned salt**
- **1 teaspoon cracked black**
  pepper

- Combine all ingredients in a large zip-lock bag or other tight sealing container large enough to accommodate your meat. Marinate in refrigerator 12 to 24 hours.

Any shrimp, chicken, or beef is great in this marinade.

Homemade Barbeque Sauce

A LOT!

- **1 gallon catsup**
- **3 pounds brown sugar**
- **5 ounces horseradish**
- **½ bottle liquid smoke**
- **10 ounces Worcestershire**
  sauce
- **1½ cups cider vinegar**
- **2 tablespoons salt**
- **2 tablespoons dry mustard**
- **1 tablespoon cayenne pepper**

- Bring to a boil and simmer five minutes.

Wonderful to have in your refrigerator for summer dinner on the grill.

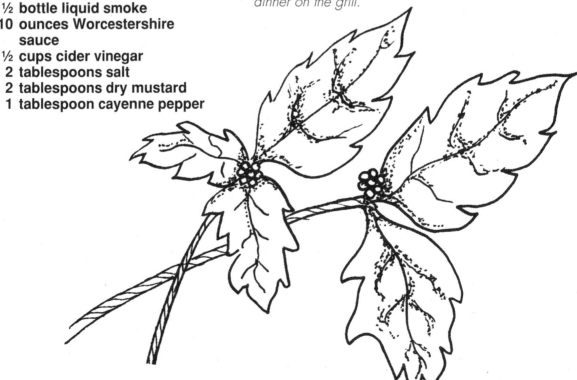

Carolina Barbeque Sauce

1 cup

- **1 cup butter**
- **4 tablespoons yellow mustard**
- **1 teaspoon salt**
- **1 tablespoon freshly squeezed lemon juice**
- **1 tablespoon white vinegar**

- Melt butter and add remaining ingredients. Stir until blended. Use to baste turkey, chicken, and pork. Put some sauce inside turkey before and during smoking.

A unique barbeque taste.

Fresh Mango Salsa

2 cups

- **2 cups fresh peeled mango, diced**
- **1 serrano pepper, seeded and finely chopped**
- **1 clove garlic, minced**
- **½ cup chopped fresh cilantro**
- **½ small red onion, chopped**
- **¼ cup fresh lime juice**
- **2 tablespoons olive oil**

- Combine all ingredients and refrigerate for at least one hour before serving.
- Chunk pineapple in its own juice may be substituted for mango.

Serve with grilled fish, chicken or pork tenderloin.

Medallions of Veal with Wild Mushroom Sauce and Sun-Dried Tomato Cream

Medallions of Veal (per serving)

- **3 ounces of veal 2½ to 3 inches high**
  fresh thyme and rosemary sprigs
- **2 slices of pancetta**
- **1 cup basic demiglace**
- **4 ounces butter**
- **2 ounces brandy**
- **4 ounces white wine**
- **½ cup mushrooms, shiitake, oyster, domestic**
- **1 ounce chopped shallots**
- **5 ounces cream**
- **1 ounce tomato paste**

- Wrap thyme, rosemary and pancetta around the veal. Skewer with toothpicks and season with salt and pepper.
- Sear on both sides.
- Finish in oven.

Served with fine herbs wrapped in pancetta, with duo of Wild Mushroom Sauce and Sun-Dried Tomato Cream, and roasted rosemary new potatoes and baby vegetables.

Wild Mushroom Sauce

- **1 ounce butter**
- **½ cup sliced mushrooms**
- **2 ounces brandy**
- **4 ounces demiglace**

- Sauté mushrooms in butter. Deglaze with brandy and add brown demiglace.

Sun-Dried Tomato Cream

- **1 ounce butter**
- **2 ounces sun-dried tomatoes, sliced**
- **4 ounces white wine**
- **4 ounces whipping cream**
- **1 ounce tomato paste**
  salt and pepper

- Sauté sun-dried tomatoes in butter. Deglaze with white wine and reduce.
- Add cream and tomato paste and season with salt and pepper.

Chef Robert Kennedy, Southern Hills Country Club

Sesame Chicken Breast with Scallion Dipping Sauce

Serves 4

4 boneless, skinless chicken breast halves, cut in 4-inch strips
½ cup coconut milk
2 shallots, peeled and chopped
1 clove garlic, peeled and chopped
1 teaspoon grated fresh ginger
1 teaspoon curry powder
1 tablespoon chopped fresh cilantro
   juice of 1 lime
2 eggs, well beaten
5 cups vegetable oil
2 tablespoons black sesame seeds
2 tablespoons white sesame seeds
1½ cups dry bread crumbs
   salt to taste

- For marinade, combine coconut milk, shallots, garlic, ginger, curry powder, cilantro, lime juice and eggs. Marinate chicken, refrigerated 2 hours.
- Heat oil to 350° in a large stock pot over high heat.
- Blend black and white sesame seeds with bread crumbs.
- Remove chicken from marinade. Roll into bread crumb mixture until coated. Place in hot oil and fry about 4 minutes or until golden brown. Remove from oil and drain. Season with salt. Serve warm with Scallion Dipping Sauce.

Scallion Dipping Sauce

½ cup sour cream
2 tablespoons sweetened rice wine vinegar
2 tablespoons mushroom soy sauce
1 teaspoon grated fresh ginger
1 shallot, peeled and finely chopped
1 clove garlic, peeled and finely chopped
1 serrano chili pepper, finely chopped
¾ cup finely chopped scallions
1 tablespoon chopped fresh mint
1 tablespoon chopped fresh cilantro
   salt to taste
   fresh lime juice to taste

- Puree all ingredients in a blender until smooth.

Chef Robert Merrifield, Ouida Kelly, Polo Grill

Chicken Margarita

Serves 1

**1 8-ounce chicken breast,
skinned and boned**
½ slice colby-jack cheese

- Marinate chicken 24 hours in marinade. Grill chicken, brushing with marinade. Top with cheese and Margarita butter and melt in oven. Serve on a dinner plate with salsa, a bread stick and garnish the chicken with a lime wheel.

Marinade

1 cup pineapple juice
3 tablespoons soy sauce

- Mix juice and sauce together.

Margarita Butter

1 tablespoon butter
**1 tablespoon Lasco lemon
cocktail mix**

- Mix until smooth.

Chef Don Conner, Full Moon Cafe.

Chicken Alfresco

Serves 4

olive oil
1 tablespoon minced garlic
**4 chicken breast halves,
skinned and boned**
½ tomato
6 mushrooms
½ zucchini, julienned
½ yellow squash, julienned
1 carrot, julienned
10 snow peas
½ cup soy sauce
½ cup white wine

- Sauté garlic in a small amount of olive oil. Add chicken, tomato and mushrooms. Simmer 10 minutes.
- Add other vegetables, soy sauce and white wine. Simmer until chicken is tender.
- Serve on bed of linguine or rice.

Chef Mohsen "Moe" Shadgoo, Nick's Supper Club.

Chicken Piccata
Serves 2

- 3 tablespoons butter, unsalted
- 1 tablespoon fresh lemon juice
- 1 cup flour
- ½ teaspoon salt
- ¼ teaspoon black pepper
- ½ teaspoon granulated garlic
- 2 6- to 8-ounce boneless, skinless chicken breasts
- 3 tablespoons vegetable oil
- ½ cup white wine
- ⅓ cup freshly grated Parmesan cheese
- ½ teaspoon freshly chopped parsley
- ½ teaspoon paprika

- Melt butter and lemon juice together and set aside.
- Place flour, salt, pepper and garlic into a small paper bag and shake to blend. Add chicken to bag and shake to coat.
- Pour oil into skillet and heat to 325°. Place chicken in pan and brown on each side. Pour wine in pan and simmer until tender.
- Top with Parmesan and place in broiler for 3 minutes to brown. Remove and top with lemon butter, parsley and paprika.

Serve on wild rice.

Chef Steve Bailey, The Green Onion Restaurant

Artichoke and Asparagus Stuffed Chicken Breast
Serves 4

- 4 large boneless, skinless chicken breast halves
- ⅓ cup minced onion
- 3 medium garlic cloves, minced olive oil
- 1 8-ounce can artichoke hearts, drained and chopped
- ½ cup bread crumbs
- ½ cup shredded mozzarella cheese
- 2 tablespoons freshly grated Parmesan cheese
- 1 teaspoon cilantro
  salt and pepper to taste
- 1 egg, beaten
- 12 asparagus spears, peeled and trimmed

- Pound chicken breasts with a tenderizing mallet. Set aside.
- Sauté onion and garlic in olive oil until tender and then add artichoke hearts. Sauté 5 more minutes. Let cool slightly then add bread crumbs, mozzarella cheese, Parmesan, cilantro, salt and pepper. Stir in egg. Form stuffing into 4 small balls.
- Fill each chicken breast half with ball of stuffing. Lay 2 or 3 asparagus spears on the chicken, roll up and secure with toothpicks. Place chicken in lightly oiled pan. Brush chicken with olive oil or melted butter. Sprinkle with paprika and bake in preheated 325° oven 30 to 40 minutes.
- Serve whole or cool slightly and cut into circles to reveal stuffing.

Chef Donn Weber, Gilcrease Rendezvous Restaurant

179

Curried Breast of Chicken with Mango Chutney

Serves 4

¼ **cup curry powder**
½ **cup mayonnaise**
⅔ **cup yogurt**
½ **teaspoon Tabasco Sauce**
½ **teaspoon white pepper**
  juice of 1 lemon
 4 **6-ounce boneless, skinless chicken breasts**
  clarified butter
  flour

- Combine curry powder, mayonnaise, yogurt, Tabasco, white pepper and lemon juice to make marinade. Add chicken breasts to marinade and coat thoroughly. Refrigerate overnight.

- Preheat a large skillet with clarified butter. Dredge chicken breasts in flour. Do not remove excess marinade. Place in heated skillet. Brown the breasts evenly by rotating their position in the skillet. When golden brown on first side, turn and place skillet in preheated 400° oven for approximately 10 to 12 minutes.

- Remove from oven and serve over steamed rice and top with Fresh Mango Chutney.

Fresh Mango Chutney

 2 **tablespoons butter**
¼ **cup diced green bell pepper**
¼ **cup diced red bell pepper**
¼ **cup diced red onions**
¼ **teaspoon salt**
⅛ **teaspoon white pepper**
⅛ **teaspoon cayenne pepper**
 2 **very ripe mangoes with stones and skins removed, diced**
 1 **tablespoon sugar**
 1 **tablespoon lemon juice**

- Heat butter in a skillet. Sauté peppers and onions with salt, pepper and cayenne. Add mangoes, sugar and lemon juice. Sauté over low heat, stirring frequently. Do not allow to boil.

- Simmer for approximately 5 minutes. Remove from heat and refrigerate chutney. Serve chilled over Curried Breast of Chicken.

Chef Gregory Huffines, Cardigan's American Bistro

Pork Savoyard

Serves 2

4 **2-ounce slices pork tenderloin, tenderized**
¼ **cup clarified butter**
¼ **cup sliced mushrooms**
⅛ **cup dry sherry**
1 **cup whipping cream**
⅛ **cup chopped scallions**
¼ **cup julienne ham**
¼ **cup grated Swiss cheese**

- Sauté pork until half done in clarified butter. Add mushrooms and cook until tender.
- Deglaze pan with sherry and add cream and scallions. Reduce until thickened.
- Place 2 slices of pork on each plate layering ham between each slice of pork.
- Pour remaining sauce over pork and put Swiss cheese on top. Melt under broiler until golden brown.
- Serve immediately.

Chef Wick Poore, Cedar Ridge Country Club

Stuffed Pork Tenderloin

Serves 3 to 4

2 **pounds pork tenderloin, trimmed**
2 **tablespoons oil or butter**
1 **small onion, diced**
2 **Granny Smith apples, peeled and diced**
1 **can plums in syrup**
2 **stalks celery, diced**
½ **cup bread crumbs**
salt and pepper to taste
½ **teaspoon cinnamon**

- Butterfly tenderloin.
- Sauté onions, apples, plums and celery in oil until slightly soft. Add bread crumbs, salt, pepper and cinnamon.
- Spread mixture evenly over pork tenderloin. Roll up pork tenderloin and roast in 350° oven 20 to 25 minutes.
- To "butterfly" pork loin halves, cut an inverted T down the length of each half and open it out flat. With a meat mallet or rolling pin, pound the pork to an even thickness. (The filling spreads smoother, and the loin rolls uniformly.) Roll jelly-roll fashion starting with long end. Tie the rolls at even intervals. Bake the loins, seam side down.

Chef Michael Hawkins, Ludger's Restaurant, Catering and Cooking School

Beef and Pasta Strudel

Serves 6

Strudel Filling

- 1 medium onion, chopped
- ½ pound mushrooms, chopped
- 2 pounds beef tenderloin, shredded
- 3 cups cooked orzo pasta
- 1½ cups whipping cream, reduced to 1 cup
- 1 teaspoon minced garlic
- 1 teaspoon marjoram
- salt and pepper to taste

- Sauté onions and mushrooms until soft. Remove from pan and drain.
- Brown tenderloin, drain and mix with pasta, vegetables and cream.
- Season with garlic, marjoram, salt and pepper

Strudel Pastry

- 12 sheets Phyllo dough
- melted butter

- Lay one sheet of dough on work surface and brush with butter. Lay 5 more sheets on top, brushing each with butter.
- Cut into 3 rectangles.
- Repeat with remaining 6 sheets of phyllo.
- Place 1 cup of filling in center of each pastry. Fold edges up and over to form pocket. Place each seam side down on baking sheet and brush again with butter.
- Bake in 350° oven 25 minutes or until golden brown.
- Serve on a pool of Tomatoes Provençal.

Tomatoes Provençal

- 2 cloves garlic, minced
- olive oil
- ½ cup red wine
- 6 medium tomatoes, coarsely diced
- 1 ounce fresh basil, julienne

- Brown garlic in olive oil and deglaze pan with wine.
- Add tomatoes and basil and simmer until just soft.

Chef Jay Edmondson, La Villa Restaurant at Philbrook

Hanover's Brisket

Serves 6 to 8

- **1 can beef consommé**
- **1 5- to 6-ounce bottle soy sauce**
- **¼ cup freshly squeezed lemon juice**
- **1 tablespoon liquid smoke garlic to taste**
- **5 pound trimmed brisket**
- **½ cup barbecue sauce**

- Combine liquid ingredients except barbecue sauce. Pour over meat and marinate overnight in non-corrosive pan.
- Bake in marinade 1 hour per pound at 275° in covered pan, basting occasionally. Remove cover during last hour or total time and pour barbecue sauce over brisket. Increase oven temperature to 350° and continue baking.

David Hanover, Hanover's Meat Market

Grilled Venison Backstrap

Serves 4

- **4 1-inch thick steaks**
- **4 strips of bacon**
- **4 ounces of Worcestershire sauce**
- **lemon pepper seasoning**
- **8 toothpicks**

- With a knife, pierce the venison to tenderize and to allow the Worcestershire to penetrate the meat.
- Wrap with a strip of bacon and secure with 2 toothpicks. Put steaks in a pan and add the Worcestershire.
- Soak the meat well; cover and refrigerate for 6 hours, turn every hour then season with lemon pepper.
- Grill until medium rare. Place on plate, remove toothpicks. Serve with Green Peppercorn Sauce.

Green Peppercorn Sauce

- **4 large mushrooms, sliced**
- **2 tablespoons chopped shallots**
- **2 tablespoons butter**
- **2 tablespoons brandy**
- **1 tablespoon green peppercorns**
- **1 cup whipping cream**
- **½ cup beef broth**
- **parsley**

- Sauté mushrooms and shallots in butter until tender. Add brandy, peppercorns, cream and broth. Bring to boil. Simmer until sauce reduces and thickens. Season to taste with salt and pepper.
- Top meat with sauce. Sprinkle with chopped parsley and serve.

Recipe also works well with beef or buffalo tenderloin or strip loin.

Chef David Rivest, The French Hen

183

Artful Dining

Built with profits from Oklahoma black gold, Tulsa transformed from a rugged pioneer town to a sophisticated petroleum center. The Tulsa Ballet Theatre, Tulsa Opera, Tulsa Philharmonic, Oklahoma Sinfonia and other groups provide a varied menu suited to current residents' wide-ranging interests.

Opportunities for creative expression in front of the footlights abound. The American Theatre Company, American Indian Theatre Company and Theatre Tulsa provide professionally acted and staged productions throughout the year. In the summer months, Discoveryland presents the ever popular OKLAHOMA! under the stars in the beautiful Osage hills. Theatre North and African-American Community Theatre present a season of children's jazz and Broadway productions.

Oilmen Waite Phillips and Thomas Gilcrease bestowed on Tulsa their great love of art with two spectacular and distinct museums.

The Philbrook Museum of Art, an ornate Italian Renaissance villa formerly the home of Waite Phillips, houses collections of American, Asian, African, European, American Indian and Ancient art, as well as sculpture.

Philbrook's Museum School offers year-round classes in many disciplines for both children and adults.

The Thomas Gilcrease Museum, devoted to American history and Western art, features numerous works by Remington, Moran, Russell, Catlin and Bierstadt. The archaeological treasures and rare documents mingle with significant collections of American Indian and Latin American pottery, silver, beadwork and art. The yearly Gilcrease Rendezvous, held on the spacious museum grounds, celebrates Oklahoma's Indian and cowboy heritage.

A showcase for the finest assemblage of Jewish art in the Southwest, the Fenster Museum features treasures that span 4,000 years and trace Jewish history. The museum focuses on all people's common values and history.

The Tulsa community continues with great generosity in the tradition set by its founders. A firm commitment by companies and individuals to the premise that the arts enhance living ensures that all of the arts remain healthy and fully integrated in Tulsans' lives.

Artful
Dining

PASTA & SEAFOOD
Our Way

Pasta

Capellini Primavera 188

Cheesy Vegetable Lasagna 194

Fettuccine with Goat Cheese and Pistachio Nut Sauce 191

Four Cheese Rigatoni 192

Garlic and Goat Cheese Pasta 191

Lemon-Garlic Angel Hair Pasta 192

Pasta Florentine 189

Pasta Lugano 187

Rainbow Rotini 190

Spaghetti alla Puttanesca 187

Spaghetti with Gorgonzola and Ricotta 193

Spinach Linguine with Spring Sauce 189

Sweet Peppers with Pasta Stuffing 195

Pasta Sauces

Alfredo Sauce 199

Fresh Pesto Sauce 198

Marinara Sauce 199

Rosemary Pasta Sauce 190

Spicy Tomato Sauce 199

Pasta with Meat/Poultry

Bacon, Tomato and Basil Fettuccine Alfredo 193

Chicken Spaghetti 198

Fettuccine with Broccoli and Chicken 196

Fettuccine with Chicken and Pecans 195

Manicotti 197

Tomato Basil Fettuccine with Italian Sausage 196

Veal...Sage, Rosemary and Time 197

Pasta with Seafood

Classic Crabmeat Fettuccine 201

Fettuccine with Scallops in Saffron Butter 202

Lemon Butter Sea Scallops with Rice Stick Noodles 202

Linguine of the Sea 200

Salmon, Peas and Sun-Dried Tomatoes 200

Shrimp Fettuccine with Tomato Basil Cream 204

Spinach Pasta with Shrimp 203

Tomato Angel Hair Pasta with Basil and Crab 201

Seafood

Baked Scallops 203

Caribbean Grilled Fish Marinade 210

Delicious Deviled Shrimp 205

Fish Florentine 207

Grilled Salmon with Sun-Dried Tomato Sauce 206

Lemon Grilled Halibut 209

Red Snapper Cancun 208

Red Snapper with Shrimp 209

Sautéed Soft Shell Crabs 205

Sea Bass with White Beans, Roasted Peppers and Fresh Herbs 210

Shrimp with Tomatoes and Feta 204

Sole en Papillote 207

Southwest Sole 206

Professional Chefs

Asparagus Lasagna 217

Bow Tie Pasta with Lobster and Asparagus 211

Chicken Primavera 213

Lobster and Crabmeat Soufflé 211

Macadamia Crusted Tiger Prawns with Amaretto Sauce 214

Pasta Maine Lobster 213

Seared Yellow-Fin Tuna with Vanilla Bean Beurre Blanc 216

Spinach Fettuccine Provençal 212

Sun-Dried Tomato Pesto 212

Tortilla Crusted Shrimp 215

Pasta Lugano

Serves 3 to 4

- 4 tablespoons olive oil
- 3 cloves garlic, minced
- 1 small onion, sliced
- ½ green bell pepper, sliced
- ½ red bell pepper, sliced
- 2 tablespoons chopped parsley
- 4 large Roma tomatoes, peeled and quartered
- 1 tablespoon dried Italian seasonings
  salt and pepper to taste
- ½ cup dry red wine
- ½ cup sliced mushrooms
- 8 to 10 ounces bow tie pasta
  freshly grated Parmesan cheese

- In a large skillet, sauté garlic, onions and peppers in olive oil until tender.
- Add parsley, tomatoes and seasonings and cook for 2 to 3 minutes.
- Add wine. Bring to rapid boil for 1 minute.
- Cover and simmer at low heat for 10 minutes.
- Add sliced mushrooms and continue to simmer 15 minutes.
- Cook bow tie pasta al dente and drain.
- Toss pasta with sauce and pass the Parmesan.

Recipe from a Trattoria on Lake Lugano, Italy.

Spaghetti alla Puttanesca

Serves 6

- 1½ tablespoons olive oil
- 3 cloves garlic, finely chopped
- 3 anchovy fillets
- 1 14-ounce can Italian plum tomatoes
- 1 cup pitted black olives, halved if large
- 4 tablespoons capers
- 1 pound spaghetti or vermicelli
  parsley
  freshly grated Parmesan cheese

- Sauté garlic and anchovy fillets in olive oil until tender.
- Add tomatoes and their juice, olives and capers. Cook 5 minutes.
- Cook pasta al dente.
- Add sauce to drained pasta. Mix well.
- Sprinkle with parsley and Parmesan.

Capellini Primavera

Serves 4 to 6

½ **cup butter or olive oil**
1½ **cups chopped onions**
¾ **cup julienne-cut carrots**
5 **cups broccoli florets, 1-inch pieces**
3 **cups sliced mushrooms**
1¼ **cups yellow squash slices, cut in half**
1 **teaspoon finely chopped garlic**
1½ **cups water**
1 **tablespoon beef or vegetable bouillon granules**
¼ **cup sun-dried tomatoes, oil-packed and minced**
1¼ **cups crushed tomatoes in puree**
1 **tablespoon snipped fresh parsley**
1 **teaspoon oregano leaves**
1 **teaspoon ground rosemary**
¼ **teaspoon crushed red pepper flakes**
1 **pound angel hair pasta, cooked and drained**
½ **cup freshly grated Parmesan cheese**

- Melt butter or heat oil in Dutch oven over medium heat. Sauté onions, carrots, and broccoli for 5 minutes. Add mushrooms, yellow squash and garlic and sauté for 2 minutes longer.
- Add remaining ingredients. Stir well and bring to a simmer. Cook for 8 to 10 minutes or until vegetables are tender and flavors are blended.
- Serve over pasta. Sprinkle with Parmesan.

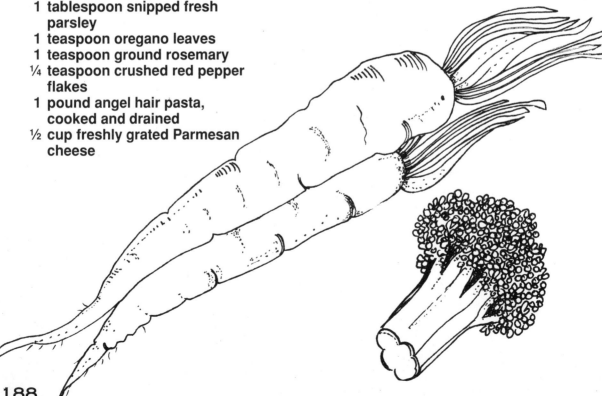

Pasta Florentine

Serves 2 to 4

4 cups chopped fresh spinach
½ pound fresh mushrooms
   juice of 1 lemon
4 tablespoons butter
1 clove garlic, minced
2 tablespoons Marsala wine
1 cup whipping cream
   salt to taste
   freshly ground pepper
½ pound linguine
¼ cup freshly grated Parmesan cheese

- Cook spinach in boiling, salted water until tender. Drain well and set aside.
- Slice mushrooms, add lemon juice and mix well.
- Melt butter in skillet. Add garlic and Marsala. Cook 3 minutes and add the mushrooms. Cook an additional 5 minutes, add the cream and bring the mixture to a boil. Add salt, then pepper liberally. Remove from heat.
- Cook pasta al dente. Drain and add spinach and mushroom mixture. Toss.
- Top with Parmesan.

Spinach Linguine with Spring Sauce

Serves 4

3 tablespoons olive oil
1 clove garlic, minced
1 cup chopped onion
1½ cups diced zucchini
1 cup diced carrots
1 16-ounce can tomatoes
½ teaspoon dried basil
½ teaspoon salt
½ teaspoon sugar
1 8-ounce package spinach linguine
¾ cup grated Parmesan cheese

- In large deep skillet, heat oil. Add garlic, onions, zucchini, and carrots. Cook, stirring occasionally, until vegetables are tender crisp.
- Stir in tomatoes and their liquid. Add basil, salt and sugar. Cover and simmer over low heat 10 to 15 minutes, stirring to break up tomatoes.
- Cook linguine al dente and drain. Add to tomato sauce along with Parmesan. Toss until well-coated.

Rainbow Rotini

Serves 4

2 **tablespoons olive oil**
1 **tablespoon butter**
2 **cloves garlic, minced**
1 **medium onion, chopped**
1 **red bell pepper, chopped**
3 **medium tomatoes, chopped**
¼ **cup chopped fresh basil**
½ **teaspoon oregano**
   salt and pepper to taste
8 to 10 **ounces rainbow rotini**
7 **ounces feta cheese, crumbled**

• Heat oil and butter over medium heat.
• Sauté garlic until brown, add onion and pepper. Cook until transparent.
• Add tomatoes and cook 5 to 10 minutes.
• Add basil, oregano, salt and pepper.
• Cook pasta al dente and drain.
• Serve sauce over pasta and top with feta cheese.

Rosemary Pasta Sauce

Serves 3 to 4

⅓ **cup olive oil**
1 **tablespoon minced garlic**
2 **teaspoons minced fresh rosemary or 1 teaspoon dried, crumbled**
1 **teaspoon crushed red pepper freshly grated Parmesan cheese**

• Combine olive oil and garlic Add herbs and heat. Simmer for 30 seconds.
• Pour over 8 ounces pasta with favorite steamed vegetables such as broccoli, zucchini, carrots or crookneck squash.
• Pass the Parmesan.

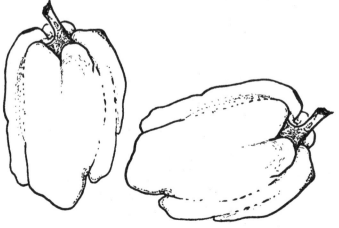

Fettuccine with Goat Cheese and Pistachio Nut Sauce

Serves 4 to 6

- **2 cups whipping cream**
  freshly ground pepper
- **½ teaspoon freshly grated nutmeg**
- **1 cup roasted pistachio nuts**
- **1 pound fettuccine**
- **½ pound goat cheese, coarsely chopped**
- **½ cup freshly grated Parmesan cheese**
- **2 tablespoons cognac**

- Simmer 1 cup cream in saucepan. Add pepper and cook 5 minutes. Add nutmeg, remaining cream, pistachios and bring to boil.
- Cook fettuccine al dente. Drain and add to sauce. Place pasta and sauce over low heat, add goat cheese and toss until cheese is melted.
- Sprinkle with additional pepper and ¼ cup Parmesan. Add cognac, toss and serve with additional Parmesan.

Garlic and Goat Cheese Pasta

Serves 2

- **1¼ cups whipping cream**
- **8 cloves garlic, minced**
- **2 ounces goat cheese**
- **2 tablespoons minced parsley or basil**
- **½ pound fresh or 6 ounces dried pasta (tomato or spinach fettuccine)**

- Bring one cup cream to a low boil in small saucepan. Add garlic and simmer 10 minutes.
- Transfer to blender and blend with goat cheese. Return to saucepan and reduce if sauce is too thin or add a bit of additional cream if too thick. Toss with herbs and cooked pasta.

This is a garlic lover's favorite, and simple to prepare. Try sautéing a few cherry tomatoes for garnish to be placed around the edge of the pasta bowls.

Lemon-Garlic Angel Hair Pasta

Serves 2 to 4

- **1 tablespoon olive oil**
- **2 cloves garlic, minced**
- **½ cup dry white wine**
- **¼ cup freshly squeezed lemon juice**
- **1 large tomato, chopped**
- **4 ounces spinach angel hair pasta**
- **¼ cup chopped fresh basil**
- **2 tablespoons freshly grated Parmesan cheese**
- **salt and pepper to taste**

- Sauté garlic in olive oil until softened.
- Remove from heat, add wine.
- Return to heat and reduce by half.
- Add lemon juice and tomato and heat gently.
- Cook pasta al dente and drain.
- Top with sauce. Sprinkle with basil and Parmesan.

Great side dish.

Four Cheese Rigatoni

Serves 6

- **1 pound rigatoni pasta**
- **½ cup butter, divided**
- **2 ounces grated Parmesan cheese**
- **2 ounces grated Gruyère cheese**
- **2 ounces grated Edam cheese**
- **2 ounces grated fontina cheese**
- **freshly ground pepper**

- Cook pasta al dente.
- Drain pasta, reserving ¼ cup water.
- Heat 2 tablespoons butter in large pan.
- Turn pasta into melted butter and gradually stir in remaining butter and cheeses.
- Remove from heat when cheeses start to melt. Continue to stir, adding water if sauce seems too dry.
- Serve at once with fresh black pepper.

Spaghetti with Gorgonzola and Ricotta

Serves 6

7 tablespoons butter
1 stalk celery, chopped
1 small onion, chopped
1¼ cups milk
5 ounces Gorgonzola cheese
10 ounces ricotta cheese
   salt and pepper
1 pound spaghetti
   freshly ground pepper

- Melt butter, add celery and onion, cook gently.
- In food processor, puree together milk, Gorgonzola, ricotta and cooked vegetables. Heat mixture, stirring occasionally. Add salt and pepper to taste.
- Cook pasta al dente and drain.
- Stir in cheese sauce and sprinkle with freshly ground pepper.

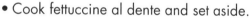

Bacon, Tomato and Basil Fettuccine Alfredo

Serves 4

12 ounces fettuccine
8 ounces bacon, cut into ½-inch pieces, fried and drained
1 cup half and half
4 tablespoons butter
¼ teaspoon salt
¼ teaspoon pepper
1 tomato, diced
¼ cup chopped fresh basil
½ cup freshly grated Parmesan cheese

- Cook fettuccine al dente and set aside.
- Place bacon, half and half, butter, salt and pepper in saucepan. Heat but do not boil.
- Combine pasta and sauce. Add tomatoes, basil and Parmesan. Toss.
- Serve immediately.

Cheesy Vegetable Lasagna

Serves 8 to 12

- 8 **ounces lasagna noodles**
- 2 **eggs, beaten**
- 2 **cups low-fat cream-style cottage cheese**
- 2 **cups low-fat ricotta cheese**
- 1 **teaspoon basil**
- 1 **teaspoon oregano**
- 2 **cups sliced fresh mushrooms**
- ¼ **cup chopped onion**
- 1 **clove garlic, minced**
- 2 **tablespoons butter**
- 2 **tablespoons flour**
- 1 **teaspoon black pepper**
- 1¼ **cups skim milk**
- 2 **10-ounce packages frozen chopped spinach, thawed and thoroughly drained**
- 1 **large carrot, shredded**
- ¾ **cup shredded fresh Parmesan cheese**
- 1 **8-ounce package shredded mozzarella cheese**

- Cook noodles according to directions and set aside.
- Mix eggs, cottage cheese, ricotta, and herbs. Set aside.
- In a large skillet cook mushrooms, onion, and garlic in melted butter until tender. Stir in flour and pepper.
- Add milk all at once. Cook and stir until thick and bubbly.
- Remove from heat and stir in the vegetables and ½ cup of Parmesan.
- To assemble, use a 13 x 9-inch glass pan and layer a third of the noodles. Spread with a third of the cottage cheese mixture, then one third of the spinach mixture. Sprinkle with one third of the mozzarella. Repeat the layers 2 more times and sprinkle with the remaining ¼ cup Parmesan.
- Bake immediately or chill for up to 48 hours.
- To serve immediately, bake uncovered in a 350° oven 35 minutes. Let stand 10 minutes before cutting.
- To make ahead, cover the lasagna with foil and chill. Bake, covered, in 350° oven 30 minutes. Uncover and bake 30 minutes more until heated through.

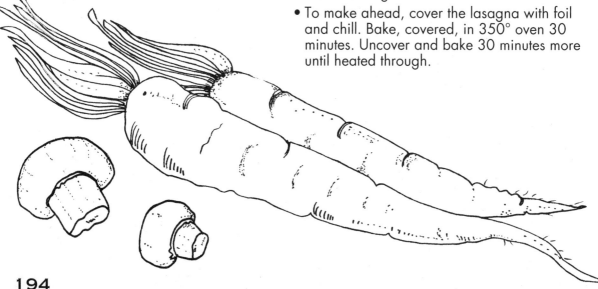

Sweet Peppers with Pasta Stuffing

Serves 6

- **6 large equal-sized sweet bell peppers**
  salt and black pepper
- **1 tablespoon olive oil**
- **7 ounces black olives, pitted and chopped**
- **⅓ cup chopped parsley**
- **1 clove garlic, minced**
- **4 anchovy fillets, chopped**
- **1 teaspoon capers**
- **8 ounces orzo pasta**
- **7 ounces mozzarella cheese, cubed**

- Cut tops off the peppers and remove the seeds. Sprinkle inside with salt, pepper and oil.
- Combine olives, parsley, garlic, anchovies and capers.
- Cook pasta al dente and drain.
- Combine pasta, chopped ingredients and cheese.
- Fill peppers with mixture and place on greased baking sheet.
- Bake in 400° oven 35 minutes. Cover if peppers start to brown too quickly.

Fettuccine with Chicken and Pecans

Serves 6

- **1 pound chicken breasts, skinned, boned and cubed**
- **¾ cup butter**
- **3 cups fresh sliced mushrooms**
- **1 cup sliced scallions**
- **¾ teaspoon salt**
- **½ teaspoon freshly ground pepper**
- **½ teaspoon garlic powder**
- **1 10 ounce package fresh fettuccine**
- **1 egg yolk**
- **⅔ cup half and half**
- **2 tablespoons chopped fresh parsley**
- **½ cup freshly grated Parmesan cheese**
- **1 cup chopped pecans, toasted**

- Melt ¼ cup butter in large skillet and sauté chicken until lightly browned.
- Remove chicken and set aside.
- Add mushrooms, scallions, ½ teaspoon salt, ¼ teaspoon pepper and ¼ teaspoon garlic powder to skillet. Sauté until mushrooms are tender. Return chicken and simmer for 20 minutes.
- Cook fettuccine al dente. Drain well.
- Melt remaining butter and combine with egg yolk, half and half, parsley and remaining salt, pepper and garlic powder.
- Stir butter sauce into fettuccine. Sprinkle with Parmesan and toss well.
- Add chicken and mushroom mixture and sprinkle all with toasted pecans.

Fettuccine with Broccoli and Chicken

Serves 4

- **1 pound fresh fettuccine**
- **½ cup sesame oil**
- **1 cup uncooked diced chicken breast**
- **2 teaspoons minced garlic**
- **2 teaspoons slivered ginger**
- **3 cups broccoli florets**
- **½ cup sherry**
- **⅓ cup soy sauce**
- **3 tablespoons butter**
- **½ cup freshly grated Parmesan cheese**
- **½ cup toasted almond slices**

- Cook fettuccine al dente. Drain and rinse with cold water. Drain again.
- Heat oil in a wok until it is smoking hot. Stir-fry chicken for 30 seconds. Add garlic, ginger, and broccoli. Stir-fry 1 minute. Add sherry and soy sauce; simmer 1 more minute.
- Add fettuccine and butter to wok. Toss. Add Parmesan and toss again. Garnish with toasted almonds. Serve with more Parmesan if desired.

Great combination of Chinese and Italian!

Tomato Basil Fettuccine with Italian Sausage

Serves 4

- **4 tablespoons olive oil**
- **1 small red onion, diced**
- **1 tablespoon minced garlic**
- **½ cup sun-dried tomatoes, chopped**
- **¾ pound Italian sausage, cooked and drained**
- **½ pound broccoli florets, blanched**
- **10 ounces tomato-basil fettuccine, cooked and drained**
- **½ cup goat cheese, crumbled**
- **1 tablespoon chopped fresh basil**

- Heat oil, sauté onion and garlic. Add tomatoes and sauté. Add cooked sausage and broccoli, sauté 2 minutes.
- Add pasta and simmer 1 minute. Place on platter and top with goat cheese. Place under broiler until cheese softens. Garnish with chopped basil and serve.

Veal...Sage, Rosemary and Time

Serves 4 to 6

¾ **cup minced green pepper**
¾ **cup minced onion**
3 **cloves garlic, minced**
1 to 2 **tablespoons butter**
2 **pounds ground veal**
1 **28-ounce can Italian
   tomatoes, chopped**
1½ **cups chicken broth**
½ **teaspoon sage**
½ **teaspoon rosemary**
½ **teaspoon fennel seed**
8 to 10 **ounces penne pasta
   freshly grated Parmesan
   cheese**

- Sauté pepper, onion, and garlic in butter until tender.
- In separate skillet brown veal and drain. Combine veal, sautéed vegetables, tomatoes, broth and herbs. Cook on stove covered on low heat 1 hour.
- Cook penne pasta until tender. Drain. Mix veal mixture and pasta together in glass baking dish. Sprinkle heavily with freshly grated Parmesan.
- Bake in 350° oven covered for 35 minutes.

Manicotti

Serves 6

1 **package manicotti noodles,
   cooked and drained**
1 **pound ground beef**
1 **pound Italian sausage**
4 **cloves garlic, minced**
1 **cup chopped onion**
1 **cup chopped green pepper**
4 **tablespoons Italian seasoning**
2 **10-ounce boxes chopped
   frozen spinach, thawed and
   drained**
2 **eggs**
3 **cups cottage cheese**
3 **cups Marinara Sauce,
   page 199**
1 **cup grated mozzarella cheese**
1 **cup freshly grated Parmesan
   cheese**

- Brown meat and drain. Add vegetables and sauté. Add seasoning, spinach, eggs, and cottage cheese.
- Cover 9 x 13-inch baking dish with thin layer of marinara sauce.
- Stuff cooked noodles and place over sauce.
- Cover with remaining sauce and sprinkle with grated mozzarella and Parmesan.
- Bake in 325° oven 45 minutes or until bubbly.

Chicken Spaghetti

Serves 16

- **6 whole chicken breasts**
- **3 tablespoons olive oil**
- **3 cloves garlic, minced**
- **1 cup chopped onion**
- **1 cup chopped celery**
- **1 cup chopped green pepper**
- **1 15-ounce can tomato sauce**
- **1 16-ounce can tomatoes**
- **1 10-ounce can Rotel tomatoes**
- **4 cups chicken broth**
- **3 tablespoons Italian seasoning**
- **5 dashes Tabasco Sauce**
- **1 teaspoon seasoned salt**
- **1 teaspoon pepper**
- **12 mushrooms, sliced**
- **1 cup sliced black olives**
- **4 cups Old English cheese**
- **8 ounces spaghetti freshly grated Parmesan cheese**

- Stew chicken breasts in salted water until tender. Tear chicken into large chunks and set aside. Reserve water
- Sauté garlic, onion, celery, green pepper in olive oil.
- Add tomato sauce, tomatoes, Rotel, broth and seasoning. Cook slowly for 1 hour.
- Add mushrooms and olives and cook for 15 minutes. Add chicken and cubed Old English and stir until melted.
- Cook spaghetti in chicken water and add to sauce.
- Place in two 9 x 13-inch baking dishes, top with Parmesan and bake covered in 350° oven 30 minutes. Uncover last 10 minutes.

Can be made ahead, a good crowd pleaser.

Fresh Pesto Sauce

1 cup

- **2 cups fresh basil leaves**
- **3 cloves garlic, minced**
- **½ cup freshly grated Parmesan cheese**
- **⅔ cup extra-virgin olive oil**
- **¼ cup pine nuts salt and pepper**

- Combine all the ingredients in food processor and blend until mixture is thoroughly combined.

Can be frozen in ice cube tray.

Extra virgin olive oil is the "first pressing" from the olives obtained without the use of heat or chemicals. Therefore it is more flavorful.

Alfredo Sauce

1 ½ cups

- **6 tablespoons butter**
- **1 cup whipping cream**
- **½ cup freshly grated Parmesan cheese**
- **freshly grated nutmeg**
- **salt and pepper**

- Melt butter over medium heat. Add cream, stir until mixture simmers.
- Remove from heat, add Parmesan a little at a time while stirring.
- Season to taste with nutmeg, salt and pepper.

Marinara Sauce

3 cups

- **1 large onion, minced**
- **3 to 4 cloves garlic, minced**
- **½ cup olive oil**
- **2 pounds ripe tomatoes, peeled, cored and cut in 1-inch pieces**
- **pinch of sugar**
- **salt and pepper**
- **Italian seasonings to taste**

- Over medium heat, cook onion and garlic in olive oil in large saucepan for 5 minutes. Add tomatoes, sugar, salt, pepper and Italian seasonings.
- Simmer covered, stirring occasionally for 25 minutes.
- Puree in food processor and then simmer the puree for 15 minutes, stirring occasionally.

Spicy Tomato Sauce

6 to 8 cups

- **3 28-ounce cans of whole Italian tomatoes**
- **7 to 10 cloves of garlic, chopped or crushed**
- **5 tablespoons olive oil**
- **2 cups water**
- **3 tablespoons dried basil**
- **1½ tablespoons oregano**
- **3 tablespoons fennel seeds**
- **3 dashes Tabasco Sauce**
- **salt and cracked pepper to taste**

- Cut tomatoes in quarters, removing the hard stem portion and retaining juice.
- Sauté garlic in olive oil for about 5 minutes using a large stainless steel pot being careful not to burn the garlic.
- Add cut tomatoes with juice to garlic and oil. Add water, herbs and Tabasco, and simmer 1 to 2 hours. Add salt and pepper to taste.
- For variety, sliced mushrooms and chopped red or yellow peppers can be added

This sauce freezes well and is generally better if allowed to rest a day in the refrigerator before serving.

Linguine of the Sea

Serves 6

1 quart half and half
3 tablespoons tomato paste
2 tablespoons unsalted butter
1 teaspoon dry mustard
large pinch freshly grated nutmeg
salt to taste
white pepper to taste
1 pound linguine
5 whole allspice
1½ pounds bay scallops
1 pound uncooked shrimp, shelled and deveined
dry white wine
freshly grated Parmesan cheese

- In medium saucepan over very low heat, simmer cream, until thickened to consistency of medium white sauce. Stir in tomato paste, butter, mustard, nutmeg, salt and pepper. Set aside over warm water.

- Cook pasta in boiling salted water until al dente. Drain, rinse and drain again. Put in large bowl. Add cream sauce and toss well.

- In deep skillet combine allspice, scallops, and shrimp with enough wine to barely cover seafood. Simmer until shrimp turn pink. Do not overcook.

- Remove seafood with slotted spoon. Add to pasta mixture and toss well. Sprinkle with Parmesan. Serve immediately.

For additional color, tiny peas, bits of dried red pepper and/or chopped parsley may be added at the final tossing.

Salmon, Peas and Sun-Dried Tomatoes

Serves 4 to 6

2 tablespoons olive oil
2 tablespoons butter
2 to 3 scallions, chopped
½ cup white wine
½ cup sun-dried tomatoes
1 cup fish stock, or clam juice, or chicken broth
1 cup whipping cream
3 tablespoons tarragon
3 tablespoons dill
1 teaspoon Worcestershire sauce
2 cups poached salmon, cubed
2 cups peas
¾ pound multi-colored pasta

- Heat oil and butter and sauté scallions. Add wine, tomatoes, stock, cream, tarragon, dill and Worcestershire.

- Simmer until thick and add salmon and peas.

- Cook pasta al dente and toss with salmon sauce.

Classic Crabmeat Fettuccine

Serves 4

- 1 **6-ounce package frozen crabmeat, thawed**
- ½ **cup butter**
- 1 **clove garlic, minced**
- ¾ **cup whipping cream**
- ½ **cup freshly grated Parmesan cheese**
- ½ **teaspoon salt**
- ½ **teaspoon black pepper**
- 1 **12-ounce package fettuccine noodles, cooked and drained**
- 1 **tablespoon chopped parsley**

- Drain crabmeat. Melt butter and sauté garlic in butter. Blend in crab, cream, Parmesan, salt and pepper. Heat while stirring constantly until blended.
- Serve over noodles and garnish with parsley.

Tomato Angel Hair Pasta with Basil and Crab

Serves 4

- 1½ **cups butter**
- 4 **teaspoons chopped fresh shallots**
- 4 **teaspoons chopped fresh basil**
- 4 **teaspoons chopped fresh parsley**
- 6 **cups chopped fresh peeled tomatoes**
- 1 **pound fresh crabmeat**
- 1¼ **pounds angel hair pasta**

- Melt butter in saucepan. Add shallots, basil, parsley and tomatoes. Bring to boil. Add crabmeat.
- Cook pasta in boiling water for 90 seconds. Drain and add to hot sauce. Serve at once.

Best when vine-ripened summer tomatoes are used.

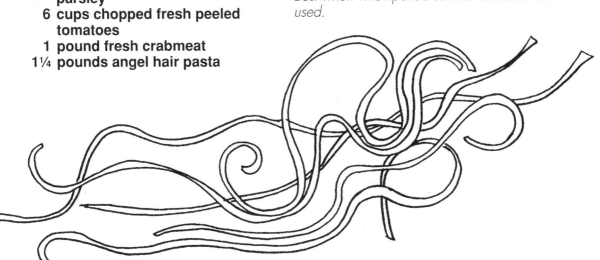

Fettuccine with Scallops in Saffron Butter

Serves 6

1½ **pound sea scallops**
1 **tablespoon olive oil**
10 **ounces pea pods**
1 **pound fettuccine**

- Sauté scallops in olive oil using large skillet.
- Cook pea pods and drain well.
- Cook fettuccine and drain well.
- Toss peas and fettuccine in skillet with scallops. Add Saffron Butter Sauce and toss. Serve immediately.

Saffron Butter Sauce

¼ **teaspoon saffron**
2 **tablespoons minced shallots**
2 **tablespoons wine vinegar**
3 **tablespoons dry white wine**
3 **tablespoons whipping cream**
   salt and pepper to taste
1 **cup unsalted butter, cut into 16 pieces**

- Combine saffron, shallots, vinegar and wine. Bring to simmer over moderate heat until reduced to 2 tablespoons. Stir in cream and simmer until reduced to 2 tablespoons. Add salt and pepper.
- Whisk in butter one piece at a time. Sauce should not get hot enough to liquefy.

Lemon Butter Sea Scallops with Rice Stick Noodles

Serves 2 to 3

1 **package Rice Stick noodles**
2 **tablespoons olive oil**
12 **large sea scallops**
2 **cups chopped green onion**
1 **cup white wine**
⅓ **cup freshly squeezed lemon juice**
½ **teaspoon salt**
½ **cup butter, softened**
¼ **cup chopped fresh parsley**
1 **lemon, sliced**
   freshly ground pepper

- To prepare rice stick noodles, ladle boiling water over noodles and let the noodles sit 5 to 10 minutes.
- In sauté pan heat oil until hot and sear scallops. Reduce heat and add onions. Cook 2 minutes. Remove scallops.
- Deglaze pan with wine. Add lemon juice, salt and butter. Cook 2 minutes more.
- Drain water from noodles. Toss with scallops, sauce and fresh parsley. Garnish with lemon slices and freshly ground pepper.

Baked Scallops

Serves 4

1 **pound bay scallops**
2 **tablespoons chopped onion**
6 **tablespoons butter**
1 **teaspoon freshly squeezed lemon juice**
½ **teaspoon garlic salt**
⅓ **cup bread crumbs**

- Wash scallops, drain and dry on paper towels. Place in casserole that has been brushed with melted butter.
- Sauté onion in 2 tablespoons butter until soft. Spread over scallops.
- Melt remaining butter, add lemon juice and garlic salt and pour over scallops.
- Sprinkle with bread crumbs and bake in 375° oven 12 to 15 minutes until scallops are tender when pierced with a knife.

Spinach Pasta with Shrimp

Serves 4

1 **pound unpeeled, raw shrimp**
5 to 6 **green onions, finely sliced, including part of green tops**
1 **clove garlic, minced**
3 **tablespoons butter**
2 **tablespoons chopped fresh parsley**
½ **teaspoon fines herbes**
1 **large tomato, peeled, seeded and chopped**
½ **cup shrimp stock (shells from one pound shrimp, boiled 5 minutes with one cup water and drained)**
½ **cup white wine cornstarch for thickening, if necessary salt and pepper freshly squeezed lemon juice**
8 **ounces spinach linguine, cooked al dente**

- Peel shrimp reserving shells for stock.
- Boil shells in 1 cup water 5 minutes. Drain, reserving shrimp stock.
- Sauté green onions and garlic in butter. Add parsley, fines herbes, tomato, stock and wine. Thicken with cornstarch, if necessary.
- Add uncooked shrimp and cook until translucent.
- Season with salt, pepper and a squeeze of fresh lemon juice.
- Toss with cooked pasta to mix.

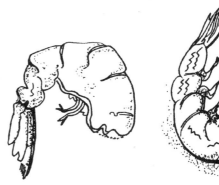

Shrimp Fettuccine with Tomato Basil Cream

Serves 4

- 10 ounces fettuccine
- 1 pound raw medium shrimp, peeled and deveined
- 3 tablespoons butter
- 1 tablespoon olive oil
- 3 ounces brandy
- 3 to 4 green onions, chopped
- 2 Roma tomatoes, finely chopped
- ½ pint whipping cream
- 4 ounces half and half
- 2 tablespoons chopped fresh basil
  freshly ground black pepper
  freshly squeezed lemon juice

- Cook pasta al dente.
- In large skillet sauté shrimp in butter and oil until just pink but not done. Add brandy and ignite, stirring until flame goes out. Remove shrimp to warm covered plate.
- Add green onions, tomatoes, cream, half and half and basil to skillet and bring to light boil. Lightly boil 3 to 4 minutes until slightly thickened. Add shrimp and pasta to skillet and toss until well coated. Top with pepper and sprinkle lightly with lemon juice.

Shrimp with Tomatoes and Feta

Serves 4

- 2 tablespoons butter
- 2 teaspoons minced garlic
- ½ cup chopped onion
- 4 cups peeled and chopped tomatoes
- 4 tablespoons fresh basil or 2 teaspoons dried
- 2 teaspoons Dijon mustard.
- 2 teaspoons sugar
- ½ cup dry white wine
- ½ cup plus 4 tablespoons minced parsley
- 2 tablespoons freshly squeezed lemon juice
- 1 teaspoon salt
  freshly ground black pepper
- 1½ pounds large shrimp, peeled and deveined
- 4 tablespoons feta cheese, crumbled

- In large skillet, melt butter. Add garlic and onions and sauté until tender. Add tomatoes, basil, mustard, and sugar. Mix well to blend. Cook over low heat for 15 minutes, stirring occasionally.
- Add wine, ½ cup parsley, lemon juice, salt and pepper.
- Increase heat to moderate, add shrimp. Cook 3 to 4 minutes. Transfer to baking dish or individual au gratin dishes. Sprinkle with feta cheese.
- Bake in 375° oven 10 minutes or until the sauce bubbles. Broil briefly to brown on top.
- Sprinkle with remaining parsley and serve immediately.

Serve with Caesar Salad and French bread.

Delicious Deviled Shrimp

Serves 4

- **1 pound fresh shrimp, peeled and deveined**
- **1 egg, slightly beaten**
- **¼ teaspoon salt**
- **½ cup fine bread crumbs**
- **¼ cup butter**
  Deviled Shrimp Sauce
- **3 cups hot cooked rice**

- Roll shrimp in mixture of egg and salt, then roll in bread crumbs.
- Brown in butter over medium heat about 10 minutes until pink.
- Remove shrimp and keep warm while preparing Deviled Shrimp Sauce.

Deviled Shrimp Sauce

- **1 cup chopped onion**
- **1 clove garlic, minced**
- **2 tablespoons butter**
- **1 10½-ounce can consommé**
- **½ cup water**
- **2 tablespoons steak sauce**
- **1½ teaspoons prepared mustard**
- **½ teaspoon salt**
- **½ teaspoon Tabasco Sauce**
  juice of 1 lemon

- Sauté onion and garlic in butter over medium heat until tender.
- Add remaining ingredients except lemon juice.
- Bring to a boil and simmer 15 minutes or until volume is reduced to one-half, about 1 cup. Add lemon juice.
- Arrange shrimp on rice and top with sauce.

Sauce can be prepared in advance.

Sautéed Soft Shell Crabs

Serves 2

- **4 soft shell crabs**
- **1 cup milk**
  juice of ½ lemon
- **5 to 6 heavy dashes Tabasco Sauce**
  seasoned flour
- **6 tablespoons butter**
- **3 tablespoons olive oil**
- **2 to 3 cloves garlic, minced**
- **2 teaspoons dried tarragon**
- **⅓ cup chopped fresh parsley plus 1 teaspoon**

- Dip crabs in mixture of milk, lemon juice and Tabasco. Dredge in seasoned flour and gently shake off excess.
- In medium skillet, melt butter with oil. Add garlic and sauté until clear and tender. Add tarragon.
- Place crabs in hot butter upside down and sauté over medium heat 3 minutes. Turn crabs and sprinkle ⅓ cup parsley over crabs and butter. Sauté 3 more minutes.
- Remove and serve immediately. Sprinkle remaining parsley over crabs and top with flavored butter from pan.

Serve with fresh steamed asparagus and small red new potatoes.

Grilled Salmon with Sun-Dried Tomato Sauce

Serves 2

2 **fresh salmon steaks**
olive oil
1 **tablespoon butter**
1 **teaspoon olive oil**
2 **tablespoons flour**
½ **cup finely chopped green onion tops**
5 to 6 **sun-dried tomatoes, finely chopped**
1 **large clove garlic**
1 **cup bottled clam juice**
10 to 12 **whole green peppercorns**
3 to 4 **ounces Marsala wine**
1 **teaspoon chopped basil**
½ **teaspoon chopped tarragon**
½ **cup whipping cream**

- Brush salmon steaks with olive oil and grill with skin on over charcoal or other grill approximately 8 to 10 minutes for each inch of thickness. Remove the skin before serving.
- Make a light roux with butter, oil and flour. Add green onion tops, sun-dried tomatoes and garlic. Add clam juice and peppercorns and bring to a boil. Reduce by ½. Add Marsala wine, basil and tarragon. Simmer a few minutes, add cream and reduce again.
- Ladle ¼ cup sauce onto each plate and place salmon steak on top of sauce. Extra sauce may be spooned on top of salmon or served on the side.

A unique combination of flavors!

Southwest Sole

Serves 4

½ **red bell pepper, seeded and julienned**
½ **yellow bell pepper, seeded and julienned**
1 **jalapeño pepper, seeded and julienned**
1 **tablespoon butter**
3 **tablespoons olive oil**
¾ **tablespoon crushed basil**
4 **sole fillets**
1 **tablespoon cilantro**
6 to 8 **cherry tomatoes, halved**
3 to 4 **sliced mushrooms**
fresh parsley

- Sauté peppers in butter and oil until peppers are soft and oil is flavored. Set peppers aside. Add basil to pan and stir.
- Sprinkle fish fillets with cilantro and sauté approximately 3 minutes depending on thickness. Turn fillets.
- Add tomatoes and mushrooms and sauté fish an additional 2 to 3 minutes. Distribute tomatoes, mushrooms and peppers on top of fish fillets, sprinkle with fresh parsley and serve.

This recipe will work well with any mild white fish.

Sole en Papillote

Serves 4

- **5 stalks celery, minced**
- **2 leeks (white portion), minced**
- **4 carrots, minced**
- **3 tablespoons butter**
  salt and freshly ground black
  pepper
- **2 pounds fillet of sole**
- **2 tomatoes, sliced**
- **1 lemon, sliced**
- **4 bay leaves**
- **¾ teaspoon fresh thyme**
  or ½ teaspoon dried
- **4 squares 12 x 1-inch aluminum**
  foil or cooking parchment

- Sauté celery, leeks, carrots in butter for 5 minutes or until tender. Season with salt and pepper.
- On each foil or parchment square, layer one-fourth ingredients in following order: sautéed vegetables, sole fillets, salt and pepper, tomato slices, lemon slices, bay leaf and thyme. Fold packets securely, tucking edges under, and place on a baking sheet. Bake in preheated 350° oven 20 minutes.
- Slit packets before serving, or allow guests to open their own.

Fish Florentine

Serves 4

- **1 pound fresh spinach**
- **¼ cup minced onion**
- **¾ cup sliced mushrooms**
  salt and pepper to taste
- **1 teaspoon vegetable oil**
- **2 tablespoons butter**
- **1½ tablespoons flour**
- **1 cup milk**
- **¼ cup dry white wine**
- **1 pound fish (orange roughy,**
  flounder, or sole)
- **½ cup grated white Cheddar or**
  Swiss cheese

- Steam spinach just until wilted and drain well.
- Place spinach in lightly oiled, shallow baking dish. Sprinkle with onion, mushrooms, salt, pepper and oil.
- Melt butter and stir in flour until smooth. Cook over low heat about two minutes. Blend in milk and stir until thickened and smooth. Add white wine and remove from heat.
- Arrange fillets over spinach and vegetables. Top with white sauce and sprinkle with cheese. Bake in 350° oven 45 minutes or until fish flakes easily with fork.

Can be prepared early and refrigerated until baking time.

Red Snapper Cancun

Serves 6 to 8

3 pounds **red snapper fillets**
1 teaspoon **salt**
½ cup **freshly squeezed lime juice**
¼ cup **olive oil**
2 cloves **garlic, crushed**
2 **onions, thinly sliced**
6 large **tomatoes**
1 tablespoon **tomato paste**
1 large **bay leaf**
½ teaspoon **dried oregano**
18 **green olives, pitted and cut in half**
2 tablespoons **capers**
1 4-ounce can **diced green chilies, drained**
¼ cup **freshly squeezed lemon juice**

- Place red snapper in a shallow 2-quart casserole.
- Rub the fish with salt and lime juice. Prick with a fork to aid in penetration of the lime juice and marinate in lime juice 3 to 4 hours, turning occasionally.
- Place olive oil in a heavy skillet. Add garlic and onion to the skillet and sauté over moderate heat 3 to 5 minutes or until tender.
- Peel, seed and coarsely chop the tomatoes. Add tomatoes, tomato paste, bay leaf, oregano, olives, capers, chilies, and lemon juice to the skillet.
- Cook, stirring, over moderate heat 10 to 15 minutes until the mixture is thick and some of the liquid has evaporated.
- Place fillets in a shallow baking dish large enough to hold them in 1 layer and cover them evenly with the tomato sauce. Bake uncovered in a preheated 325° oven 20 to 30 minutes or until the fish flakes easily when tested with a fork.

Red Snapper with Shrimp

- 2 **tablespoons butter**
- 5 **cloves garlic, minced**
- 2 **cups small shrimp, peeled, deveined, and cooked**
- 1 **cup toasted bread cubes**
  salt and pepper to taste
- 2 **pounds red snapper fillets**
- 8 **ounces tomato sauce**
- ½ **cup dry vermouth**
- 1 **teaspoon sugar**
- ⅛ **teaspoon cayenne**

- Melt the butter in a heavy skillet. Add the garlic to the butter and cook gently over low heat for 2 to 3 minutes. Add the shrimp, bread cubes, and salt and pepper to taste. Combine these ingredients gently and quickly. Remove the pan from heat.
- Arrange one half the fish fillets on the bottom of a buttered, shallow 2-quart baking dish. Top the fish with an even layer of the shrimp and bread cube mixture. Arrange the remaining fish fillets over the shrimp and sprinkle the fish lightly with salt.
- Combine tomato sauce, vermouth, sugar and cayenne. Pour over the fish. Bake uncovered in preheated 350° oven 30 minutes, basting occasionally.

Lemon Grilled Halibut

- ½ **cup freshly squeezed lemon juice**
- 1 **tablespoon lemon zest**
- ¼ **cup Dijon mustard**
- 3 **tablespoons freshly chopped tarragon or 1½ teaspoons dried**
- 2 **tablespoons finely chopped chives or scallions**
- ¼ **cup olive oil**
- ¼ **teaspoon freshly ground black pepper**
- 6 **8-ounce halibut steaks or 3 pounds of fillets**

- Combine lemon juice, zest, mustard, tarragon and chives in small mixing bowl. Slowly whisk in olive oil until well blended. Add pepper.
- Arrange fish in shallow glass dish. Cover with marinade, coating all pieces evenly. Marinate 1 to 2 hours.
- Grill fish 5 to 7 minutes per side, until desired doneness. Garnish with lemon slices and parsley.

Serve with Almost Wild Rice, page 130.

Sea Bass with White Beans, Roasted Peppers and Fresh Herbs

Serves 4

- 2 fresh thyme sprigs
- 2 fresh rosemary sprigs
- 7 tablespoons extra-virgin olive oil
- 3 ounces bacon, diced
- ½ white onion, diced
- 2 cloves garlic, diced
- 3 cups chicken broth
- 1½ cups water
- ¾ cup dried Great Northern beans, soaked overnight
- ½ cup chopped tomato
- 1 tablespoon minced fresh thyme
- ½ teaspoon minced fresh rosemary
- 1½ pounds sea bass
- 1 red bell pepper, roasted and julienned
- 1 yellow bell pepper, roasted and julienned
- 4 ounces prosciutto, julienned
- 1 teaspoon balsamic vinegar

- Rub herb sprigs between your fingers and combine with olive oil in a bowl. Let sit at room temperature for several hours. Discard herbs reserving oil.
- Heat 1 tablespoon herb oil in a large pot. Add bacon and cook until brown. Add onion and garlic and sauté 5 to 6 minutes. Add broth, 1½ cups water, beans, tomato and the minced herbs. Simmer until beans are tender, 1½ to 2 hours. Drain bean mixture.
- Heat 2 tablespoons herb oil in a large skillet. Cook fish about 4 minutes per side. Transfer to a platter and keep warm.
- Add bell peppers and prosciutto to the pan and heat through.
- Mix in vinegar.
- Spoon beans onto plates. Top with fish and peppers. Spoon remaining herb oil around the beans.

Fish may be grilled. Swordfish, orange roughy or halibut may be used.

Caribbean Grilled Fish Marinade

Marinade for 6 fish steaks

- 3 large cloves garlic, chopped coarse
- 1 teaspoon salt
- 1 teaspoon dried thyme
- ¼ teaspoon ground allspice
- ¼ cup freshly squeezed orange juice
- 2 to 3 tablespoons lemon juice
- 2 tablespoons dry white wine, optional
- ¼ teaspoon Tabasco Sauce
- ¼ cup olive oil

- Combine all ingredients.
- Marinate fish steaks at least one hour before grilling.

Use grouper, swordfish or mako shark.

Lobster and Crabmeat Soufflé

Serves 4

> soft butter, for coating
> 4 6-ounce soufflé ramekins
> parchment paper
> 4 ounces butter
> 4 ounces flour
> 2 cups half and half
> 1 tablespoon Minor's lobster base
> 1 cup grated cheddar cheese
> 8 egg yolks
> salt and white pepper, to taste
> Tabasco Sauce, to taste
> 4 ounces lobster meat, chopped
> 4 ounces crab meat, chopped
> 8 egg whites

- Spread a little butter in four individual soufflé ramekins. Make four inch-high collars from parchment paper and secure them with scotch tape.
- Melt 4 ounces butter in saucepan. Add the flour and stir over medium heat to form a roux. Add the half-and-half and the lobster base. Cook until thick, stirring constantly.
- Remove pan from heat, add cheddar cheese and beat in egg yolks. Stir in seasonings, then lobster meat and crab meat.
- In a separate bowl, beat egg white until they hold stiff peaks. Gently fold egg whites into soufflé base.
- Spoon mixture into soufflé dishes and bake in preheated 375° oven for approximately 30 minutes.
- When done, the centers will be semi-firm and moist. Serve immediately.

Chef Richard J. Clements, Tulsa Country Club

Bow Tie Pasta with Lobster and Asparagus

Serves 4

> 3 cups whipping cream
> 1 cup dry sherry
> 1 cup diced tomatoes, seeded
> 2 cups diced lobster meat
> ½ cup chopped scallions
> salt and white pepper
> 4 cups bow tie pasta, cooked
> 1 bunch fresh asparagus, blanched

- Reduce cream by half over low heat. At the same time in a separate pan, cook tomatoes and lobster meat in the sherry. Add the scallions, cream, salt and pepper.
- Toss the pasta in hot water and drain well. Add to the lobster mixture and heat through.
- Garnish with fresh blanched asparagus. Serve immediately.

Chef Jacques Lissonnet, Bravo, Adams Mark Hotel

Sun-Dried Tomato Pesto

1 cup

- **12 sun-dried tomatoes, soaked in hot water for 15 to 20 minutes**
- **2 cloves garlic**
- **2 tablespoons walnuts**
- **2 tablespoons freshly grated Parmesan cheese**
- **½ cup olive oil**
- **¼ cup chicken stock**
- **1 tablespoon freshly squeezed lemon juice**
- **1 teaspoon salt**
- **½ teaspoon freshly ground pepper**

- Place tomatoes, garlic, walnuts and Parmesan in a food processor with a little oil and puree. With motor running add remaining oil, chicken stock, lemon juice, salt and pepper. Puree until smooth.
- Place in airtight container and refrigerate. Can be held up to a month under refrigeration.

Use on pizza or pasta—yummy!

Chef Keith Lindenberg, Cooking School of Tulsa

Spinach Fettuccine Provençal

Serves 4 to 6

- **1 pound spinach fettuccine**
- **2 tablespoons extra virgin olive oil**
- **1 red pepper, julienned**
- **1 green pepper, julienned**
- **⅛ cup sun-dried tomatoes**
- **¼ cup diced fresh tomatoes**
- **1 caccatori sausage, sliced (pepperoni may be substituted)**
- **2½ cups tomato sauce**
- **10 herb-cured olives**

- Cook fettuccine in boiling salted water until done. Prepare remaining ingredients while pasta is cooking.
- In hot sauté pan, add olive oil. Sauté peppers lightly and add tomatoes and sausage. Sauté lightly and add tomato sauce and olives.
- Let simmer 5 minutes.
- Serve on top of fettuccine.

Chef Matt Kelley, Cascia Hall Class of 1986

Pasta Maine Lobster

Serves 2

- 1 tablespoon butter
- ½ cup sliced fresh mushrooms
- ½ cup cooked lobster
- 1 cup Madeira
- 1½ cups whipping cream
- 3 cups cooked pasta (penne, fusilli or rotini)
- 2 tablespoons freshly grated Parmesan cheese
  salt and pepper to taste

- Sauté mushrooms and lobster in butter.
- Add Madeira, cream and reduce.
- Simmer for 3 minutes.
- Add pasta and Parmesan.
- Salt and pepper to taste.

Chef John J. Briscoe, McGill's Restaurant

Chicken Primavera

Serves 4

- ½ cup olive oil
- 1 medium onion, diced ½ inch
- 1 medium carrot, sliced thin
- ½ medium red pepper, diced ½ inch
- 1 medium green pepper, diced ½ inch
- 20 medium pitted black olives
- 1 medium zucchini, diced ½ inch
- 1 medium tomato, diced ½ inch
- 2 8-ounce chicken breasts, cooked and diced
- 2 large cloves garlic, crushed
- ½ cup dry white wine
- 3 tablespoons fresh parsley, chopped fine
- 2 tablespoons fresh basil, chopped fine
  salt and pepper to taste
- 8 ounces fettuccine noodles, cooked and drained

- In large sauté pan over high heat, add olive oil. Add onion, carrots, red and green pepper and black olives. Stir constantly. After 2 minutes add zucchini and cook 1 minute. Add tomatoes and diced chicken breast. Stirring 1 more minute, add crushed garlic and sauté for 30 seconds. Add wine, parsley and basil. Season with salt and pepper to taste. Stir frequently until most of the white wine is evaporated.
- Toss with pasta or pour over the four portions of pasta. Top with freshly grated Parmesan.

Chef John Fard, Ti Amo Ristorante Pizzeria

Macadamia Crusted Tiger Prawns with Amaretto Sauce

Tempura Batter

Serves 4

pinch cayenne pepper
1 cup flour
2 teaspoons baking powder
1 teaspoon salt
1 cup ice cold water
1 egg, beaten
bowl of ice

- Combine flour, baking powder and salt in stainless steel bowl and mix well. Place bowl on top of ice. Add ice water, stirring constantly. Add beaten egg and mix until consistency is smooth.

Tiger Prawns

12 4- to 6-ounce tiger prawns, peeled and deveined
1 cup flour
Tempura Batter
clarified butter

- Clean shrimp, then dust with flour. Dip shrimp in tempura batter and place in medium to hot skillet with heated clarified butter (enough to cover shrimp one-half to three-quarters). Sauté shrimp to a golden brown, turning once. Set them on a plate.

Amaretto Sauce

2 cloves garlic, minced
1 teaspoon shallots
½ cup chopped macadamia nuts
2 teaspoons butter, divided
¼ cup amaretto
6 ounces whipping cream
salt and pepper

- Sauté garlic, shallots and macadamia nuts in ½ teaspoon butter. Add amaretto. Flambé on low heat reducing liquid to half, then add cream. Slow simmer reducing to half again, then add remainder of butter. Salt and pepper to taste.

Chef Daniel Broyles, Warren Duck Club

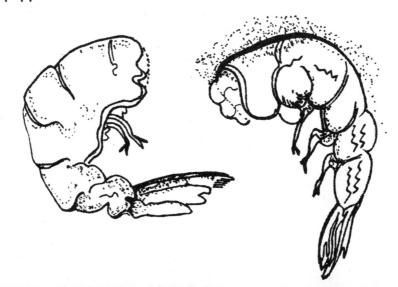

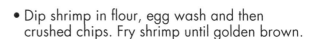

Tortilla Crusted Shrimp

Serves 4

20 shrimp, peeled and deveined
4 tablespoons flour, seasoned
1 ounce egg wash
½ cup crushed white tortilla chips
Spicy Peanut Sauce

Spicy Peanut Sauce

2½ tablespoons olive oil
1 large onion, diced
10 cloves garlic, minced
5 serrano chili peppers, seeded and minced
2 cups chicken broth
⅓ cup molasses
¼ cup soy sauce
¼ cup freshly squeezed lemon juice
1 pound crunchy peanut butter
½ cup cilantro

- Dip shrimp in flour, egg wash and then crushed chips. Fry shrimp until golden brown.
- Glaze plate with Spicy Peanut Sauce and present shrimp with fresh vegetable and starch.

4 cups

- Sauté onion, garlic and chilies in olive oil until softened. Add remaining ingredients and beat until warmed.
- Place mixture in food processor and blend until smooth.

Chef Ling Pham, Doubletree Hotel Downtown, "The Grille"

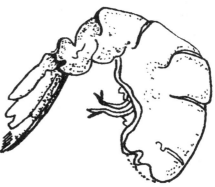

Seared Yellow-Fin Tuna with Vanilla Bean Beurre Blanc

Serves 4

- 1 pound yellow-fin tuna
  olive oil
- ½ teaspoon cayenne pepper
- 1 teaspoon crushed red pepper
- 1 teaspoon white pepper
- 1 teaspoon black pepper
- 2 teaspoons whole rosemary
- 2 teaspoons sweet basil
- 2 teaspoons whole thyme
- 2 teaspoons oregano
- ½ teaspoon chili powder
- 1 teaspoon ground cumin
- 1 teaspoon granulated onion
- 1 teaspoon granulated garlic
- 4 teaspoons paprika
- 1 teaspoon Kosher salt
- 1 teaspoon salt
- 2 teaspoons whole fennel seed
  Vanilla Bean Beurre Blanc
  Sauce

- Mix all well and completely cover center-cut very fresh yellow-fin tuna loin that has been coated with olive oil to hold the spice. Sear rare on all sides on a hot cast iron skillet. Set aside to cool and slice very thin.

Vanilla Bean Beurre Blanc

- 1 shallot, chopped
- 1 vanilla bean, split
- 2 cups white wine
- ½ cup whipping cream
- 1 cup unsalted butter, softened
  salt to taste
- 2 teaspoons white wine vinegar

- Sauté shallot and vanilla bean until shallot is translucent.
- Add wine and reduce completely.
- Add cream and reduce by half.
- Remove from heat and whip in butter. Strain and season with salt and vinegar.
- Serve sauce warm and tuna at room temperature.
- Place Beurre Blanc in center of plate and arrange sliced tuna in shingled pattern to show the contrast of the cooked sides and raw center.

Chef Timothy A. Inman, Bodean Seafood Restaurant

Asparagus Lasagna

Serves 10

- **24 lasagna pasta strips**
- **7 ounces goat cheese**
- **4½ cups whipping cream, divided**
- **zest and juice of 2 lemons**
- **1 teaspoon white pepper**
- **3 teaspoons salt**
- **30 fresh asparagus spears, stems removed**
- **1½ cups grated mozzarella cheese**
- **½ cup freshly grated Parmesan cheese**

- Cook lasagna strips al dente and shock with cold water and oil. Remove to colander.
- Blend goat cheese with 4 cups cream, stir and simmer until smooth. Add lemon zest and juice, pepper and salt. Keep warm.
- Blanch asparagus and shock in cold water. Remove to colander to drain. Diagonally slice asparagus with ½-inch cuts and reserve.
- Lay pasta strips lengthwise in 9 x 13-inch glass baking dish bringing the noodles up over edges. Ladle ⅓ of the sauce over pasta, layer ½ of the asparagus and sprinkle with ½ of the mozzarella. Repeat for second layer. For third layer, finish with pasta, remaining sauce and Parmesan. Whip remaining ½ cup cream and spread over sauce.
- Bake in 350° oven until bubbles form around the sides and the top is light brown.
- Chill overnight and reheat for easy serving.

Crab meat with the asparagus makes this very interesting. Also, this can be served chilled in ½-inch slices with roast pepper puree as a summer lunch entrée or dinner appetizer.

Chef Rick Kamp, RJK Enterprises

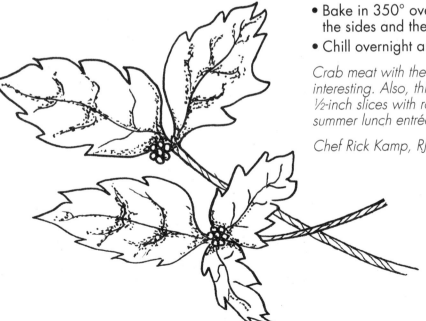

Tulsa Sunsets

Will Rogers once remarked, "Tulsa is a real town. It was founded on the spirit of its people." The city gives testimony to the American dream, to individualism, to hard work, pride, home, family, faith and philanthropy. The pioneer spirit that helped to settle Oklahoma still burns strongly in its volunteers whose creativity and self-reliant attitude reflect that of their ancestors.

Individuals and companies in Tulsa continue a history of generous support to numerous national organizations, as well as to area hospitals, recreation centers, community theatre, the Tulsa City County libraries, museums, the Tulsa Zoo, numerous social service agencies and the Tulsa Garden Center.

Tulsa volunteers also respond, with gracious hospitality and frontier practicality, hosting various functions, such as the national Governors' Conference, small groups of foreign professionals and the U. S. Open Golf Tournament.

Cascia Hall, recognizing each individual's potential impact on the community, directs its students toward sharing their time and abilities through its Community Service program. Cascia's young people have volunteered thousands of hours at nursing homes, programs for the physically challenged, social service agencies, laboratories, legal service offices, area hospitals and veterinary hospitals.

Through community service, Cascia men and women have grown in their respect and understanding of their fellow man. This is an invaluable adjunct to classroom learning and a life lesson that will hasten their growth into mature members of society.

Tulsa Sunsets

Pear Tart

Pâté Sucree

- 1¾ **cups flour**
- 10 **tablespoons plus 2 teaspoons unsalted butter, well chilled**
- ¼ **cup sugar**
- 2 **egg yolks**
- ¼ **teaspoon water**
- 4 **drops of vanilla**

Filling

- 1 **cup plus 3 tablespoons sugar**
- 6 **tablespoons flour**
- 3 **eggs**
- ¾ **cup butter, melted**
- 2 **Bartlett pears, peeled, cored, and quartered lengthwise**
  powdered sugar

- Combine flour, butter and sugar in processor and mix using on and off turns until mixture resembles coarse meal, about 45 seconds.
- Add yolks, water, vanilla and continue mixing until dough is crumbly. Work into a ball. Flatten into a disc and freeze 30 minutes. (Dough can be prepared ahead and frozen for several months.)

- Combine sugar, flour and eggs and whisk until smooth. Whisk butter into sugar mixture and set aside.
- Roll out dough on floured surface to ⅛-inch thick. Press into an 11-inch tart pan with removable bottom. (Place in refrigerator.)
- Cut pears cross wise ⅛-inch thick and gently open into a fan shape. Arrange pears in crust in flower petal pattern.
- Pour filling into tart shell over pears.
- Bake in preheated 375° oven 35 to 40 minutes until crust and filling are brown.
- Sprinkle with powdered sugar.

A dessert to impress!

Fresh Strawberry Almond Pie

Serves 6 to 8

Crust

- **2 cups crushed shortbread cookies**
- **¼ cup finely chopped blanched whole or slivered almonds**
- **5 tablespoons butter, melted**

Filling

- **6 cups strawberries, hulled**
- **1 cup sugar**
- **3 tablespoons cornstarch**
- **⅓ cup water**
- **¼ teaspoon salt**
- **½ teaspoon almond extract sweetened whipped cream**

- In small bowl stir together all crust ingredients. Press on bottom and sides of 9-inch pie pan. Bake in preheated 350° oven 8 minutes. Cool completely.

- Mash enough strawberries to equal 1 cup.
- In saucepan combine sugar and cornstarch. Stir in mashed strawberries and water. Cook over medium heat, stirring constantly, until mixture thickens and comes to a full boil, 8 to 15 minutes. Boil 1 minute and remove from heat. Stir in salt and almond extract, cool 10 minutes.
- Fill baked crust with remaining strawberries. Pour cooked mixture over strawberries.
- Refrigerate at least 3 hours. Garnish with sweetened whipped cream before serving.

Fab Frozen Brandy Alexander Pie

Serves 6 to 8

- **1 14-ounce can sweetened condensed milk**
- **2 tablespoons crème de cacao**
- **2 tablespoons brandy**
- **1 cup whipping cream, whipped**
- **1 9-inch graham cracker crust shaved chocolate for garnish**

- Combine milk, crème de cacao and brandy. Fold mixture into whipped cream carefully. Pour into crust and freeze 4 to 6 hours overnight until firm.
- Garnish with shaved chocolate.

French Silk Pie

Crust

- ½ **cup butter**
- ½ **cup flour**
- ⅓ **cup flaked coconut**
- 2 **tablespoons brown sugar**

Filling

- 1 **cup powdered sugar**
- ½ **cup butter, softened**
- 3 **ounces unsweetened chocolate, melted**
- 1 **teaspoon vanilla**
- 2 **eggs**
- ½ **pint whipping cream, whipped**
- **chopped walnuts or pecans**

- Melt butter and add flour, coconut and sugar
- Cook over medium heat; stirring constantly 3 to 4 minutes until mixture begins to brown and all butter is absorbed.
- Press into bottom and sides of 9-inch pie dish. Cool.

- Blend sugar, butter, chocolate, vanilla and eggs. Beat 2 minutes at highest speed.
- Pour into crust and chill 2 hours. Garnish with whipped cream and nuts.

The coconut crust makes this special!

German Chocolate Angel Pie

- 3 **egg whites, room temperature**
- ¼ **teaspoon salt**
- ¼ **teaspoon cream of tartar**
- ¾ **cup sugar**
- ¾ **teaspoon vanilla**
- ¾ **cup chopped pecans**
- 1 **4-ounce bar German chocolate**
- 3 **tablespoons water**
- 1 **teaspoon vanilla**
- 1 **cup whipping cream**

- Beat egg whites with salt and cream of tartar until foamy. Add sugar 2 tablespoons at a time, beating well after each addition. Continue beating until stiff peaks form. Fold in vanilla and pecans. Spoon into 9-inch lightly greased glass pie plate and form nest-like shell.
- Bake in preheated 300° oven 50 to 55 minutes. Cool.
- Melt chocolate in water. Cool. Add vanilla. Whip cream and fold into cooled chocolate. Spoon into meringue shell. Freeze.
- Thaw slightly to serve.

Store in freezer. Excellent dessert that can be made several days ahead.

Pineapple-Lime Pie

Serves 6 to 8

- 1 **9-inch pie crust, baked and cooled**
- 1 **can sweetened condensed milk**
- ½ **cup fresh lime juice**
- 1 **15-ounce can crushed pineapple, drained**
- ½ **teaspoon almond extract**
- 1 **cup whipping cream, whipped**
- 4 **kiwi fruit**

- Combine milk and lime juice.
- Add pineapple and almond extract.
- Pour into cooled pie crust. Refrigerate.
- To serve, cover with whipped cream and arrange peeled, sliced kiwi on whipped cream.

A pretty, refreshing summer dessert.

Frangipane Tart with Strawberries and Raspberries

Serves 8 to 10

Tart

- 1¼ **cups flour**
- 6 **tablespoons cold unsalted butter**
- 2 **tablespoons cold solid shortening**
- ¼ **teaspoon salt**
- 2 **tablespoons ice water**

Filling

- 6 **tablespoons unsalted butter**
- ½ **cup sugar**
- 1 **large egg**
- ¾ **cup blanched almonds, finely ground**
- 1 **teaspoon almond extract**
- 1 **tablespoon amaretto liqueur**
- 1 **tablespoon flour**
- ¼ **cup strawberry or raspberry jam**
- 2 **cup strawberries**
- 2 **cups raspberries**

- Place tart ingredients in food processor and mix until blended. Add more ice water if needed to form ball. Chill 1 hour, wrapped in wax paper.
- Roll out dough ⅛-inch thickness. Fit into 11 x 8-inch rectangular or 11-inch round tart pan. Chill.

- In small bowl cream together butter, sugar and beat in the egg, almonds and almond extract, amaretto liqueur and flour.
- Spread filling evenly on bottom of tart shell and bake in preheated 375° oven 20 to 25 minutes.
- Remove from oven and let tart cool. Brush tart with 3 tablespoons jam.
- Cut strawberries lengthwise ⅛-inch slices and arrange overlapping in long rows. Alternate rows with whole raspberries.
- Brush top with remaining jam for glaze.

Lovely for a summer dinner party.

Lemon Angel Pie

4 **eggs, separated**
½ **teaspoon cream of tartar**
⅛ **teaspoon salt**
1½ **cups sugar**
   grated rind of 1 lemon
1 to 2 **tablespoons freshly squeezed lemon juice**
1 **cup whipping cream, whipped**
   toasted sliced almonds

- Beat 4 egg whites until frothy and add cream of tartar, salt and 1 cup sugar. Beat until stiff and spread in a buttered 9-inch pie pan.
- Bake in preheated 275° oven 1 hour.
- Beat 4 egg yolks until pale yellow and add rind, lemon juice and remaining ½ cup sugar. Beat to combine and place in the top of a double boiler and cook until thick.
- Cool and spread in cooled crust.
- Top with whipped cream and toasted almonds.

Lemon Buttons

1 **3-ounce package cream cheese**
½ **cup butter**
1 **cup flour**
2 **eggs, beaten**
2 **tablespoons flour**
2 **tablespoons freshly squeezed lemon juice**
1 **cup sugar**
½ **teaspoon baking powder**

- Blend cheese, butter and flour together. Shape into 24 1-inch balls. Press into mini-muffin tins to form crust.
- Beat eggs, flour, lemon juice, sugar and baking powder. Place 1 tablespoon of filling into each mini-crust. Bake in preheated 350° oven 15 minutes.

Frosting

¼ **cup butter**
1 **teaspoon freshly squeezed lemon juice**
1 **cup powdered sugar**

- Blend butter, lemon juice and sugar and frost.

Perfect Apple Pie

9-inch pie

Perfect Pie Crust
3 tablespoons flour
1½ cups sugar
3 tablespoons butter
6 to 7 Golden Delicious, Rome or Granny Smith apples, peeled, cored and sliced cinnamon
½ teaspoon sugar

- In unbaked 9-inch pie crust, sprinkle two tablespoons flour and ½ cup sugar. Dot with butter. Add apple slices. Pour 1 cup sugar over apples. Sprinkle with 1 tablespoon flour and dust with cinnamon.
- Cover with top crust. Seal edges. Cut 6 to 7 small slits in top crust. Bake in preheated 400° oven one hour. Cool on rack and sprinkle top crust with ½ teaspoon sugar while pie is hot.

The Flag, Apple Pie and Mom!

Perfect Pie Crust

Four 9-inch pie crusts

4 cups flour, sifted
1 level cup cold vegetable oil
⅔ cup cold water

- Pour flour into large mixing bowl. Add oil. Cut mixture with pastry cutter until fine. Add water. Mix with fork. Form into large ball. Cut ball into quarters. Form each quarter into ball. Roll each ball into individual crust.

Black Bottom Peanut Butter Pie

Serves 6 to 8

½ cup peanut butter
½ cup milk
½ cup powdered sugar
1 3-ounce package cream cheese
1 8-ounce container whipped topping
1 prepared chocolate crumb crust

- Place peanut butter, milk, sugar and cream cheese in blender. Blend until smooth. Stir in whipped topping. Pour into crust. Freeze two hours.

Pretty garnished with chocolate curls.

Pumpkin Chiffon Pie

Serves 6 to 8

- 1 **envelope unflavored gelatin**
- ¾ **cup brown sugar, firmly packed**
- ½ **teaspoon salt**
- 1 **teaspoon cinnamon**
- ½ **teaspoon ginger**
- ¼ **teaspoon cloves**
- 1 **16-ounce can pumpkin**
- 2 **egg, separated**
- ½ **cup milk**
- ⅓ **cup sugar**
- 1 **teaspoon grated orange rind**
- ½ **cup sour cream**
- 1 **baked 9-inch pie crust**

- Combine gelatin, brown sugar, salt, cinnamon, ginger, cloves, pumpkin, egg yolks and milk in saucepan. Cook over medium heat, stirring constantly, until mixture comes to a boil. Do not boil. Cool. Chill until mixture is thoroughly cold and will mound when spooned. Fold in orange rind and sour cream.
- Beat egg whites until soft peaks form. Add sugar slowly and continue beating until mixture is stiff and glossy.
- Fold into pumpkin mixture. Spoon into crust. Chill several hours or overnight until set.
- Garnish with orange slices and additional sour cream if desired.

Grand finale to Thanksgiving Feast.

Southern Sweet Potato Pie

Serves 6 to 8

- 3 **medium sweet potatoes, boiled**
- 3 **eggs, separated**
- ½ **cup butter**
- 1 **cup sugar**
- 1 **cup evaporated milk**
- 1 **teaspoon vanilla**
- ½ **teaspoon nutmeg**
  9-inch unbaked pie crust

- Cool and peel sweet potatoes. Mash potatoes and add egg yolks, butter, sugar, milk and spices.
- Beat egg whites until peaks form. Fold egg whites into potato mixture.
- Pour into 9-inch unbaked pie crust. Bake in preheated 375° oven 45 minutes or until slightly brown.

A tradition in most Tulsa kitchens.

Chocolate Nut Torte To Diet For

Serves 8

Torte

- **4 squares semi-sweet chocolate**
- **1¾ cups pecans**
- **2 tablespoons plus ½ cup sugar**
- **¼ cup unsalted butter at room temperature**
- **3 large eggs at room temperature**
- **1 tablespoon Grand Marnier or rum**

- Generously grease 8-inch round cake pan, then cut a circle of wax paper to fit the bottom of the pan. Then grease the paper.
- Melt the chocolate in the top of a double boiler. Set aside.
- Place nuts and 2 tablespoons of the sugar in a food processor. Pulse on and off until the nuts are ground. Remove to a bowl.
- Process butter and ½ cup sugar until blended. Add chocolate and process until smooth. Add eggs and Grand Marnier or rum and mix. Add nuts pulsing once or twice.
- Pour into the cake pan and bake in preheated 375° oven 25 minutes. Cake will be soft when removed but will firm as it cools. Cool 20 minutes on wire rack. Invert the cake onto the rack, remove paper, and cool completely.

Unglazed torte can be kept tightly covered at room temperature for up to 2 days or frozen in tightly wrapped aluminum foil.

Glaze and Garnish

- **22 pecan halves**
- **6 squares semi-sweet chocolate**
- **6 tablespoons unsalted butter**

- Bake pecan halves on baking sheet at 350° for 10 to 15 minutes, stirring occasionally.
- Melt the chocolate and butter. Stir until smooth. Dip end of each pecan into the chocolate and put on wax paper to dry.
- Set the rest of the glaze aside to thicken slightly. It should be soft enough to pour, but thick enough to coat the cake.
- Holding the cake on the rack over a sink or waxed paper, pour the glaze onto the middle of the cake and tilt the cake so that the glaze runs evenly down all sides and covers them completely. A knife dipped in hot water will smooth sides if necessary. Put the pecans in a circle on the top of the torte around the edge. (May be held overnight uncovered at room temperature.)

At our holiday parties, this dessert was always the first to go. Out of desperation to have my very own slice, I made it for a dinner party. After the other guests left, a good friend and I stood in the kitchen and finished off every last morsel of the torte, consoling ourselves with the thought that the calories would not count since no one else saw us.

Commando Chocolate Cake

Cake

- 2½ **cups flour**
- ½ **cup unsweetened cocoa powder**
- 2 **teaspoons baking soda**
- ¾ **teaspoon salt**
- 2¼ **cups sugar**
- 1 **cup unsalted butter, at room temperature**
- 2 **large eggs**
- 2 **cups buttermilk**
- 1 **teaspoon vanilla**

- Butter three 9-inch round pans. Line with buttered wax paper.
- Mix flour, cocoa, baking soda and salt. Set aside.
- Beat sugar, butter and eggs until creamy.
- With mixer running, add buttermilk and vanilla. Then add flour mixture. Blend until incorporated. Do not overmix.
- Divide batter evenly between three pans.
- Bake in preheated 350° oven 30 minutes or until cake tests done.
- Cool in pans 10 minutes. Invert onto wire racks, remove wax paper and cool completely.

Buttercream Icing

- 6 **ounces unsweetened chocolate, processed in food processor until fine**
- ½ **cup butter at room temperature**
- 1 **tablespoon vanilla**
- 1½ **cups sugar**
- 1 **cup whipping cream**

- Place chocolate in food processor and blend until fine. Add butter and vanilla. Blend and set aside.
- Bring sugar and cream to a boil in heavy saucepan.
- Reduce heat and simmer 6 minutes, stirring frequently.
- Remove from heat. Add chocolate mixture, stir until melted. Cover and refrigerate until thoroughly chilled.
- Beat frosting with mixer to soften prior to spreading on cooled cake.

Cherries and pecans or almonds may be added to each layer after frosting and to top of cake.

Mocha Magic Cake

Two-layer 9-inch cake

1¾ **cups flour**
2 **cups sugar**
¾ **cup unsweetened cocoa**
2 **teaspoons baking soda**
1 **teaspoon baking powder**
1 **teaspoon salt**
2 **eggs, slightly beaten**
1 **cup strong coffee**
1 **cup buttermilk**
1 **teaspoon vanilla**
½ **cup vegetable oil**

- Sift dry ingredients. Add eggs, coffee, buttermilk, vanilla and oil. Beat at medium speed for 2 minutes.
- Pour into 2 greased and floured 9-inch pans. Bake in preheated 350° oven 30 to 40 minutes.

This recipe is from the 1920's. It is a dark rich cake that should not be overcooked. It is lovely with chocolate buttercream frosting. See Commando Chocolate Cake for frosting, page 229.

Coconut Lemon Pound Cake

Serves 12 to 16

1 **cup butter**
⅔ **cup solid shortening**
3 **cups sugar**
5 **eggs**
3 **cups flour**
1 **teaspoon baking powder**
1 **cup milk**
1 **3½-ounce can coconut**
2 **teaspoons lemon extract**
zest of 1 lemon
powdered sugar

- Cream butter and shortening with sugar until fluffy. Add eggs, one at a time.
- Add 2 cups flour and baking powder, beat well. Beat in remaining 1 cup flour and milk. Add coconut, lemon extract and zest.
- Bake in greased and floured 10-inch tube pan in preheated 350° oven 1½ hours. Cool.
- Remove from pan and dust with sifted powdered sugar before serving.

A delicious, old-fashioned pound cake.

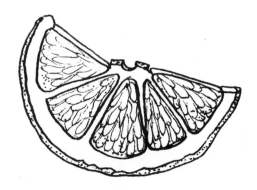

Classic Pound Cake

Serves 12 to 16

1 cup butter, softened
3 cups sugar
6 eggs
½ pint whipping cream
3 cups flour
1 teaspoon vanilla
1 teaspoon almond extract

- Cream butter and sugar. Add eggs, one at a time, beating after each addition.
- Add cream and flour alternately. Add flavorings. Pour in buttered Bundt pan.
- Place in COLD oven at 325° and bake 1¼ hours (may take a bit longer).
- Cool 10 or 15 minutes in pan and then cool on rack.

Serve with Luscious Lemon Sauce or Grand Marnier Sauce.

Luscious Lemon Sauce

1 cup sugar
½ cup butter
¼ cup water
1 egg, well-beaten
1 teaspoon grated lemon peel
3 tablespoons fresh lemon juice

- Combine all ingredients in medium saucepan.
- Heat to boiling over medium heat, stirring constantly. Serve warm.

Can be prepared in advance, refrigerated and warmed when ready to serve.

Grand Marnier Sauce

2 egg yolks
¼ cup sugar
2 tablespoons Grand Marnier
½ cup whipping cream

- Place yolks and sugar in top of double boiler. Start beating vigorously with a wire whisk, making certain to scrape the pan well. Set over boiling water and continue beating constantly and vigorously until the yolks are quite thick and pale yellow.
- Remove from heat and add Grand Marnier. Scrape the mixture into a cold bowl. Chill in freezer but do not allow to freeze.
- Whip cream until stiff. Fold into chilled sauce.

Serve over fresh berries, poached pears or, for a truly special dessert, fill meringue shells with vanilla ice cream and top with berries and sauce.

Chocolate Fondue

**3 squares semi-sweet
   chocolate
1 tablespoon milk
1 tablespoon rum or 1
   teaspoon rum extract
1 cup whipping cream
2 tablespoons powdered sugar**

- Melt chocolate with milk over low heat, and stir in rum. Cool.
- Whip cream and sweeten with powdered sugar.
- Fold cooled chocolate into whipped cream. Chill.

Great dip for strawberries, bananas, pineapple and angel food cake squares.

Peach Upside-Down Cake

Serves 8

**8 ripe peaches, peeled and
   sliced
3 tablespoons plus
   6 tablespoons butter
1 cup sugar, divided
1 egg
1 teaspoon vanilla
1 cup flour
1½ teaspoons baking powder
½ cup milk
   brown sugar**

- Butter a 9-inch round cake pan with 3 tablespoons butter and sprinkle with ½ cup sugar.
- Arrange peaches decoratively in concentric circles.
- Cream 6 tablespoons butter with ½ cup sugar. Add egg and vanilla.
- Sift flour and baking powder. Stir flour mixture into egg mixture ½ at a time alternating with the milk. Arrange batter over peaches, smoothly.
- Set on baking sheet in middle of preheated 350° oven and bake 1 hour until cake tests done.
- Cool 10 minutes. Invert onto ovenproof plate, releasing edges with knife. Sprinkle with brown sugar and broil until peaches are browned. Serve warm with whipped cream.

This is a wonderful way to use Porter peaches.

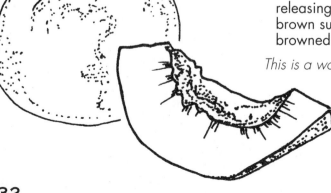

Serves 10 to 12

Apple Cake

1¾ **cups flour**
2 **teaspoons baking powder**
3 **large eggs**
1½ **cups sugar**
5 **Granny Smith apples**
½ **cup unsalted butter, melted**
⅔ **cup firmly packed dark brown sugar**
1 **teaspoon cinnamon**

- Sift together flour and baking powder.
- Beat eggs and sugar until the mixture is thick and pale. Beat in the flour gradually until the batter is smooth. Pour batter into well-greased 9 x 13-inch pan.
- Arrange the apples peeled, cored and cut into ¼-inch slices in one layer on top of batter. Overlap the slices. Drizzle butter over apples.
- Stir together the brown sugar and cinnamon and sprinkle over the apples.
- Bake in preheated 350º oven 45 minutes or until tester comes out clean.

This cake is best served warm. Great with morning coffee or as a winter dessert.

Piña Colada Cake

Serves 12 to 15

1 **18½-ounce package yellow cake mix**
1 **3¾-ounce package instant vanilla pudding**
1 **cup piña colada drink mix, divided**
½ **cup white run**
⅓ **cup vegetable oil**
4 **eggs**
1 **cup flaked coconut**
1 **8-ounce can crushed pineapple, undrained**
1 **cup sifted powdered sugar**

- Place cake mix, pudding, ½ cup piña colada mix, rum, oil and eggs in bowl. Beat for 2 to 5 minutes. Add coconut and pineapple.
- Bake in buttered and floured Bundt pan in preheated 350º oven 55 minutes.
- Cool in pan 15 minutes.
- Turn out and drizzle top with powdered sugar mixed with remaining piña colada mix.

Pineapple Special Occasion Cake

Serves 12

1 box yellow pudding recipe cake mix
1 15-ounce can crushed pineapple, drained
1 large container whipped topping
Buttercream Frosting

- Prepare cake mix as directed, baking two 9-inch layers.
- Cool layers and split horizontally. Put one layer, cut side up on cake plate.
- Spread whipped topping about ½-inch thick over layer. This is easier if topping is slightly frozen. Using about ⅓ of the pineapple, place little bits over the whipped topping.
- Repeat with remaining layers. Put cake into freezer briefly to firm up the layers.

Buttercream Frosting

2 tablespoons flour
½ cup milk
½ cup unsalted butter
1½ cups sifted powdered sugar
¼ teaspoon almond extract
fresh sliced strawberries or pineapple

- In a small saucepan, blend flour with milk. Cook over low heat, stirring constantly until very thick. Cool completely.
- Cream butter, sugar and extract until light and fluffy. Add cooled flour mixture and beat until smooth.
- This makes a small amount of frosting. Use it only on the sides of the cake and put strawberries or pineapple on the top. The frosting is not very sweet and has interesting texture.

This cake is the definitive birthday cake. Gets rave reviews every time!

Italian Cream Cake

Three-layer 9-inch cake

Cake

- 2 cups sugar
- 1 cup butter
- 5 eggs, separated
- 2 cups sifted flour
- 1 cup buttermilk
- 1 teaspoon baking soda
- 1 cup flaked coconut

- Cream sugar and butter.
- Add egg yolks one at a time, flour, buttermilk, soda and coconut. Beat well.
- Beat egg whites, and fold into batter.
- Pour into three greased and floured 9-inch round pans. Bake in preheated 350° oven 25 minutes.
- Cool and frost.

Frosting

- 1 8-ounce package cream cheese
- ½ cup butter
- 1 teaspoon vanilla
- 1 cup chopped pecans
- 1 box powdered sugar

- Beat ingredients and frost only the tops of each layer, leaving sides bare like a torte.

Makes a wonderful celebration cake.

Heavenly Pumpkin-Pecan Roll

Serves 8

3 **eggs**
1 **cup sugar**
⅔ **cup pumpkin**
1 **teaspoon lemon juice**
¾ **cup flour**
1 **teaspoon baking powder**
2 **teaspoons cinnamon**
1 **teaspoon ginger**
½ **teaspoon nutmeg**
½ **teaspoon salt**
1 **cup finely chopped pecans**

Filling

1 **cup powdered sugar**
2 **3-ounce packages cream cheese**
4 **tablespoons butter**
½ **teaspoon vanilla**

- Beat eggs on high speed 5 minutes. Gradually beat in sugar. Stir in pumpkin and lemon juice.

- Stir dry ingredients together. Fold in pumpkin mixture.

- Spread in greased 15 x 10-inch pan that has been completely lined with greased aluminum foil. Top with pecans.

- Bake in preheated 375° oven 15 minutes. Turn out on towel that has been sprinkled heavily with powdered sugar. Roll towel and cake together, cool and unroll.

- Combine all ingredients. Beat until smooth. Spread over cake and roll again without towel. Chill.

Freezes well. Sure to impress your holiday guests!

Pumpkin Spice Cake

1 bundt cake

- 3 **cups sugar**
- 1 **cup solid shortening**
- 3 **eggs**
- 1 **16-ounce can pumpkin**
- 3 **cups sifted flour**
- 1 **teaspoon baking soda**
- 2 **teaspoons baking powder**
- 1 **teaspoon ground cloves**
- 1 **teaspoon nutmeg**
- 1 **teaspoon cinnamon**
- 1 **teaspoon allspice**
- 1 **teaspoon vanilla**

- Cream together sugar and shortening; add eggs and pumpkin.
- Sift together dry ingredients; add to creamed mixture. Add vanilla.
- Bake in a greased and floured Bundt pan in a preheated 350° oven 1 hour to 1 hour and 15 minutes.
- Cool 30 minutes and remove from pan.

Glaze

- ½ **cup brown sugar**
- 2 **tablespoons melted butter, cooled**
- 1 **cup sifted powdered sugar**
- 1 **tablespoon milk for spreading consistency or more if needed**
  pecan halves

- Blend ingredients together and drizzle over cooled cake.
- Decorate with pecan halves.

Freezes well and improves with age. Wonderful in the Fall and at Halloween.

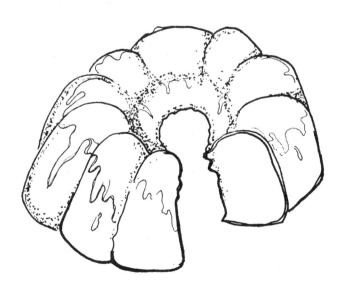

Royal Banana Crêpes

Serves 8

Dessert Crêpes

4 eggs
1 cup sifted flour
½ teaspoon salt
1 cup milk
2 tablespoons butter, melted
2 tablespoons brandy
¼ teaspoon lemon rind
1 tablespoon sugar

- Combine all ingredients. Beat until smooth with beater or blender.
- Refrigerate mixture at least one hour before making crêpes.
- Warm a 10-inch skillet over moderate heat, and brush lightly with oil. Pour about ¼ cup of the batter into the hot pan, tilting to coat evenly with a thin layer of batter; pour out any excess. Cook until lightly browned on the bottom, about 2 minutes. Flip the crêpe and cook until brown spots begin to appear on the second side, 15 to 30 seconds longer. Remove the crêpe from the pan and let cool. Repeat with the remaining batter and oil to make 16 crêpes.

Sauce and Filling

½ cup butter
½ cup brown sugar, packed
½ teaspoon cinnamon
½ teaspoon nutmeg
8 large bananas
½ cup light cream
whipped cream or ice cream
for topping
pecans

- Melt butter in heavy skillet. Stir in sugar and spices. Cut bananas in halves, lengthwise Add to sauce and coat.
- Stir in cream and cook until thickened. Remove from heat and roll bananas in crêpes, reserving sauce. Place seam side down in baking dish.
- To serve, warm crêpes in 350° oven about 5 to 7 minutes or briefly in microwave.
- Cover with warm sauce. Top with whipped cream or ice cream and sprinkle with pecans.

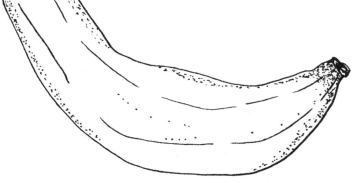

Cobbled Blueberries

Serves 8

⅓ **cup butter**
1 **cup flour**
¾ **cup brown sugar**
1½ **tablespoons baking powder**
¾ **cup milk**
2 **cups blueberries**
⅓ **cup brown sugar**
½ **teaspoon cinnamon**

- Melt butter in a 8 x 8-inch baking pan.
- Mix flour, brown sugar, baking powder and milk. Pour batter over butter in pan. Do not stir.
- Sprinkle blueberries over batter.
- Combine ⅓ cup brown sugar and cinnamon. Sprinkle over fruit.
- Bake in preheated 350° oven 30 minutes.
- Serve warm or cold with vanilla frozen yogurt or ice cream.

Apple Yoda

Serves 6 to 8

¼ **cup sugar**
1 **teaspoon cinnamon**
¼ **teaspoon nutmeg**
½ **cup water**
2 **teaspoons freshly squeezed lemon juice**
6 **large tart apples (McIntosh, Jonathan or Granny Smith)**
1 **8-ounce package cream cheese**
½ **cup butter**
¾ **cup sugar**
¾ **cup flour**
¼ **teaspoon salt**

- Mix ¼ cup sugar, cinnamon and nutmeg together and set aside. Mix water and lemon juice in another bowl and set aside.
- Lightly butter a soufflé dish.
- Peel, core and slice apples into prepared dish. Sprinkle with sugar and spice mixture. Pour water and lemon juice mixture over all.
- Blend cream cheese, butter and ¾ cup sugar, flour and salt in food processor.
- Spread over apples and bake in preheated 350° oven approximately 1 hour or until brown.

Great for apple pie and cheesecake lovers.

Fresh Berry Clafouti

Serves 6 to 8

1½ cups sugar, divided
2 to 3 cups fresh fruit (sliced berries or peaches in season)
1 cup flour
2 teaspoons vanilla
¾ cup unsalted butter, melted
2 eggs, beaten

- Pour ½ cup sugar over fresh fruit. Butter pie pan and fill with fresh fruit.
- Mix 1 cup sugar, flour, vanilla, butter and eggs. Pour over fruit. Bake in preheated 325° oven 40 minutes or until golden brown on top.

Rhubarb Raspberry Crisp

Serves 4

1½ pounds rhubarb, cut into 1-inch pieces, about 4 cups
⅔ cup sugar
   zest and juice of 1 orange
1 cup flour
½ cup dark brown sugar
½ teaspoon cinnamon
8 tablespoons cold, unsalted butter, cut into small pieces
½ cup rolled oats
¼ cup hazelnuts, skinned, toasted and chopped
1 pint fresh raspberries

- Combine rhubarb, sugar, orange zest and juice in a large bowl. Stir.
- In another bowl, combine flour, brown sugar, and cinnamon. Rub butter into flour mixture with your fingers until it is well incorporated and large crumbs form. Add oats and nuts.
- Turn rhubarb into a 1½-quart baking dish, scatter raspberries evenly over surface and cover with crumb topping.
- Bake in preheated 350° oven 45 minutes until toppings brown and crisp and juices are bubbling. Let cool slightly before serving.

Rhubarb is delicious paired with sweet fruits such as raspberries, strawberries or peaches to temper its tartness.

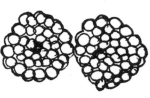
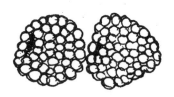

Brownie Pizza with Fruit

Serves 10

1 15-ounce package brownie mix
⅓ cup water, brought to a boil
¼ cup oil
2 eggs
1 8-ounce package cream cheese, softened
¼ cup sugar
1 teaspoon vanilla
strawberry slices
banana slices
2 1-ounce squares semi-sweet chocolate, melted
fresh mint leaves, optional

- Combine brownie mix, water, oil and 1 egg in large bowl and stir until well blended. Pour into greased and floured 12-inch pizza pan. Bake in preheated 350° oven 25 minutes.
- Beat cream cheese, sugar, 1 egg and vanilla in small mixing bowl at medium speed until well blended. Pour over crust. Bake 15 minutes. Cool.
- Top with fruit and drizzle with chocolate.

Garnish with mint leaves.

Lemon Cloud

Serves 8

4 eggs, separated
1 teaspoon cream of tartar
1½ cups plus 2 teaspoons sugar, separated
2 teaspoons sugar
juice and zest of 1½ lemons
1¼ cups whipping cream

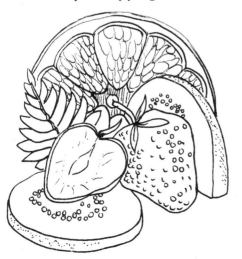

- Beat egg whites until foamy, add cream of tartar, beat until stiff. Gradually add 1 cup sugar. Spread into a buttered 9 x 9-inch glass pan. Bake in preheated 250° oven 1 hour. Cool.
- Beat 4 egg yolks lightly. Add ½ cup sugar, lemon juice and zest. Stir and cook until thick. Set aside to cool.
- Beat cream and add 2 teaspoons sugar.
- When lemon mixture is cool, fold in ⅓ of the whipped cream. Spread half of remaining cream over meringue and cover with lemon mixture. Top with remaining cream. Refrigerate at least 12 hours before serving. Best made a day ahead.

A refreshing summer dessert. This can be easily doubled and made in a 9 x 13-inch pan.

Lemon Soufflé Flips

Serves 8

- 1 **cup sugar**
- ¼ **cup flour**
- ⅛ **teaspoon salt**
- 2 **tablespoons butter, melted**
- 5 **tablespoons lemon juice**
- 1 **tablespoon grated lemon rind**
- 3 **eggs, separated**
- 1½ **cups milk**
- 1 **cup whipping cream, whipped and sweetened**

- Blend sugar, flour and salt; add melted butter, lemon juice and rind. Mix well. Whisk in well beaten egg yolks and milk.
- Beat egg whites until they begin to form peaks. Fold into batter and pour into buttered custard cups.
- Place custard cups in pan of water and bake in a preheated 350° oven 45 minutes.
- Flip the soufflés onto a plate. The lemon pudding will be on the top and the cake on the bottom.
- Serve with a dollop of whipped cream.

Also great with fresh raspberries on top. This is a light and special dessert.

Bourbon Street Bread Pudding

Serves 6

- ½ **pound very fresh French baguette bread, torn in pieces**
- 5 **cups milk**
- 2 **cups sugar**
- 2 **teaspoons vanilla**
- 3 **eggs, beaten**
- ¾ **cup raisins**

Bourbon Sauce

- ½ **cup unsalted butter**
- 1 **cup sugar**
- ⅛ **cup bourbon**
- 1 **egg, beaten**

- Butter shallow baking dish and fill with bread.
- Whisk together milk, sugar, vanilla, eggs and raisins and pour over bread. Let sit until bread is soft.
- Bake in preheated 350° oven 1 hour until set.

- Melt butter. Add sugar, heating slowly until dissolved. Add bourbon and egg. Heat, stirring constantly until thickened.
- Serve warm sauce over pudding.

Bread Pudding with St. Cecilia Sauce

Serves 6

- **1 cup raisins**
- **1 24-inch loaf, stale French bread, crust removed or several day-old croissants, broken into several pieces**
- **4 large eggs**
- **1 cup sugar**
- **4 tablespoons unsalted butter, melted**
- **1 quart milk**
- **1 ounce dark rum**

- Generously butter a 6-cup soufflé dish and cover bottom with raisins. Layer bread pieces over the raisins.
- Combine eggs, sugar and butter in large bowl. Add milk and rum. Mix well. Pour mixture over bread and raisins. Allow to sit until liquid has been absorbed, about 30 minutes.
- Preheat oven to 350°. Place dish of pudding mixture in another oven-proof dish or pan of boiling water, so the casserole is surrounded with hot water about halfway up its sides. Bake for 1 hour and 15 minutes or until mixture is firmly set and browned on top.

St. Cecilia Sauce

- **3 large egg yolks**
- **⅔ cup powdered sugar**
- **1 cup whipping cream**
- **½ teaspoon vanilla**

- Whisk egg yolks with powdered sugar. Set aside. Whip cream with vanilla until peaks form. Fold the egg-sugar mixture into the whipped cream. Serve the bread pudding, warm or cooled, in small dishes with a dollop of cream sauce on top.

A favorite dessert from a former Tulsa restaurant, La Cuisine.

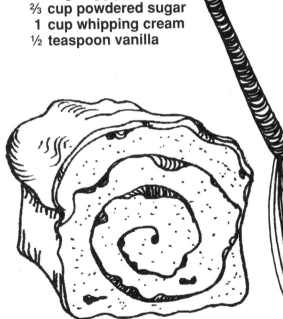

Christmas Plum Pudding

Serves 12

- ½ **pound currants**
- ½ **pound raisins**
- ½ **pound golden raisins**
- 8 **ounces plus 3 tablespoons Bushmill whiskey**
- ½ **pound brown sugar**
- ½ **pound butter**
- 4 **eggs**
- ½ **pound bread crumbs**
- 1 **tablespoon flour**
- ¼ **teaspoon salt**
- ½ **teaspoon ginger**
- ½ **teaspoon nutmeg**
- ½ **teaspoon cinnamon**
- ½ **teaspoon allspice**
- **juice of ½ lemon**
- **juice of ½ orange**
- 2 **ounces mixed peel**
- ½ **ounce ground almonds**
- 1 **ounce whole almonds**
- 4 **ounces milk**
- 1 **teaspoon baking powder**

- Combine dried fruits in a bowl. Add 8 ounces whiskey and mix well. Allow to stand 12 hours, stirring occasionally.
- Cream sugar and butter until soft. Add eggs and mix well.
- Combine bread crumbs, flour, salt and spices. Add soaked fruits, juices, grated peels and nuts. Stir well and add to batter mixture.
- Heat milk and mix with baking powder. Pour into mixture, mixing well.
- Place in well greased 1-quart mold. Cover mold with two layers of aluminum foil tightly secured with string. Place mold on trivet in deep saucepan. Add boiling water ⅔ up the side of mold and bring to a boil. Reduce heat and cover saucepan. Boil 7 hours, adding more water as necessary. Uncover, cool, and cover again.
- Store in refrigerator until ready to serve. Before serving, steam for two hours to heat through. Unmold. Warm 3 tablespoons whiskey, ignite and pour over pudding. Serve immediately with Hard Sauce. Garnish with a sprig of holly.

Hard Sauce

- ½ **cup butter**
- 1 **cup powdered sugar**
- 1 **teaspoon vanilla or teaspoon bourbon**

- Cream butter and sugar. Add vanilla or bourbon. Chill.

Sr. Mary's famous Christmas Tradition.

Date Nut Pudding

Serves 6

1 cup white sugar
2 cups brown sugar, divided
2 cups boiling water
3 tablespoons butter
1 cup milk
2 cups flour
2 teaspoons baking powder
1 teaspoon vanilla
1 cup chopped pecans
1 cup chopped dates

- Boil white sugar, 1 cup brown sugar and water for 10 minutes. Pour into glass baking dish or loaf pan. Set aside.
- Combine 1 cup brown sugar, butter, milk, flour, baking powder, vanilla, pecans and dates. Stir until smooth.
- Drop the batter by spoonfuls on syrup.
- Bake in 300° oven 50 minutes.

Bolivian Rice Pudding

Serves 8

6 cups milk
1 cinnamon stick
1 piece orange peel
1 cup rice, not instant
1 cup sugar
1 teaspoon vanilla
1 egg yolk
¼ cup raisins
¼ cup slivered almonds

- Bring milk to boil and add cinnamon, orange peel and rice. Simmer 20 to 25 minutes stirring constantly.
- Add sugar and vanilla, gradually. Continue to stir 5 to 10 minutes on low heat. Stir in egg yolk. Pudding will thicken as it cools.
- Remove orange peel and cinnamon stick. Add raisins and almonds. Cool. Pour into glass bowl. Refrigerate. Glass preserves the flavor.

To serve hot, add teaspoon of butter, stir to melt.

Traditional South American Dessert.

Caramel Flan

Serves 8 to 10

1½ **cups sugar, divided**
1 **can evaporated milk**
1 **can sweetened condensed milk**
2½ **cups whole milk**
1 **teaspoon vanilla**
9 **eggs**
dash salt

- In small saucepan, melt 1 cup sugar, stirring constantly. Do not burn.
- Pour caramel in bowl and turn to cover bottom and sides. May need to warm again. Use hot pads because pan becomes hot from sauce.
- Heat milk, vanilla and ½ cup sugar until steam rises. Take off stove and cool.
- Beat eggs with salt until well mixed. Pour cooled milk into eggs and mix.
- Pour custard on top of caramel. Cover with aluminum foil.
- Bake in a pan of water for 1½ hours in preheated 325° oven.
- Cool completely and turn out on a plate.

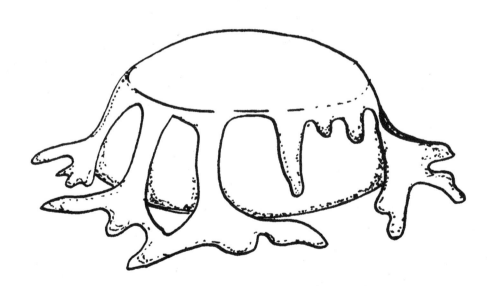

Caribbean Rum Cheesecake

Serves 12

Crust
- **15 graham crackers, crumbled**
- **½ cup sugar**
- **1 teaspoon cinnamon**
- **½ cup butter, melted**

• Mix dry ingredients and add butter. Press on bottom and sides of 9-inch springform pan. Reserve a few crumbs for topping.

Filling
- **3 8-ounce packages cream cheese**
- **1 3-ounce package cream cheese**
- **¾ cup sugar**
- **4 eggs**
- **1 tablespoon rum**

• Blend cheese, sugar, eggs and rum in food processor until smooth. Pour into crust and bake in preheated 375° oven 25 minutes.

Topping
- **1 cup sour cream**
- **¾ cup sugar**
- **1 tablespoon rum**

• Combine ingredients and spread over top. Sprinkle with reserved crumbs. Bake an additional 5 minutes.

Use Puerto Rican rum for the best results. Delicious!!

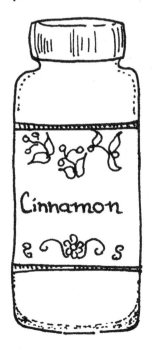

Simply Cheesecake

Serves 12

- **4 whole graham crackers, broken into pieces**
- **2 tablespoons sugar**
- **2 tablespoons unsalted butter, melted**
- **3 large eggs**
- **1½ cups sugar**
- **1 tablespoon pure vanilla extract**
- **5 8-ounce packages cream cheese, cut into 1-inch cubes**

- Process graham crackers in a food processor until finely chopped. Add sugar and butter and process to combine.
- Place a baking sheet on the center rack of the oven and preheat oven to 350°.
- Press crust onto bottom of a lightly oiled 9-inch springform pan and set aside.
- Process eggs and sugar in a food processor until smooth. Add the vanilla and process. Remove liquid and set aside.
- Process half the cream cheese until smooth. Remove to a large mixing bowl. Repeat with the remaining cream cheese and egg/sugar mixture. Add to mixing bowl and stir to combine the two batches.
- Pour filling into springform pan. Place on baking sheet and bake until the edge has risen slightly and cheesecake is firm to the touch, but the center is still soft, 30 to 45 minutes.
- Cool on a wire rack. Cover and refrigerate overnight.

Delicious served with Luscious Lemon Sauce or Grand Marnier Sauce, page 231.

Crème de Cacao Cheesecake

10-inch cheesecake

Crust

- 2 **cups finely ground chocolate wafer cookie crumbs**
- ¼ **cup granulated sugar**
- 6 **tablespoons butter, melted**
- 1 **cup semi-sweet chocolate chips**

- Combine crumbs and sugar in large bowl. Add butter and stir until mixture resembles coarse meal.
- Press into bottom and up sides of 10-inch springform pan. Bake in preheated 325° oven 7 to 10 minutes.
- Remove from oven and sprinkle chocolate chips over crust.

Filling

- 4 **8-ounce packages cream cheese, room temperature**
- 4 **eggs**
- 1 **cup sugar**
- ½ **cup crème de cacao**
- 5 **ounces white chocolate, melted**

- Beat cream cheese until soft. Add eggs and sugar and beat until smooth. Add liqueur and white chocolate and beat again.
- Pour over crust.
- Bake until edges of filling are puffed and dry looking and center is just set or about 50 minutes. Cool.

Ganache

- 1 **cup whipping cream**
- 5 **ounces German sweet chocolate**
  chocolate curls

- Bring cream to a boil. Add chocolate and stir until melted. Pour into bowl and refrigerate for several hours.
- Beat until fluffy and pipe around edges of dessert. Garnish with chocolate curls.

A delight to the eye and so very good.

Eclair Cake Extraordinaire

Serves 10

        1 **cup water**
       ½ **cup soft butter**
       ¼ **teaspoon salt**
        1 **cup flour**
        4 **eggs, room temperature**
        2 **packages instant vanilla**
          pudding
      2½ **cups cold milk**
        1 **8-ounce package cream**
          cheese, softened
        1 **12-ounce container of**
          whipped topping
       ½ **cup chocolate chips**
        2 **tablespoons soft butter**
        1 **cup powdered sugar**
3 to 4 **tablespoons milk**

- Bring water and butter to boil. When all butter is melted, add salt and flour and mix by hand until mixture forms a ball that leaves side of pan.
- Add eggs one at a time and beat thoroughly after each egg.
- Spread glue-like mixture into an ungreased 15 x 10-inch jelly roll pan and bake in preheated 400° oven 30 minutes. Pierce bubbles with a fork and cool completely.
- Mix pudding with milk, add cream cheese and beat thoroughly. Spread over crust and then spread whipped topping over pudding mixture.
- Melt chocolate chips and butter over low heat. Mix in powdered sugar and milk alternately and stir until a thin glaze forms. Pour over whipped topping. Refrigerate for at least one hour before serving.

Pavé Au Chocolat

Serves 6 to 8

       ½ **cup butter**
       ¾ **cup powdered sugar**
        4 **egg yolks**
        4 **squares unsweetened**
          chocolate, melted
        4 **tablespoons dark rum**
       ¾ **cup water**
        2 **2½-ounce packages lady**
          fingers

- Cream butter and sugar. Beat in egg yolks one at a time. Add melted chocolate.
- Combine rum and water in a flat dish. Dip lady fingers one at a time in the rum mix.
- Make a row of lady fingers on serving dish. Spread with chocolate mixture. Add two more layers, alternating lady fingers with chocolate, covering sides and top with chocolate.
- Allow to mellow and do not refrigerate.
- Garnish with candied violets or chopped nuts.

Chocolate Sin

Serves 8 to 10

10 ounces semi-sweet chocolate
1 cup plus 4 tablespoons unsalted butter at room temperature
1½ cups sugar
8 large eggs

- Liberally butter a 9-inch round cake pan. Line the bottom with buttered wax paper.
- Melt the chocolate in the top of a double boiler. Add butter and stir until butter has melted and the mixture is smooth. Remove from heat. Whisk the sugar gradually into the chocolate until mixture is thick.
- In a separate bowl, beat the eggs until they are foamy. Stir them into the chocolate batter until they are well incorporated.
- Pour batter into prepared pan and place pan in a 14 x 11-inch baking pan. Add enough boiling water to come halfway up the side of baking pan. Bake in the center of preheated 350° oven 1½ hours.
- Remove the cake and let sit for 10 minutes. Invert onto a plate. Serve at room temperature with Coffee Whipped Cream

Coffee Whipped Cream

1 cup whipping cream
2 tablespoons powdered sugar
1 tablespoon strong coffee

- Beat cream until it just begins to hold shape. Sift sugar over the top and beat until cream holds soft peaks. Stir in coffee. Spoon onto each serving.

Chocolate Toffee Trifle

Serves 8 to 10

- 1 **box Devils Food cake mix**
- 1 **small package instant chocolate pudding**
- 1½ **cups milk**
- ½ **cup Kahlúa**
- 6 **1⅛-ounce Heath bars, frozen**
- 1 **16-ounce container whipped topping**

- Bake cake according to package directions. Cool and cut into 1-inch cubes.
- Combine pudding, milk, Kahlúa and mix well.
- Crush candy bars.
- In large glass trifle bowl, layer in order, half cake, half pudding, half whipped cream and half candy bars. Repeat layers. Cover with plastic wrap and refrigerate overnight.

A pretty buffet dessert and always a hit!

German Chocolate Mousse

Serves 8 to 10

- 1 **4-ounce bar German sweet chocolate**
- ½ **cup butter**
- 3 **eggs, separated**
- 1 **cup powdered sugar**
- 1 **teaspoon vanilla**
- 1 **pint whipping cream, whipped**
- 1 **10-ounce box vanilla wafers**

- Melt chocolate and butter together.
- Beat egg yolks and combine with chocolate. Mix in ⅔ cup sugar and vanilla. Chill, then fold in whipped cream.
- Beat egg whites until they form peaks. Add remaining ⅓ cup sugar to egg whites and fold into chocolate cream.
- Crush vanilla wafers and line 9 x 9-inch deep dish with part of crumbs. Spread 2 cups chocolate mousse over crumbs. Repeat until all the mousse is used. Top mousse with crumbs.
- Refrigerate 24 hours before serving.

May also be prepared in a trifle bowl. The layering looks pretty.

Marvelous Mocha Mousse

Serves 12

- 1 **cup chopped pecans**
- 1 **square unsweetened chocolate**
- 2 **eggs, separated**
- 2 **cups powdered sugar, divided**
- ½ **cup butter**
- 2 **tablespoons instant coffee**
- ½ **teaspoon salt**
- 3 **teaspoons milk**
- 1 **teaspoon vanilla**
  vanilla wafer crumbs

- Toast pecans. Melt chocolate over low heat and cool.
- Beat egg whites until foamy. Add ¼ cup sugar (2 tablespoons at a time) beating well after each addition.
- Add ¼ cup sugar to egg yolks and blend well.
- Cream butter. Sift coffee, salt and remaining 1½ cups sugar together and add to butter. Mix well and blend in melted chocolate, milk and vanilla.
- Add egg yolks and toasted pecans. Fold in egg whites.
- Sprinkle vanilla wafer crumbs over bottom of lightly buttered soufflé dish. Pour mousse over crumbs. Sprinkle with additional crumbs and chill in refrigerator.

Extremely easy and extremely good.

Awesome Brownies

2 dozen

- 4 **squares unsweetened chocolate**
- 1 **cup butter**
- 2 **cups sugar**
- 4 **eggs**
- 2 **teaspoons vanilla**
- 1 **cup flour**
  pinch of salt
- 1 **12-ounce package semi-sweet chocolate chips**
- 2 **cups miniature marshmallows**
- 1½ **cups chopped pecans**
  powdered sugar

- Melt chocolate and butter together. Add sugar. Cool.
- Add eggs one at a time, beating well. Add vanilla, flour and salt; mix until well blended. Stir in chocolate chips and marshmallows.
- Pour into a greased 9 x 13-inch baking pan. Sprinkle with chopped pecans. Bake in preheated 350° oven 30 to 35 minutes. Do not overbake. The top will look bubbly.
- Dust well with powdered sugar. Best if made a day in advance and allowed to stand overnight. These are too gooey to cut right away. Can be frozen.

Named by teenaged sons—enough said!

World Famous Brownies

2 dozen

- **1 cup butter**
- **2 squares unsweetened chocolate**
- **2 squares semi-sweet chocolate**
- **4 eggs, beaten**
- **2 cups sugar**
- **1 cup flour**
- **1 teaspoon baking powder**
- **2 teaspoons vanilla**
- **2 cups chopped pecans**

- Melt butter and chocolate. Add eggs, sugar, flour, baking powder, vanilla and pecans. Stir until well blended. Pour into greased 9 x 13-inch pan and bake in preheated 350° oven 30 to 45 minutes. They should not be overcooked. Cool and cut into squares.

A neighbor brought these over the day we moved into our house, and we have been best friends ever since.

Peppermint Brownies

2 dozen

- **1 box fudge brownie mix with can of chocolate**
- **1½ cups powdered sugar**
- **1½ tablespoons milk**
- **5 tablespoons butter, softened, divided**
- **1 teaspoon peppermint extract dash of salt**
- **2⅔ tablespoons cocoa**

- Bake brownie mix as directed and let cool.
- Mix sugar, milk, 3 tablespoons butter, extract and salt. Spread over cooled brownies.
- Mix cocoa with remaining butter and swirl through icing.

Blonde Brownies

2 dozen

- **1 box Golden Butter Cake mix**
- **½ cup butter, melted**
- **3 eggs**
- **1 cup chopped pecans**
- **1 8-ounce package cream cheese**
- **1 box powdered sugar**
- **1 teaspoon vanilla**

- Combine cake mix, butter, 1 egg and pecans. Press into a greased 9 x 13-inch pan.
- Mix cream cheese, sugar, 2 eggs and vanilla. Pour over crust.
- Bake in 350° oven 45 minutes.

Kahlúa Party Bars

35 to 40 bars

- 1½ **cups graham cracker crumbs**
- 1 **cup chopped toasted almonds**
- ½ **cup plus 1½ tablespoons butter**
- ¼ **cup sugar**
- ⅓ **cup cocoa**
- 1 **egg, slightly beaten**
- 1½ **teaspoons vanilla**
- 6 **tablespoons Kahlúa, divided**
- 6 **tablespoons unsalted butter**
- 1 **tablespoon milk or cream**
- 1¾ **cups powdered sugar**
- 4 **ounces semi-sweet chocolate**

- In a 7 x 11-inch baking pan, combine graham cracker crumbs and almonds, and set aside.

- In a small saucepan, combine ½ cup butter, sugar, cocoa, egg and vanilla and mix well. Cook slowly, stirring about 4 minutes until thickened. Pour over crumb mixture and mix thoroughly. Press into bottom of pan. Drizzle with 3 tablespoons Kahlúa and place in freezer.

- Cream the unsalted butter until fluffy. Add milk and 3 tablespoons Kahlúa and blend. Gradually add powdered sugar, mixing until smooth and creamy. Spread on the chilled graham cracker layer and return to freezer until firm.

- Melt 1½ tablespoons butter and the semi-sweet chocolate in a small saucepan over very low heat. Stir to blend. Using a knife or spatula, spread in a thin layer over the chilled powdered sugar layer. The chocolate hardens quickly so work fast. Slice into 35 to 40 small bars to serve.

The Kahlúa bars may be made ahead, tightly wrapped and frozen.

Rocky Road Fudge Bars

24 bars

1 **cup flour, lightly spooned into cup**
½ **cup butter**
1 **square unsweetened chocolate**
1 **teaspoon baking powder**
1 **cup sugar**
2 **eggs**
1 **teaspoon vanilla**
½ **to 1 cup chopped pecans**

- Grease and flour 9 x 13-inch pan.
- Melt butter and chocolate together. Combine with remaining ingredients and mix well.
- Spread in pan and set aside.

Filling

1 **8-ounce package cream cheese, softened**
½ **cup sugar**
2 **tablespoons flour**
4 **tablespoons butter, softened**
1 **egg**
½ **teaspoon vanilla**
¼ **cup chopped pecans**
2 **cups mini marshmallows**
1 **cup semi-sweet chocolate chips**

- Reserve 2 ounces cream cheese for frosting.
- Blend 6 ounces cream cheese, sugar, flour, butter, egg and vanilla until smooth.
- Stir in pecans. Spread over bar mixture in pan.
- Bake in preheated 350° oven 25 minutes or until inserted toothpick comes out clean. Sprinkle with marshmallow and chocolate chips.
- Return to oven and bake 2 minutes. Remove from oven.

Frosting

4 **tablespoons butter**
1 **square unsweetened chocolate**
2 **ounces reserved cream cheese**
¼ **cup milk**
1 **pound powdered sugar**
1 **teaspoon vanilla**

- In a large pan over low heat, melt butter, chocolate and remaining cream cheese with milk.
- Stir, and sift in powdered sugar and add vanilla.
- Beat with mixer on low until smooth.
- Spread frosting on top of bars. Store in refrigerator. Freezes well.

Jamaican Butterscotch Bars

24 bars

1 **cup butter**
1 **box light brown sugar**
2 **cups flour**
1 **teaspoon baking powder**
2 **eggs**
½ **teaspoon almond extract**
1 **teaspoon vanilla**
7 **ounces flaked coconut**
½ **cup chopped pecans**

- Melt butter in large saucepan.
- Add remaining ingredients and stir well.
- Pour into greased 9 x 13-inch baking pan.
- Bake in preheated 350° oven 30 minutes or until cake begins to pull away from edges of pan.
- Cool and cut into squares or bars.

These are best baked a day ahead or early enough to cool thoroughly. This recipe was given to me by a friend in her eighties, and our family has enjoyed the results for over twenty-five years.

Fresh Lemon Delights

24 bars

Crust

1 **cup butter**
½ **cup powdered sugar**
2 **cups flour**

- Mix crust ingredients together with a pastry blender and press into a 9 x 13-inch dish. Bake in preheated 350° oven 15 minutes.

Filling

4 **eggs, beaten**
1 **teaspoon baking powder**
1 **tablespoon freshly squeezed lemon juice**
2 **cups sugar**
4 **tablespoons flour**
½ **teaspoon salt**
  grated zest of 1 lemon

- Beat eggs, add baking powder, juice, sugar, flour, salt and zest. Pour over HOT crust and bake in 350° oven 25 minutes.

Frosting

1½ **cups powdered sugar**
3 **tablespoons melted butter**
4 **tablespoons freshly squeezed lemon juice**

- Whisk sugar, butter and juice over low heat until sugar dissolves. Pour over bars while hot. Tilt pan to spread evenly.
- Cool and refrigerate.

Deluxe and delicious.

Apricot Bars

24 bars

Crust

3 cups flour
2 teaspoons baking powder
2 cups firmly packed brown sugar
1 cup dry quick oats
1½ cups butter
½ cup chopped pecans

- Combine dry ingredients and cut in butter. Press half into 9 x 13-inch baking dish. Add pecans to other half of dough. Set aside.

Filling

1½ cups apricot jam
1 tablespoon warm water

- Heat jam and water together until jam thins and can be spread over crust easily. Cover with remaining dough.
- Bake in preheated 350° oven 30 minutes or until brown. Cool and cut into bars.

Chocolate Chocolate Chip Cookies

3 dozen

1 cup butter, softened
1½ cups sugar
2 eggs
2 teaspoons vanilla
2 cups flour
⅔ cup cocoa
¾ teaspoon baking soda
¼ teaspoon salt
2 cups semi-sweet chocolate chips
½ cup walnuts, coarsely chopped

- In a large bowl, beat butter, sugar, eggs and vanilla until light and fluffy.
- In a separate bowl, mix flour, cocoa, baking soda and salt. Add to butter mixture. Stir in chips and nuts.
- Drop rounded teaspoonfuls onto ungreased cookie sheets. Bake in preheated 350° oven 8 to 10 minutes. Take out while still a little moist looking for soft cookies.

A favorite cookie at Cascia Open House and Teacher's Luncheon.

Cascia Chip Cookies

3 to 4 dozen

1½ **cups flour**
 1 **teaspoon soda**
 ½ **teaspoon salt**
 ½ **cup butter**
 ½ **cup solid shortening**
 1 **cup brown sugar**
 1 **cup white sugar**
 2 **eggs**
 3 **cups quick cooking oats**
 1 **cup chopped pecans**
 1 **cup chocolate chips**
 1 **tablespoon vanilla**

- Sift flour, soda and salt.
- Cream together butter, shortening and sugars. Add eggs and sifted ingredients.
- Stir in oats, pecans, chips and vanilla.
- Drop by rounded tablespoon onto greased cookie sheet.
- Bake in preheated 375° oven 8 to 10 minutes. Bake underdone because they continue baking after being removed from oven.

Lip Smackin' and Teeth Chompin' Cookies

3 to 4 dozen

 ¾ **cup brown sugar**
 ¾ **cup white sugar**
1½ **cups solid shortening**
 3 **eggs**
2¼ **cups flour**
 ½ **teaspoon baking soda**
 ½ **teaspoon salt**
 3 **cups oats**
 ½ **cup chopped pecans**
 ½ **cup peanut butter**
1½ **teaspoons vanilla**
 1 **cup chocolate chips**

- Cream together sugars and shortening. Add eggs and beat.
- Sift together flour, soda and salt. Add to creamed mixture.
- Stir in oats, pecans, peanut butter, vanilla and chocolate chips.
- Drop rounded teaspoons of dough about 2 inches apart on a lightly greased cookie sheet.
- Bake in preheated 350° oven 10 to 15 minutes.

Best-Ever Cookies

5 dozen

  1 **cup butter**
  1 **cup white sugar**
  1 **cup brown sugar**
  1 **cup vegetable oil**
  2 **eggs**
  1 **teaspoon vanilla**
3½ **cups flour**
  1 **teaspoon salt**
  1 **teaspoon baking soda**
  1 **teaspoon cream of tartar**
  1 **cup crisped rice cereal**
  1 **cup oats**
  1 **cup coconut**
  ½ **cup pecans**

- In a large bowl cream butter and sugars. Add oil, eggs and vanilla.
- Combine flour, salt, soda and cream of tartar and add to first mixture.
- Add cereal, oats, coconut and pecans.
- Make one-inch balls and flatten with fork.
- Bake in preheated 350° oven 12 minutes.

Traditional Butter Cookies

2 to 3 dozen

  1 **cup butter, room temperature**
1½ **cups powdered sugar**
  1 **egg**
  1 **teaspoon vanilla**
2½ **cups flour**
  ¼ **teaspoon salt**
  1 **teaspoon cream of tartar**
  1 **teaspoon baking soda**

Icing
  ½ **cup powdered sugar**
  2 **tablespoons milk**
    food coloring

- Cream butter and sugar. Add egg, vanilla and dry ingredients. Chill and roll to ¼-inch thickness. Cut in desired shapes.
- Bake on lightly greased cookie sheets in preheated 350° oven for 10 to 12 minutes. Cool and ice.

- Mix sugar and milk to spreading consistency and add food coloring such as green for shamrocks or Christmas trees. Spread on cooled cookies.

Date Pinwheels

Cookie Dough

2 cups flour
½ teaspoon baking soda
½ teaspoon salt
½ cup butter
½ cup brown sugar
½ cup white sugar
1 egg, well beaten

- Sift together flour, baking soda and salt.
- Cream butter and sugars. Add egg. Beat in dry ingredients.
- Chill dough.

Filling

½ pound pitted dates, finely chopped
¼ cup sugar
⅓ cup water
¼ cup pecans, finely chopped
½ teaspoon salt

- Cook dates, sugar and water for about five minutes.
- Remove from heat, add pecans and salt. Cool.
- Roll dough into rectangle ¼-inch thick. Spread date mixture over dough. Roll like jelly roll and wrap in wax paper. Refrigerate overnight or longer.
- Slice and bake on greased cookie sheet in preheated 350° oven 10 minutes.

A great treat for a Christmas Openhouse. Fun to bake and send to your college student.

Nana's Sugar Cookies

1 cup butter
3 cups flour
½ teaspoon baking soda
½ teaspoon baking powder
¾ teaspoon salt
2 eggs
1 cup sugar
1 teaspoon vanilla
sugar

- Blend butter with dry ingredients. Beat eggs, adding sugar and vanilla. Combine with butter mixture. Refrigerate until firm.
- Roll thin, cut into shapes and dust with sugar.
- Bake on lightly greased cookie sheets in preheated 375° oven 8 minutes, until golden. Frost with colored icings and decorative sprinkles.

A classic! Easy to handle dough. A true summertime treat with lemonade...to say nothing of years of Christmas tradition.

Scottish Shortbread

Serves 6 to 8

1 cup butter
½ cup powdered sugar
1 teaspoon vanilla
2 cups sifted flour

- Cream butter, sugar, and vanilla. Mix in flour.
- Turn out on cookie sheet. Pat into a circle ¾-inch thick and 7 inches in diameter. Pinch edges to decorate. Prick with a fork. Chill 30 minutes.
- Bake in preheated 375° oven 5 minutes. Reduce heat to 300° and bake 45 minutes longer.
- Shortbread should be a pale golden, not brown. While warm, cut into wedges.

This is wonderful served with strawberries and whipped cream.

Ginger Snaps

8 dozen

1 cup butter
2 cups sugar
2 eggs
½ cup molasses
½ teaspoon salt
1 teaspoon cinnamon
2 teaspoons ginger
½ teaspoon cloves
4 teaspoons baking soda
3½ cups flour

- Cream together butter and sugar. Add eggs. Stir in dry ingredients.
- Chill dough several hours. Flour hands and shape dough into little balls. Bake on ungreased baking sheet in preheated 350° oven 8 to 10 minutes or until brown.

Husbands love these.

Oreo Ice Cream Dessert

Serves 12

30 **Oreos, crushed**
4 **tablespoons butter, melted**
½ **gallon vanilla ice cream**
⅔ **cup sugar**
2 **ounces semi-sweet chocolate, 2 squares**
4 **tablespoons butter**
1 **small can evaporated milk, ⅔ cup**
1 **teaspoon vanilla**
whipped cream or whipped topping

• Combine cookies and melted butter. Place in bottom of 9 x 13-inch pan. Soften ice cream, spread on top and freeze.

• Melt sugar, chocolate and butter together. Gradually add evaporated milk and stir until thickened. Add vanilla and cool. When cool, spread over ice cream. Freeze. When chocolate layer is frozen, add a layer of whipped cream or whipped topping.

A big hit with teenagers.

Caramel Crunch Ice Cream Squares

24 squares

1 **cup flour**
½ **cup rolled old fashioned oats**
⅓ **cup brown sugar**
½ **cup butter**
½ **cup chopped pecans**
1 **jar caramel ice cream topping**
1 **quart caramel fudge ice cream, softened**

• Blend flour, oats, sugar and butter until crumbly. Add pecans and mix. Crumble mixture onto a cookie sheet and bake in 400° oven 12 to 15 minutes. Let it brown lightly. With a fork, further crumble the mixture. Reserve ⅓ cup for sprinkling on top. Pat remaining mixture into a 9 x 13-inch pan.

• Pour 1 jar of caramel ice cream topping over crumb base. Spoon 1 quart softened caramel fudge ice cream over topping. Sprinkle remaining crumbs on top. Freeze until firm. Cut into squares and serve.

Will remind you of a "Nutty Buddy".

Chocolate Orange Sorbet

Serves 6

- ¾ **cup sugar**
- ⅔ **cup Dutch baking cocoa (Droste)**
- 1½ **cups water**
- 1 **ounce bittersweet or semi-sweet chocolate**
- ¼ **cup freshly squeezed orange juice**
- 1 **tablespoon orange zest**

- Combine sugar and cocoa in a saucepan over low heat. Slowly stir in water.
- Chop chocolate and add to pan. Cook until chocolate melts and sugar dissolves.
- Increase heat and boil 1 minute, stirring constantly.
- Pour into a bowl and stir in orange juice and zest. Refrigerate until well chilled.
- Transfer to an ice cream maker and process according to manufacturer's instructions. Cover and freeze overnight to allow flavors to mellow.

For an elegant presentation, serve in hollowed-out orange shells.

Orange Cups

Serves 8

- 8 **large navel oranges**
- 1⅓ **cups sugar**
- 2 **tablespoons cognac**
- 2 **envelopes unflavored gelatin**
- ½ **cup cold water**
- 1½ **cups whipping cream shaved chocolate**

- Cut thick slice from navel end of orange (about ¼ of orange). Juice oranges and set aside. Scoop out orange pulp and discard. Flute edges of the orange. Place orange cups in shallow dish.
- Strain juice into 1-quart measuring cup. There should be 3 cups juice. If necessary, add orange juice. Stir sugar and cognac into juice.
- Sprinkle gelatin over cold water in top of double boiler and heat until dissolved. Pour into medium bowl. Slowly stir juice mixture into dissolved gelatin. Stir in ¾ cup whipping cream and ladle into orange cups. Chill until firm.
- Whip remaining ¾ cup cream and put a dollop of cream on each chilled orange cup. Garnish with shaved chocolate.

Mediterranean Coolers

1 12-ounce package phyllo
    dough
4 to 5 tablespoons melted butter
2 cups pecans, chopped
½ cup sugar
1 tablespoon orange blossom
    water
2 tablespoons rose water
4 tablespoons melted butter
    ice cream

- Cut dough in 6 x 6-inch squares. Brush individual molds (can use custard cups) with butter. Layer 6 to 8 squares of dough in mold, brushing each layer with butter.
- Combine pecans, sugar, waters and butter. Place 2 to 4 tablespoons of filling in the bottom of the phyllo cup.
- Bake in preheated 325° oven until dough is brown.
- Cool. Serve while shells are still warm with a dip of your favorite ice cream in center of cup.

Can be prepared ahead and frozen. If frozen, remove and briefly warm at 325°.

Baskin Robbins contest winner!

Tulsa Truffles

1 pound semi-sweet chocolate,
    melted
1 cup butter, room temperature
6 egg yolks
6 tablespoons rum
    cocoa

- Combine chocolate, butter and egg yolks in a food processor; add rum. Refrigerate two hours.
- When workable, shape into 1-inch balls and roll in cocoa. It will be messy. Refrigerate or freeze.

Easy Christmas Hostess gift and so appreciated!

New Orleans Pralines

20 large pralines

- **3 cups sugar**
- **½ pound butter**
- **pinch salt**
- **2 tablespoons white corn syrup**
- **1 cup buttermilk**
- **1 teaspoon baking soda**
- **3 teaspoons vanilla**
- **3 cups pecan halves**

- Mix sugar, butter, salt and corn syrup. Dissolve baking soda in buttermilk and add to sugar mixture. Cook over medium heat until it forms a firm ball when dropped into cold water (about 25 minutes). If using a candy thermometer, cook to 250° or firm ball stage, stirring constantly.
- Add vanilla and pecans and beat rapidly.
- Plunge pan into a sink of cold water and stir until mixture begins to thicken.
- Drop quickly by spoonfuls onto buttered wax paper placed over sheet of aluminum foil.

English Toffee

2 dozen

- **1½ cups chopped pecans or almonds**
- **1½ cups butter**
- **1½ cups light brown sugar**
- **1½ cups chocolate chips**

- Butter 9 x 13-inch pan. Sprinkle finely chopped nuts in bottom.
- In a saucepan, mix butter and brown sugar. Bring to boil on medium heat stirring constantly. Immediately pour over nuts. Sprinkle chocolate chips over toffee. Cover with foil and let chocolate chips melt 10 to 15 minutes.
- Remove foil and spread chocolate with spatula. Slice while warm or let cool and break into pieces.

Buttermilk Fudge

2 dozen

- **2 cups white sugar**
- **2 tablespoons white corn syrup**
- **1 cup buttermilk**
- **2 teaspoons baking soda**

• Combine all ingredients over low to medium heat in heavy saucepan. Cook until soft ball stage, stirring constantly. Beat. Pour into greased 9 x 13-inch glass baking dish. Cool.

Holiday Peanut Brittle

1 pound

- **1 cup raw peanuts**
- **1 cup sugar**
- **½ cup white corn syrup**
- **⅛ teaspoon salt**
- **1 teaspoon butter**
- **1 teaspoon vanilla**
- **1 rounded teaspoon baking soda**

• Combine peanuts, sugar, corn syrup and salt in a deep 2-quart glass measuring bowl. Microwave on high for 8 minutes, stirring well after 4 minutes. Stir in butter and vanilla. Microwave on high 2½ minutes. Gently stir in baking soda until light and foamy. Pour onto greased cookie sheet. Cool. Break in small pieces.

Easy Christmas candy.

Christmas Popcorn Balls

1 dozen

- **3 quarts popcorn, popped**
- **1 cup sugar**
- **½ cup water**
- **¼ cup light corn syrup**
- **½ teaspoon salt**
- **1 teaspoon vinegar**
- **½ teaspoon vanilla**
  green and red food coloring

• Boil all ingredients except popcorn until hard ball stage. After 3 to 4 minutes, add desired food coloring. Pour over popcorn. Butter hands lightly and shape into balls. Wrap each in plastic wrap.

Chocolate Mocha Pudding

Serves 8

½ **cup butter**
8 **ounces chopped semi-sweet chocolate**
½ **teaspoon instant coffee crystals**
2 **cups whipping cream**
4 **tablespoons sugar**
4 **egg yolks**

- In a saucepan, melt together butter, chocolate and coffee crystals. Stir constantly and do not boil. Remove from heat and beat until smooth. Let stand 2 minutes to cool
- In bowl, whip cream with 2 tablespoons sugar until soft peaks form.
- In separate bowl, place egg yolks and 2 tablespoons sugar, whip until fluffy.
- Fold egg yolk mixture into chocolate, blending well. Next fold in whipped cream.
- Pour into dessert dishes and chill until ready to serve.
- Serve with a dollop of whipped cream and chocolate curls.

Fountains Restaurant

Coffee Ice Cream Pie with Amaretto Chocolate Sauce
Serves 8

1½ **cups crumbled Oreo cookies**
¼ **cup butter, melted**
1½ **pints coffee ice cream, softened**
1½ **cups angel coconut, toasted**
4 **tablespoons sweetened condensed milk**
2 **cups whipping cream, chilled**
½ **teaspoon vanilla**
½ **teaspoon amaretto or Frangelico liqueur**
½ **cup slivered almonds, toasted**

- Place cookies in food processor and process until finely chopped. Slowly add melted butter until mixed well. Pat mixture into the bottom of a lightly oiled 8-inch springform pan and freeze until firm.
- Spread coffee ice cream evenly on the cookie crust. Freeze until firm. Combine coconut and condensed milk and mix until coconut is coated. Set aside.
- Beat the cream until soft peaks form. Add vanilla and liqueur and beat until stiff. Gradually fold in coconut mixture and spread on coffee ice cream. Sprinkle with toasted almonds. Cover with plastic wrap or foil and freeze for at least 4 hours or overnight.
- To serve, wrap a warm dampened kitchen towel around the side of the pan, remove the side. Cut the cake into wedges with a knife dipped in hot water and serve on a plate of chocolate sauce.

Amaretto Chocolate Sauce
3 cups

1½ **cups whipping cream**
⅔ **cup brown sugar**
4 **ounces unsweetened chocolate**
3 **ounces semi-sweet chocolate**
¼ **cup butter, softened**
1 **tablespoon amaretto or Frangelico liqueur**

- Combine cream and brown sugar in double boiler. Stir occasionally, dissolving brown sugar. Add unsweetened and semi-sweet chocolate and whisk mixture until chocolate is melted.
- Whisk in butter and liqueur until sauce is smooth. Cool slightly. This sauce will last for a week if covered and chilled.
- Reheat sauce over very low heat or hot water, stirring occasionally, until it is warm.

Jarrett Farm Country Inn

Chocolate Nut Steamed Pudding with Chocolate Creme Anglaise

Pudding

Serves 6 to 8

- 3 **tablespoons unsalted butter, softened**
- 6 **tablespoons powdered sugar**
- 4 **large egg yolks**
- 2 **ounces semi-sweet chocolate, melted and cooled slightly**
- 4 **egg whites, large**
- 3 **tablespoons granulated sugar**
- 5 **tablespoons bread crumbs, dried fine white (1 ounce)**
- 40 **hazelnuts, toasted with skins removed and ground (1¼ ounces)**
- ¼ **lemon rind, grated**
   additional flour and butter for greasing and dusting molds
   sauce and/or whipped cream

- Preheat oven to 350°.
- Cream the softened butter with powdered sugar. Add egg yolks slowly, one at a time until blended.
- Add melted chocolate and continue to cream.
- In a separate bowl, whip egg whites with granulated sugar until soft peaks form.
- Carefully blend the bread crumbs, nuts and lemon rind into the chocolate mixture.
- Lightly fold in egg whites.
- Fill individual timbales (see note) which have been well buttered and dusted with flour to within ⅛ inch from the rim.
- Set timbales into slightly simmering water bath (select deep casserole or pan). Cover the entire pan with foil.
- Bake for 15 minutes.
- Remove from oven and turn out timbales onto individual serving dishes and top with chocolate sauce.

This will keep out of the oven in warm water for one hour.

Timbales are small domed-topped metal cups which hold from ½ to ⅓ cup. Chinese handle-less tea cups work well for substitutes. Small ramekins will work, but baking time may vary and the shape will be flatter.

Continued on next page

Chocolate Creme Anglaise

- **2 egg yolks**
- **2 tablespoons sugar**
- **⅛ teaspoon grated lemon zest**
- **½ teaspoon cornstarch**
- **2 cups half and half**
- **2 ounces semi-sweet chocolate, chopped**
- **1 teaspoon vanilla extract**

- In a stainless steel bowl, whisk egg yolks, sugar, lemon zest and cornstarch until pale ribbons form when the mixture falls from the lifted whisk.
- Heat the half and half with the chocolate. Stir until the chocolate is melted. Add a small amount to the above mixture. Whisk in remaining cream in a thin stream. Place in the top of a double boiler over barely simmering water stirring until sauce is creamy and coats a spoon.
- Stir in vanilla.

This sauce can be made without the chocolate and varied with liqueurs or extracts to taste. It can be made ahead and served cold or gently reheated in a double boiler.

Suzan Schatz, Soigne Sweets

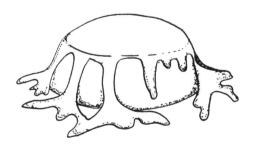

Raspberry Sour Cream Cake

9-inch cake

½ cup softened butter
1 cup sugar, divided
1 egg
1½ cups flour
1½ teaspoons baking powder
1 teaspoon vanilla extract
4 cups fresh raspberries
16 ounces sour cream
2 egg yolks

- Cream butter and gradually add ½ cup sugar, beating on medium to high speed with electric mixer. Add egg, beating well. Combine flour and baking powder. Add to mixer ingredients and mix just enough to blend ingredients. Stir in vanilla.
- Spread into a 9-inch springform pan. Sprinkle with raspberries.
- Combine sour cream, egg yolks, ½ cup sugar and pour over raspberries.
- Bake in 350° oven 60 minutes or until edges are lightly brown. Middle of cake will still appear to be soft but will become firm as cake cools.
- Serve with whipped cream and fresh raspberries.

Chef Gregory Huffines, Cardigan's American Bistro

Party Pecan Cookies

A LOT

1½ pounds sugar
1 pound cake flour
1¾ pounds shortening
2¼ pounds pecans
8 ounces egg whites
pinch salt
1 ounce vanilla

- Mix all together in large bowl. Form into logs. Yield is large even by restaurant standards and may be frozen. Wrap in plastic bags for another day. Slice as needed.
- Bake in preheated 375° oven 10 to 15 minutes until just brown around edge.

Chef Rock Backwards

Christmas Toffee

3 to 4 dozen

1 pound butter
2⅔ cups light brown sugar
1½ cups sliced almonds with skins, lightly toasted and crushed
1 cup chocolate chips, melted
1 cup chopped almonds

- In a heavy pot, bring butter and brown sugar to a slow boil.
- Cook to 290° on candy thermometer and remove from heat. Add crushed almonds.
- Pour onto cookie sheet. Cool. Cover with chocolate while still warm and sprinkle with chopped almonds.

Chef Rock Backwards

Tim's Hot Fudge

2 cups

5 ounces butter
½ cup cocoa, sifted
4 squares bitter-sweet chocolate (1-ounce each)
1½ cups sugar
1⅓ cups evaporated milk
1 teaspoon vanilla

- Mix all ingredients in a heavy pot and bring just to a boil.
- Keeps forever in the refrigerator if you are on a diet.

Great on vanilla frozen yogurt or ice cream.

Chef Tim Fitzgerald

CONTRIBUTORS

Cascia Parent Faculty Association wishes to thank these friends who contributed to GOURMET OUR WAY.

Gayle Allen
Eileen Anderson
Bette Arnett
Bill Arnett
Melissa Atkinson
WynDee Baker
Marci Barlow
Patrice Barnes
Mary Beth Bartkus
Sharon Beavers
Sharon Birkeland
Barbara Bishop
Adele Blom
Barbara Boone
Cherry Bost
Phil Braiser
Sam Bratton
Denice Brice
Janet Briggs
Jim Brownlee
Patti Burns
Jodie Burt
Judy Burton
Lynne Butterworth
Jane Butts
Jane Callahan
Belinda Clark

Cindy Clements
Kathy Collins
Deborah Constantine
Francie Conway
Dell Coutant
Lois Cox
Martha Creasy
Pam Cremer
Donna Cropper
Candy Dalesandro
Ronnie Davidson
Betty Jean DeFreece
Diane Dericks
Barbara Dismukes
Ronnie Donnelly
Catherine Doyle
Stan Doyle
Joyce Driver
Debbie Dunham
Sally Dutton
Chris Edwards
Coby Edwards
Mary Elliott
Maxine Elliott
Pam Eslicker
Judy Ewing
Jennie Fadem

Leah Farish
Barbara Farrell
Mary Fitter
Bernadette Flowers
Viva Foy
Lynn Frame
Sally Frazier
Jill Sullivan-Freeland
Lela French
John Gaberino
Marge Gaberino
Peggy Gaffke
Chris Garber
Karen Garren
Susie Geiger
Sally Gibbon
Beverly Gooch
Diana Gotwals
Sherry Grant
Edie Gregory
Pauline Grimm
Sharon Grimm
Colleen Harris
Mona Hatfield
Cheryl Hawkins
Marion Heatherman
Martha Heinsius

Bonnie Henke
Sarah Hipsher
Blossom Horton
Brad Horton
Jola Houchin
Margie Huffman
Tracy Hull
Molly Huth
John Jarboe
Sally Jarboe
Sarah Jarboe
Sandy Jilton
Dr. Johnson
Ed Johnson
Terry Jones
Joyce Kaiser
Barbara Kalmbach
Elmera Kelley
Dr. Vincent Kelly
Kathryn Kenney
Mary Kessler
Charlene King
Johnny L. King
Lulu M. King
Margaret Koro
Jeannie LaFortune
Linda LaFortune

Rosie LaFortune
Jim Lambert
Linda Lambert
Phyllis Lauinger
Connie Leos
Ann Lipton
Kathy Taylor Lobeck
Mark Malaby
Martha Malaby
Betty Maney
Betsy Manis
Linda Mann
Sally Martin
Marie Mattes
Marilyn Matulis
Sandy McBratney
Tracy McCormack
Janice McKee
Jennifer McNamara
Mary McNamara
Nancy Meinig
Annabelle Miller
Kathy Miller
Anne Millspaugh
Diana Millspaugh
Rosa Moncada
Judie Moore
Janice Morgan
Jane Moynihan
Dotti Murdock

Sr. Mary Murrihy
Franky Neal
Lavada Nicholls
Kris Nichols
Mary Niedermeyer
Ruth Nowlin
Cindy Otey
Mardeen Olmstead
Kim Osgood
Peggy Padalino
Risa Parker
Rosanne Pasco
Mary Pearson
Rhonda Pederson
Margaret Peters
Walt Peters
Belinda Phillips
Pam Pickard
Sara Pilgrim
Tom Pipal
Allison Pringle
Brady Pringle
Pam Proctor
Madeleine Ramey
Madeleine Reilly
Maria Reinoso
Beth Rengel
Gwen Reno
Sally Rippey
Judy Rogers

Kathleen Rooney
Michelle Rooney
Annette Rosenheck
Nancy Rutledge
Beth Sachse
Mary Sadler
Susan Schloss
Bettye Schneider
Kay Schroeder
Anne Schwerdt
Diane Seebass
Lyndell Shackelford
Fr. Jim Sheridan
Margaret Sherry
Trish Sherry
Pat Shollmier
Milann Siegfried
Kay Simmons
Rita Singer
Jennifer Sisk
Mary Doug Sisk
Nancy Sixsmith
Rosabelle Skidmore
Mary Snow
Terry Stamile
Linda Stearns
Linda Stoesser
Susan Suliburk
Theresa Sulton
Mary Swartz

Shelly Swartz
Barbara Taylor
Anita Thomas
Dorie Thompson
Nancy Tidwell
Denise Towsley
Marjorie Tracy
Sabrina Triplett
Barbara VanHanken
Elizabeth Vautrain
Ginger Veitch
Marina Vitanza
Dana Waggoner
Karen Walker
Ann Warren
Dick Watt
JoEdith Watt
Beverley Wayman
Dr. David Wayman
Louise Wayman
Mary White
Donna Wilkes
Margaret Williams
Debbie Wilson
Peggy Woods
Becky Wright
Debbie Zanovich
Bill Zikmund
Noah Zikmund
Sybil Zikmund

CONTRIBUTORS

Professional Chefs

Rock Backwards

Steve Bailey, The Green Onion Restaurant

John J. Briscoe, McGill's Restaurant

Daniel Broyles, Warren Duck Club

Bill Chambers, The Oaks Country Club

Richard J. Clements, Tulsa Country Club

Don Conner, Full Moon Cafe

Buzz Dalesandro, Dalesandro's Restaurant

Jay Edmondson, La Villa Restaurant at Philbrook

John Fard, Ti Amo Ristorante Pizzeria

Tim Fitzgerald

Fountain's Restaurant

Michael Fusco, Michael's

Chuck Gawey, Albert G's Bar-B-Q

David Hanover, Hanover's Meat Market

Michael Hawkins, Ludger's Restaurant and Catering

Curt Herrmann, Montrachet Restaurant

Gregory Huffines, Cardigan's American Bistro

Timothy Inman, Bodean's Seafood Restaurant

Jarrett Farm Country Inn

Rick Kamp, RJK Enterprises

Matthew Kelley

Robert Kennedy, Southern Hills Country Club

Barbara Lander and Jean Paulsen, Cornucopia Catering

Devin Levine, Southern Hills Country Club

Keith Lindenberg, Cooking School of Tulsa

Jacques Lissonnet, Bravo Restaurant, Adams Mark Hotel

Vikki Martinus, Felini's Bakery and Deli

Neil McCarley, Bodean's Seafood Restaurant

Robert Merrifield and Ouida Kelly, The Polo Grill

Cindy Payne, Summit Tower

Pepper's Restaurant

Ling Phan, The Grille, Doubletree Hotel Downtown

Wick Poore, Cedar Ridge Country Club

David Rivest, The French Hen

St. Michael's Alley Restaurant

Suzan Schatz, Soigne Sweets

Harry Schwartz

Moshen "Moe" Shadgoo, Nick's Supper Club

Laura K. Shaw, Cafe Olé

Sherry Swanson, The Bistro at Brookside

Enrique Villananueva, Casa Laredo Mexican Restaurant

Donn Weber, Gilcrease Rendezvous Restaurant

Ruth Young, Queenie's

INDEX

INDEX

INDEX